ESCAPE VELOCITY

ESCAPE

VELOCITY

American Science Fiction Film, 1950–1982

Bradley Schauer

WESLEYAN UNIVERSITY PRESS / MIDDLETOWN, CONNECTICUT

Wesleyan University Press
Middletown CT 06459
www.wesleyan.edu/wespress

Manufactured in the United States of America
Designed by Eric M. Brooks
Typeset in Skolar by Passumpsic Publishing

Library of Congress Cataloging-in-Publication Data
NAMES: Schauer, Bradley.
TITLE: Escape velocity: American science fiction film, 1950–1982 / Bradley Schauer.
DESCRIPTION: Middletown, Connecticut: Wesleyan University Press, [2016] | Series: Wesleyan film | Includes bibliographical references and index.
IDENTIFIERS: LCCN 2016005817 (print) | LCCN 2016008370 (ebook) | ISBN 9780819576583 (cloth: alk. paper) | ISBN 9780819576590 (pbk.: alk. paper) | ISBN 9780819576606 (ebook)
SUBJECTS: LCSH: Science fiction films — United States — History and criticism.
CLASSIFICATION: LCC PN1995.9.S26 S25 2016 (print) | LCC PN1995.9.S26 (ebook) | DDC 791.43/615 — dc23
LC record available at http://lccn.loc.gov/2016005817

5 4 3 2 1

For my parents

Contents

Acknowledgments

I have been very fortunate over the last ten years to receive a great deal of assistance from a great many people, without whom this book could never have been published. To begin, I would not know the first thing about teaching or writing film history without the examples set by a number of extraordinary scholars at the University of Wisconsin–Madison. I'd like to acknowledge Lea Jacobs, Vance Kepley, Ben Singer, Chris Livanos, and particularly Jeff Smith for their comments on early versions of this manuscript. I'm also grateful for the guidance of Tino Balio, Kelley Conway, Michael Curtin, Julie D'Acci, and Kristin Thompson. Special thanks to J. J. Murphy for encouraging me to apply to grad school, and to David Bordwell, whose mentorship and friendship have had a profound impact on my life.

Thank you to my friends in graduate school (and beyond) for their camaraderie and feedback on my work, especially Masha Belodubrovskaya, Colin Burnett, Casey Coleman, Kaitlin Fyfe, Heather Heckman, Derek Johnson, Pearl Latteier, Charlie Michael, Caryn Murphy, Katherine Spring, Billy Vermillion, and Tom Yoshikami. Thanks in particular to Anne Stancil for her crucial support during the early stages of this project, to Dave Resha for recommending Wesleyan University Press and for his guidance with the publication process, to Jake Smith for his critical perspective and enthusiasm for science fiction films, and to Mark Minett for the innumerable insights and recommendations he shared over the long gestation of this book.

I would also like to thank my Film & Television colleagues at the University of Arizona: Jacob Bricca, Bruce Brockman, Sergio Cañez, Josh Gleich, Yuri Makino, Michael Mulcahy, Shane Riches, Beverly Seckinger, Lisanne Skyler, Erica Stein, and Cody Young. Special thanks to Mary Beth Haralovich and Barbara Selznick for their ardent support and mentorship. I'm also grateful to my students at the U of A for their many valuable comments in class, and for tolerating my sometimes-obsessive focus on this genre and time period.

A number of generous people made my archival research as simple and productive as possible. Thank you to Barbara Hall and the staff at the Margaret Herrick Library at the Academy of Motion Picture Arts and Sciences, the staff of the UCLA Film and Television Archive, Sandra Joy Lee Aguilar and the staff at the Warner Bros. Archive at USC, Ned Comstock at the USC Cinematic Arts Library, and Maxine Fleckner Ducey, Amy Sloper, and the staff at the Wisconsin Center for Film and Theater Research.

Chapter 1 contains material from a previously published essay of mine: "The Greatest Exploitation Special Ever: *Destination Moon* and Postwar Independent Distribution," in *Film History* 27, no. 1 (2015). Thank you to editor Gregory A. Waller and the anonymous reviewer of that essay.

Working with Wesleyan University Press has been invigorating. My editor Parker Smathers has been both helpful and encouraging throughout the process. Additional thanks go to Glenn Novak for his skilled copyediting. I am also grateful to Lisa Dombrowski and Scott Higgins for expressing an interest in this project, and to the two anonymous reviewers for their very useful recommendations.

I was lucky enough to meet Erin Treat while working on this book. Her kindness, patience, and respect for my work have been so important during this time. I look forward to watching some of these movies with her (especially *Zardoz*). Finally, I'd like to thank my family. My regular phone conversations with my brother Matt about academia (and more importantly, the Milwaukee Bucks) have been fun and therapeutic. He and my sister-in-law Shelley have always been supportive of me, and generous hosts when I visit them. This book is dedicated to my parents, Jeff and Gail, who have stood by me from the very beginning, even when film studies seemed like something of a questionable career choice. They have always believed in me without hesitation. Any success I may have achieved, personally and professionally, is due to their love and example.

ESCAPE VELOCITY

Introduction

SF AND THE AMERICAN FILM INDUSTRY

On Wednesday, May 25, 1977, the Twentieth Century-Fox science fiction (SF) film *Star Wars* premiered in thirty-two theaters around the United States.[1] Despite this limited release, within a matter of days the studio realized it had an extraordinary success on its hands. Box office records were broken at a number of prominent theaters, including Mann's Chinese Theatre in Hollywood, and exhibitors described ticket queues stretching around the block.[2] Reviews were overwhelmingly positive, and the film received an unusual amount of repeat business, with many moviegoers returning to experience it again and again.[3] The adventures of Luke Skywalker and friends had clearly struck a chord with American audiences. Fox gradually expanded the film's release to over nine hundred theaters, and in November *Star Wars* surpassed *Jaws* (1975) as the highest-grossing film in the history of the American film industry.[4] By the end of 2005, the year in which the sixth Star Wars film, *Revenge of the Sith*, was released (on over thirty-five hundred screens in the United States), the series had grossed nearly $4.3 billion at the worldwide box office.[5] In 2012, the Walt Disney Company purchased *Star Wars* director George Lucas's production company Lucasfilm for $4 billion, intending to release new Star Wars films annually beginning in 2015.[6]

Given *Star Wars*'s inescapable impact upon American popular culture since 1977, it might seem in hindsight that the success of the first film was inevitable. In fact, its record-breaking box office performance shocked the industry, including Twentieth Century-Fox and Lucas himself. *Star Wars* represented a substantial gamble on Fox's behalf; Lucas had struggled to persuade any major studio to invest in the space fantasy. Both United Artists and Universal passed on *Star Wars* before Fox eventually agreed to finance and release it.[7] Part of the studios' reluctance was due to Lucas's unproven track record; his first feature, *THX 1138* (1971), had flopped, and his next film, *American Graffiti*, had not yet become the sleeper hit of 1973. But *Star Wars* was also considered a risk because of its genre. In 1973, when the contract for *Star Wars* was signed, SF films were considered to have limited appeal, mainly to children and a niche audience of SF fans. Modest successes like *Westworld* and *Battle for the Planet of the Apes* (both 1973) were profitable only because their production costs were relatively small. *Star Wars*, on the other hand, featured spectacular space battles sequences and an epic story line that called for a much larger budget. Lucas himself estimated the film would make only $16 million domestically,[8] so when *Star Wars* went over budget at $11.3 million, both studio and filmmaker were justifiably concerned.[9] Only a few weeks before the film's release, Fox attempted to sell *Star Wars* to a tax-shelter group, essentially trying to wash its hands of what it saw as Lucas's folly.[10]

The surprise success of *Star Wars* led to a dramatic reconfiguration of the major film studios' approach to SF, as Lucas's film overturned conventional industry wisdom about the commercial reach of the genre. A number of big-budget SF films were quickly put into production, as studios raced to tap into *Star Wars* mania. One of the most remarkable aspects of the film was its unabashed embrace of old SF tropes like robots, space battles, and grotesque aliens. The plot of *Star Wars* was rooted in culturally debased antecedents like pulp magazines, comic books, movie serials, and low-budget "exploitation films"—so named because their colorful, gimmicky, and sometimes lurid contents facilitated effective marketing (or "exploitation," in industry parlance). This pulp SF paradigm, often mixed with the horror genre, came to define SF in the post–World War II period, in films like *The Day the Earth Stood Still* (1951) and *Forbidden Planet* (1956). But it had been avoided by mainstream filmmakers for decades, as pulp

SF was considered unsophisticated and childish, and thus unsuitable for general audiences. *Star Wars* convincingly demonstrated that this assumption was incorrect, and by the early 1980s theaters were filled with blockbusters driven by pulp SF narratives, like *Flash Gordon* (1980) and *The Thing* (1982). In 1982 Steven Spielberg's family SF film *E.T. the Extra-Terrestrial* broke *Star Wars*'s box office records; a year later, four of the ten highest-grossing films of all time were SF. In their emphasis on spectacular special effects, their accessible, family-friendly content, and their sentimental, escapist narratives, films like *Star Wars* and *E.T.* provided the model for the contemporary blockbusters that are the economic engines of today's film industry.

The SF genre remains dominant at the box office today with films like *Avatar* (2009) and *Guardians of the Galaxy* (2014); only a few decades earlier, films with similar story lines would not even have been released to first-run theaters. The "upscaling" of exploitation genres like SF is widely understood as part of an important trend in American genre filmmaking that began in the 1970s. With films like *The Exorcist* (1973) and *Jaws* (1975), genres once limited primarily to drive-ins and dilapidated grind houses began to shatter box office records. The trend continues today; it has become something of a truism that contemporary blockbusters are simply, in the words of historian Richard Maltby, "big budget versions of 1950s exploitation cinema."[11] But what accounts for this phenomenon? How did SF cinema ascend, both economically and culturally, from its small-scale exploitation origins in the early 1950s to the blockbuster juggernauts of the early 1980s? I believe that we can best understand SF's trajectory over those thirty years by studying determinants within the American film industry and their impact on the production strategies of filmmakers and studios.

Academic studies of SF film are often largely theoretical in focus, emphasizing textual analysis that applies critical theories such as postmodernism and psychoanalysis to select films. Other works connect filmic content to broad cultural contexts. Annette Kuhn writes, "There is a notion that the overt contents of science fiction films are *reflections* of social trends and attitudes of the time, mirroring the preconceptions of the historical moment in which the films were made."[12] For instance, in an influential 1965 article, "The Imagination of Disaster," Susan Sontag argued that SF cinema's preoccupation with scenes of alien invasion and disaster reflected deep cultural fears about nuclear destruction and the dehumanizing effects of modern technology. Thus, the 1950s SF cycle is seen as both symptomatic of national trauma and an attempt to attenuate or exorcise that trauma.[13]

I intend to build upon this prior work by connecting cultural contexts to industrial and economic determinants, to reveal how these have interwoven to shape the development of the SF film genre in America. I explore factors such as the structure of the industry, distribution and marketing strategies, budget categories, target audience, technological innovations, and self-regulation. I have consulted a variety of forms of industrial discourse, such as trade and popular newspapers, promotional materials, and internal studio documents and financial ledgers. These sources provide insights into a film's production context, production costs, patterns of distribution, and reception by moviegoers and exhibitors. By establishing this historical context, and analyzing the production, distribution, and exhibition of key SF films, I explain the shifts in SF film production from 1950, when SF was first recognized by the industry as a distinct genre, to 1982, when the genre reached a commercial and critical apex, as *E.T. the Extra-Terrestrial* became both the highest-grossing film of all time and a Best Picture nominee. After 1982, the structure of the contemporary blockbuster was firmly established, with future blockbusters for the most part only intensifying the existing formula.

My account does not ignore the role of the artist; indeed, the SF genre's changing reputation hinges on a few groundbreaking films, including *2001: A Space Odyssey* (1968) and *Star Wars*, that were driven by a visionary auteur. Yet the production of these films was contingent on specific industrial environments and market conditions that allowed Stanley Kubrick and George Lucas to successfully achieve their visions. The analysis of industrial determinants has tremendous explanatory power, but is only beginning to be applied to the history of genre cinema. Kevin Heffernan's book *Ghouls, Gimmicks, and Gold: Horror Films and the American Movie Business, 1953–1968* is a pioneering study in the industrial historiography of American genre filmmaking and a key influence on my work.[14] More recently, scholars such as Blair Davis, Richard Nowell, James Chapman, and Nicholas J. Cull have written industrial analyses of horror and

SF films, reinforcing the importance of economic factors behind genre film production.[15]

An emphasis on industrial determinants does not mean that culture's role is neglected; on the contrary, the study of a genre's position within the film industry is ultimately inseparable from the study of its larger cultural status. Studio production strategies are based in part upon the perception of the genre's place in American popular culture, which in turn can be affected by the success or failure of certain films. Therefore, this book also charts the interrelationship and mutual influence of the film industry and American popular culture, as they help to shape the status of the SF genre. To do this, I analyze discourse within the American popular press related not only to SF film, but SF in other media such as literature and television. Reviews are particularly useful. This is not because they necessarily represent the opinions of average moviegoers; as we shall see, there are a number of instances where films that are panned by critics become hits, and vice versa. But critics function as cultural representatives who, in the words of Barbara Klinger, "offer a program of perception to the public, comprising a set of coordinates that map out and judge the significant features of a film. These coordinates, whether moviegoers agree or disagree, help to establish the terms of discussion and debate."[16] Regardless of individual critical evaluations, the overall tenor of the public discourse about a genre, when taken in aggregate, illuminates the way that genre is understood by "official" mainstream culture.

Klinger goes on to say that reviews "signify the cultural hierarchies of aesthetic value reigning at particular times."[17] Similarly, in her study of 1920s American cinema, Lea Jacobs examines trade press discourse to learn "the systematic assumptions and categories that structured film preference. According to what logic were films ranked? What was their cultural status?"[18] By surveying a large number of reviews of hundreds of SF films, I trace the development of popular critical attitudes toward the genre, as critics gradually transition from condescending dismissal to acceptance of SF cinema as important cultural texts, and sometimes as works of art. I also go beyond popular reviews to examine criticism in academic journals and specialized film magazines. While this type of critic tends to attack Hollywood genre cinema as creatively formulaic and reinforcing the dominant ideology, in some instances sources like *Film*

Comment and *Cineaste* are willing to analyze SF films at a length and level of detail that mainstream critics are not. The same leftist ideological lens that makes these specialized critics skeptical of popular cinema can also allow them to identify subtextual meanings that elude reviewers who write for a mass audience. Finally, I also examine fanzines, which provide a sense of how the SF fan subculture received SF cinema. In particular, I am interested in the way the relative sophistication of fan criticism, when compared to popular criticism, laid the groundwork for the serious critical consideration of American SF cinema.

My history is organized into a series of production cycles, understood as patterns of formal innovation followed by imitation, which run until they have been exhausted economically, if not creatively. Recent work by Amanda Ann Klein and Richard Nowell has demonstrated the value of cycle studies for the historian. As Klein writes, "Cycle studies' focus on cinema's use value — the way that filmmakers, audiences, film reviewers, advertisements, and cultural discourses interact with and affect the film text — offers a more pragmatic, localized approach to genre history."[19] A focus on production cycles also allows me to largely avoid thorny issues of generic definition that have preoccupied many critics and theorists. Innovative films that initiate genre cycles can be used as prototypes, or ideal examples, against which other films can be defined. For instance, *The Thing from Another World* (1951) can be considered an SF film prototype, as it was a relatively original film, identified as SF at the time, which led to a host of imitations. Therefore, subsequent films that deal with the invasion of Earth by hostile, monstrous aliens can also be considered SF, even if they contain elements that cross over into the horror genre.

Using a core/periphery model based on prototypes allows me to take an inclusive approach to generic definition while still labeling some films as better examples of a genre than others. A film genre is thus a "fuzzy category" that privileges certain films over others based on the extent to which they satisfy particular expectations.[20] I supplement my use of prototypes with Rick Altman's "discursive approach" to genre definition, in which films are categorized not according to their formal properties alone, but also by their status within certain discursive groups, including critics, spectators, and filmmakers.[21] I take the generic definitions found in the trade press and in studio marketing materials as representative of the industry's categorization of specific films, while also noting the instances where industry discourse is inconsistent or contradictory. A definition of SF rooted in both industrial discourse and production cycles avoids ahistorical, essentialist models and recognizes that genre is a fluid, historically contingent construct.

It is typical for a film cycle to take a sharply different approach to the genre than the preceding cycle, in order to differentiate it from films that have become outmoded. For American SF cinema, I argue that each successive cycle is a response to the previous cycle's relationship to pulp SF, the most commercially viable form of the genre because of its emphasis on spectacle and action, but also one that is closely associated with exploitation filmmaking. Certain economic crises in the American film industry, namely in the postwar period and the late 1960s, led the major studios to appropriate production, distribution, and marketing strategies from independent exploitation studios. But owing to what I call "the pulp paradox," the majors' attitude toward exploitation tactics has historically been volatile and ambivalent. Studios could attract audiences by playing up the more sensational qualities of a genre like SF, but also had to face the associated cultural fallout that would occur when less reputable variations of a genre began to dominate the market. Therefore, throughout the period covered in this book, the major studios alternatively embraced, selectively adopted, or rejected outright the tropes of the pulp SF model used by exploitation filmmakers.

This distinction between independent exploitation cinema and the mainstream genre films it influenced is crucial. Some have sought to explain the dramatic ascent of the SF genre in Hollywood as a matter of changing audience taste in the late 1970s; exhausted by the political conflicts of Vietnam and Watergate, American moviegoers retreated into the comforting arms of juvenile fantasies like *Star Wars*. For instance, critic Robin Wood sees the success of Lucas's film as symptomatic of a "regression to infantilism" and evacuation of political critique characteristic of Reagan-era America.[22]

We can go beyond this broad zeitgeist argument and more precisely explain the popularity of blockbusters like *Star Wars* by examining factors such as shifts in Hollywood's perception of its audience, the increased social acceptance of the SF genre, and, most importantly, changes in the way the genre was presented (in terms of content, marketing, and distribution) to moviegoers.

For Wood, modern SF blockbusters differ from the low-budget children's SF serials of the 1930s and '40s only in the sophistication of their special effects.[23] Even within the industry itself, an anonymous Universal executive remarked to the *New York Times* in 1975, "What was *Jaws* but an old Corman monster-of-the-deep flick—plus about $12 million more for production and advertising?"[24] This perspective fails to consider the extent to which budgeting utterly transforms a film. If exploitation producer Roger Corman had had a $12 million budget in 1975, his work would have been altered not only qualitatively, but structurally as well—particularly in terms of its audience appeals. The large budgets of blockbusters demand that they appeal to a wide general audience that employs evaluative criteria different from those of the niche subculture that enjoys low-budget exploitation films. Therefore, a process of translation must inevitably occur when exploitation-type narratives are brought into mainstream cinema.

All major SF films employ strategies of legitimation meant to differentiate them from exploitation cinema and render them accessible and socially acceptable for consumption by mainstream audiences. These strategies are the foundation of the genre's gradual progression to the forefront of American popular culture, and crucial to its eventual critical acclaim. Depending on the historical period, different strategies have risen to prominence, including an emphasis on scientific accuracy, the use of art cinema style and narration, political content, spectacular special effects, greater psychological complexity and nuanced characterization, the involvement of major stars, the guidance of an auteur director, the avoidance of camp, and fantasy world-building through production design. This book traces these different legitimating tactics, linking production analysis with industrial and social context.[25]

Chapter 1 positions the 1950s SF boom within the postwar trend toward "topical exploitation films." SF was growing increasingly prominent in American culture owing to rising interest in SF literature, rocketry, atomic energy, and the UFO phenomenon. However, the genre was still widely understood to be frivolous and juvenile. In order to attract adult audiences, studios needed to differentiate their SF films from the pulp stories, comics, and film serials of the time. The chapter offers a case study of the independent film *Destination Moon* (1950), which emphasized scientific realism as a means of legitimation. However, its "semi-documentary" mode was soon corrupted as studios began to emphasize more sensational SF story lines. As chapter 2 relates, big-budget SF productions were box office disappointments in the early-to-mid-1950s, as the use of pulp tropes violated the norms of A-movie filmmaking and repelled general audiences. The majors soon acquiesced and began producing the low-budget, lurid exploitation fare that had proven lucrative for independent studios like American International Pictures. By the late 1950s, SF was associated almost exclusively with cheap, culturally disreputable horror films.

SF cinema was resuscitated in 1968 by *2001: A Space Odyssey* and *Planet of the Apes*, two major-studio A films that firmly established SF as a viable mainstream genre. Chapter 3 deals with how *2001*'s unexpected popularity with the counterculture, as well as its connection to art cinema, avant-garde film, and New Wave SF literature, led critics to reassess not only Kubrick's film, but the entire genre. By the early 1970s, the serious critical study of SF film was well under way. In the wake of *2001* and *Planet of the Apes*, SF enjoyed enhanced critical and cultural cachet, but was still not considered a reliable big-budget genre. Rather, as chapter 4 discusses, most SF films from the late 1960s to mid-'70s were examples of the low-risk genre "programmers" that provided the backbone of most studio schedules at the time. The two primary strategies used by the studios to distance their films from the culturally debased pulp SF tradition were the dilution and assimilation into the mainstream of *2001*'s radical formal innovations, and the use of political themes as a marker of relevance. A case study of Norman Jewison's *Rollerball* (1975) reveals the blurring boundaries between art cinema, exploitation, and mainstream filmmaking that characterize this period of American film.

Ironically, while most SF films of the 1970s actively avoided space opera and other forms of pulp SF, it was two films that embraced that tradition, 1977's *Star Wars* and *Close Encounters of the Third Kind*, that established SF as the quintessential contemporary blockbuster genre. Both films used high production values, cutting-edge special effects, and a keen sense of verisimilitude and narrative world-building to ward off a camp response and encourage viewers to become emotionally involved in the drama. While mainstream critics and audiences responded with enthusiasm to the return toward family-oriented entertainment begun with *Star Wars* and continuing with *E.T. the Extra-Terrestrial*, others expressed concern about the juvenilization and overcommercialization of American mass art. As the conclusion discusses, these trends would only intensify in the years to come. Even though the SF genre has reached widespread cultural acceptance and economic preeminence, the strategies of legitimation I discuss throughout remain evident today. As the mainstream American film industry grows closer to being defined almost exclusively by spectacular, action blockbusters, it becomes clear that the story of SF cinema from the 1950s to the 1980s is also the story of the birth of contemporary Hollywood.

1

REALIZING THE FUTURE

///

SF in the Postwar American Marketplace

We can trace the history of SF film in America nearly to the origins of the medium. Films about interplanetary travel and speculative futures were exhibited as early as 1903, when bootleg prints of Georges Méliès's *Le voyage dans la lune* (1902) circulated throughout the country. Other nations, such as Germany (*Metropolis*, 1927, and *Frau im Mond*, 1929), the Soviet Union (*Aelita*, 1924), and Great Britain (*Things to Come*, 1936), produced extravagant SF epics when the genre was practically nonexistent in the United States. This particular history of SF film begins in 1950, the first year SF was recognized as a distinct, relatively stable genre by the American film industry. Before 1950, films with SF elements tended to be one-off oddities like the futuristic musical *Just Imagine* (1930), or mad scientist tales like *The Man They Could Not Hang* (1939), which were produced, marketed, and received as horror films. While a number of SF film serials like *Flash Gordon* (1936) were released in the classical studio era, the marginal industrial status of the sound serial limited its influence on feature filmmaking until the blockbusters of the late 1970s and '80s.

Three American SF features were released in 1950, part of what *Variety* identified as "a new interplanetary film cycle."[1] Five years later, approximately 25 SF films premiered in American theaters, and by the end of the '50s over 150 SF films had been released. As Patrick Lucanio argues, "Never in the history of motion pictures has any other genre developed and multiplied so rapidly in so brief a period."[2] This proliferation is particularly noteworthy considering the near absence of SF from American screens in the prior decades. Scholars typically attribute the explosion of SF production in the 1950s to the genre's sociocultural timeliness, its ability to tap into the currents of "Cold War anxiety" that rippled through American culture in the postwar era. For instance, Victoria O'Donnell argues, "The near deluge of 1950s science fiction films was part of a fearful and anxious American cultural climate."[3] We can also look at more directly influential factors, namely the epochal changes occurring in the American film industry in the postwar period. A sharp decline in box office attendance led studios to pursue new production strategies based on novel concepts and spectacular imagery; SF was an obvious topic for producers to pursue, because of its increasing cultural prominence. However, the genre was widely understood as juvenile and trivial, a serious obstacle faced by Eagle-Lion Films as it produced and distributed the first major SF film of the era, *Destination Moon* (1950). While Eagle-Lion was a relatively short-lived entity, the influence of *Destination Moon* is apparent in the many of the innumerable SF films to follow, particular its use of realism as a legitimating tactic.

SF as Topical Exploitation Cinema

The emergence of SF in the 1950s was greatly facilitated by the changes that transformed Hollywood after the end of the Second World War. The 1946 attendance peak of ninety million tickets sold per week, spurred by the hordes of returning servicemen and the postwar surge in disposable income, provided a false sense of security to an industry that was headed for a steep decline. Within a few years, theatrical attendance had plummeted; in 1951 only sixty-four million tickets were sold per week.[4] Studio profits shriveled from $120 million in 1946 to only $30.8 million in 1950.[5] Television is often cited as the primary culprit in this recession, but as Tino Balio notes, the box office slump was under way years before television was popularized in the mid-1950s.[6] With war's end, a galaxy of entertainment opportunities was suddenly available to average Americans, including radio, records, outdoor activities, and vacationing. Furthermore, the middle class began to migrate to the suburbs, where it was no longer convenient to attend the large downtown theaters that generated most of the industry's revenue.

These cultural shifts alone ensured the eventual overhaul of the American film industry. But a momentous United States Supreme Court ruling expedited the transition. The 1948 "Paramount decision" formally dismantled the classical studio system, which was declared an illegal oligopoly.[7] The court recognized that the success of the largest studios in the 1930s and '40s (Paramount, MGM, RKO, Twentieth Century-Fox, and Warner Bros.) was directly tied to their vertically integrated organization. The "Big Five" maximized profits and dominated their independent competitors through the ownership of not only production studios, but also distribution networks and theaters. The studios' prolific production slates were funded by distribution fees and box office receipts from their first-run picture palaces, which charged a premium for admission. The majors' affiliated theaters received priority bookings over independent exhibitors, who were prohibited from showing major releases until they had finished their initial runs. Additionally, while the studios tended to book their best films into one another's theaters, independents were forced to rent in multi-film packages, often containing an entire year's schedule of films. This practice, known as block booking, ensured that all major studio product would be exhibited, regardless of quality.

The studio oligopoly was challenged as early as 1938 by a Department of Justice that, under Thurman Arnold, was aggressively pursuing antitrust suits against a variety of American industries.[8] A series of compromises and consent decrees proved unsatisfactory to all parties, until in 1948 the Supreme Court determined that the majors were operating in restraint of trade, and ordered the divorcement of the exhibition branch from production and distribution, and the divestiture of their affiliated theaters. Unfair practices like block booking and blind bidding (the sale of films to exhibitors sight unseen) were also forbidden. The decision was intended to stimulate competition and level the playing field for independent producers and exhibitors, the victims of the majors' monopolistic tactics. Although the studios hung on to their theaters for several more years (MGM did not sign a consent decree until 1959), Hollywood's business model was drastically altered by the Court's order.

The box office slump of the late 1940s, combined with the elimination of block booking, contributed to important changes in film content. Not only were audiences becoming more discriminating as a result of the increase in entertainment options, but exhibitors also had more control over which films they booked for their theaters. With block booking, studios could package several less appealing features with a single blockbuster, guaranteeing that even the weakest films were exhibited. Under the new government-ordered à la carte distribution system, exhibitors bid for films singly. This placed a new burden on the producer to ensure that each film could stand alone as an attractive entertainment option to audiences, and as a valuable commodity to theater owners.

With no theaters of their own to fill, the major studios focused on fewer, more expensive films meant to draw audiences for prolonged theatrical runs.[9] As I discuss in the next chapter, B films were gradually phased out, replaced by more expensive "programmers" and more provocative, sensational exploitation films. Adapting to the new, more selective market, big-budget A films began to privilege visual splendor and spectacle more than in prior decades. As Peter Lev notes, "Television was limited by a small screen, poor visual definition, black and white (rather than color), and mediocre sound quality. Film could do better in all these areas."[10] Color cinematography, once reserved for only the most expensive films, became almost routine, especially with the popularization of the cheaper one-strip Eastmancolor process in the early 1950s. By 1954, 58 percent of films in production were shot in color.[11] Other strategies intended to enhance visual grandeur included location shooting in exotic locales; widescreen processes like CinemaScope; 3-D cinematography; and innovative special effects.

Certain genres rose to new prominence. For instance, the historical epic had been a Hollywood hallmark since the teens, but beginning in 1949 with Cecil B. DeMille's *Samson and Delilah* it was emphasized like never before. Biblical epics like *Samson* and *The Robe* (1953) offered towering, ornate sets, extravagant costumes, and astonishing set pieces like the Circus Maximus sequences in *Quo Vadis* (1951). While SF did not attain the historical epic's level of popularity in the '50s, in theory it was well positioned to take advantage of the new demands of the marketplace owing to its striking iconography like flying saucers, rocket ships, and robots. Color and widescreen would only enhance the impact of these spectacular images, and studio special effects departments could be put to work designing elaborate scenes of disaster, or creating the landscapes of distant planets.

SF also offered many colorful and weird story ideas, from space travel to alien invasions to brain transplants, which distributors and theaters could use in promotion. Films with unusual concepts or scenarios were another important point of emphasis in postwar Hollywood. In 1949, *Variety* noted that the studios were "concentrating upon exploitation pictures to a degree seldom reached in the past . . . in a bid for new audiences and to maintain business already at hand."[12] This particular definition of "exploitation film" referred not to the lurid, underground "classical exploitation films," nor the low-budget genre films that would be popularized in the mid-to-late '50s.[13] Rather, *Variety* referred to mainstream films that had an interesting, timely narrative angle or concept that could facilitate promotion — or "exploitation," to use industry parlance. This broad definition covered films as varied as RKO's giant-ape film *Mighty Joe Young* (1949), the independent auto-racing drama *The Big Wheel* (1949), and Fox's gritty World War II picture *Halls of Montezuma* (1950).[14] The trade press at the time also highlighted "gimmick pictures" or "topical films" as "the dominant category of product that has been scoring at the b.o." Again, the definition — films that "are off the beaten path" — was expansive, but generally referred to political or social-problem films like *The Snake Pit* (1948) or *All the King's Men* (1949).[15]

This new emphasis on timely or exploitable concepts represented an important shift in major studio production strategies. The industry recognized that "with a sagging boxoffice, new means must be employed to lure patrons into theatres."[16] Classical Hollywood cinema had generally relied on the star system for its primary appeals, but in the postwar era, novel story lines could be as valuable, or more valuable, than star casting. Social-problem films like *Pinky* (1949) and lighter fare like *Cheaper by the Dozen* (1950) were hits on the basis of their concepts (racial "passing" and a family with twelve children, respectively) rather than their actors. Traditionally, stars helped differentiate major studio product from more marginal independent films; beginning in the immediate postwar period the boundaries between these disparate production modes began to blur. As *Variety* astutely noted in 1946: "In [the] past, films with some timely or currently controversial subject which can be . . . capitalized on in publicity and advertising, were the product mostly of the smaller companies. . . . It was more propitious for studios with shorter budgets to concentrate on this type of production, letting the majors turn out films with draw names to top them. Recognizing the terrific profits such exploitation pictures made for their studios, major lots decided to cash in."[17] This adoption of independent studio production strategies by the majors was a trend that would continue throughout the decade.

Rather than just a manifestation of national sociopolitical anxieties, the SF production cycle of the 1950s can be understood as part of this new emphasis on topicality in Hollywood. SF concepts were culturally prominent in America for a number of reasons in the postwar period. First, new technologies like rocketry and the atomic bomb were highly visible in American culture, and interest in popular science had reached new levels. According to Paul S. Boyer, initial fears about the dangers of the atomic bomb had been "muted" by the late 1940s, owing in part to aggressive government propaganda efforts that emphasized the many positive benefits of nuclear energy.[18] Carroll Pursell argues that magazines like *Popular Mechanics* worked to demystify and therefore domesticate an atomic technology that seemed "magical in the sense that though it appeared to work, most people could not explain how."[19] Rocket scientists like Wernher von Braun became media celebrities, promoting the scientific and cultural importance of rocketry and the burgeoning space program. In January 1949 *Life* magazine published a heavily illustrated article titled "Rocket to the Moon," which argued that "engineers believe that a manned rocket . . . may get to the moon within the next 25 years."[20] The article's illustrations appear to be an influence on the rocket design and lunar imagery of early '50s SF films like *Destination Moon* and *Rocketship X-M* (1950).

New technologies were also closely bound to the tremendous increase in consumer spending that occurred once wartime rationing ceased. Suburban homes came equipped with all the latest appliances, including refrigerators, garbage disposals, and climate control, and do-it-yourself projects equated masculinity with a mastery of technologies like electric drills.[21] Economists and business leaders celebrated the merging of technology with capitalism, arguing that America was rapidly headed toward utopia — perhaps as early as 1980![22] These attitudes exhibit more than a little Cold War nationalism, but also indicate the extent to which rapid technological innovation had become an expected part of everyday life in America. The speculative technologies and gadgets of SF could tap into and exploit this technophilic euphoria.

SF was also a hot topic in the late 1940s and early '50s because reports of flying saucer sightings had proliferated across the mainstream American press. The UFO craze began in June 1947 when the national media picked up the story of pilot Kenneth Arnold, who reported seeing disc-shaped objects moving through the air at high speeds while he was flying near Mount Rainier. Hundreds of individual sightings soon followed, and in January 1948 the U.S. Air Force opened an official investigation, originally called Project Sign.[23] In April and May 1949 the popular general-interest magazine the *Saturday Evening Post*, in cooperation with the government, published a lengthy two-part article that attempted to debunk the UFO phenomenon.[24] These efforts only served to intensify the resolve of those who believed in the flying saucers' existence. In January 1950 ex-Marine aviator and pulp SF writer Donald E. Keyhoe argued in the men's magazine *True* that the military had been covering up information proving that flying saucers were indeed extraterrestrial. Keyhoe quickly expanded his sensationalist article into a book that sold over half a million copies.[25]

The UFO phenomenon arguably reached its apex in April 1952 when *Life*, perhaps the most respected popular magazine in the country, published a lengthy, seemingly well-researched article implying that the "flying saucers" were of extraterrestrial origin.[26] While it is unlikely that a majority of Americans truly believed aliens were visiting Earth, historians Patrick Lucanio and Gary Coville argue that fears of Soviet invasion, combined with rapid innovations in military technology, left the public vulnerable to suggestions of this kind.[27] For Hollywood producers, of course, the mere circulation of the question in the national discourse was sufficient to warrant pursuing the topic. Flying saucers quickly became an indelible part of SF iconography.

AUTHOR'S COLLECTION

The inaugural issue of *Fate* magazine in March 1948 featured an article by Kenneth Arnold, whose June 1947 flying saucer sighting initiated the UFO craze of the late '40s and '50s.

Finally, SF topics were exceedingly exploitable in the postwar period because SF literature, in the form of pulp magazines and hardcover anthologies, was more culturally prominent and popular than ever. Before World War II, SF was limited almost exclusively to stories in pulp magazines. So named because of the poor quality of their paper, pulp magazines date back to the late nineteenth century, although titles specifically devoted to SF did not arrive until Hugo Gernsback founded *Amazing Stories* in 1926. The (literally) cheap thrills of the pulps' adventure and mystery stories appealed largely to the working class, particularly men — readers who were not served by the more reputable "slick" magazines like the *Saturday Evening Post*, which targeted a more sophisticated, wealthier family audience.[28] Compared to the slicks, some of which sold millions of copies per month, SF pulps were niche publications; even the most popular SF magazines sold fewer than two hundred thousand copies an issue.[29] The wartime rationing of paper and ink led to attrition in the publishing industry, and by the late 1940s only a handful of the best-selling SF pulp titles remained.[30]

Although the pulp market was in decline in the postwar period, SF was on the brink of a new respectability. A key figure was John W. Campbell, who had assumed editorial control of the SF magazine *Astounding Stories* (quickly renaming it *Astounding Science-Fiction*) in 1937. Campbell's goal was nothing less than the mainstream legitimation of the genre. As pulp historian Mike Ashley writes, Campbell wanted adults "to openly purchase and read the magazine rather than smuggle it around as if it were something bought for their kid brother."[31] To this end, he placed a strong emphasis on scientific accuracy and literary skill. The quality of work published by Campbell was such that a handful of contributors to *Astounding* were able to sell SF stories to the slicks, a proposition that would have seemed like a pipe dream only a few years earlier. In 1946 Robert A. Heinlein, who would soon become a major player in the birth of '50s SF film, sold "Green Hills of Earth" to the *Saturday Evening Post*. SF work from writers such as Ray Bradbury and John Wyndham would follow in *Maclean's* and *Collier's*, respectively. These stories introduced SF to a large new audience that would have avoided the culturally disreputable pulps.

Also important was the introduction of thick hardcover anthologies that collected pulp stories, such as *Adventures in Time and Space*, edited by

Raymond J. Healy and J. Francis McComas, and released in 1946 by Random House. The stories were culled primarily from *Astounding*, but as Ashley remarks, "It's quite possible that many who read the stories in the anthologies had no idea they came from the pulp magazines."[32] In 1949, SF publishing reached further respectability with the introduction of an original hardcover SF line by Doubleday, featuring titles like Bradbury's *The Martian Chronicles* (1950). By the late '40s new SF books were being reviewed regularly in the *New York Times*, and by the early '50s the pulp magazines had been almost entirely supplanted by mainstream publications, including the new pocket-size paperback, as the novel became the prevailing form of SF literature.[33]

SF also began to receive academic attention beginning in the late '40s. University of North Carolina literature professor J. O. Bailey published the first critical survey of the genre, *Pilgrims through Space and Time: Trends and Patterns in Scientific and Utopian Fiction*, in 1947. A year later, writing in the *American Scholar*, Harrison Smith, editor of the *Saturday Review of Literature*, anticipated Susan Sontag by arguing that fantastic fiction helped the reader cope with a modern world that had come unmoored as a result of aspects of modern life ranging from the threat of atomic warfare to the decline of religion and the rise of psychiatry. Smith wrote, "The scientific fantasy story may, indeed, be explained as a necessary device. It has offered an imaginatively conceivable development into the future of everything menacing that science can invent. . . . [These stories] are, in a way, a buffer against known and more conceivable terrors."[34]

Despite SF's higher profile in the late '40s, it must be noted that even its admirers still generally regarded the genre as little more than a light diversion. SF was considered escapism along the lines of mystery novels, to which the genre was often compared in the press. When the *New York Times* praised Groff Conklin's pioneering 1946 anthology *The Best of Science Fiction*, it made clear the stories were "first-rate examples of pure storytelling *designed for entertainment only*" [my emphasis].[35] The author bio on the dust jacket of Fredric Brown's 1958 mainstream novel *The Office* says it all: "Fredric Brown is the popular author of more than twenty science fiction and mystery stories. This is his first serious novel."[36] This low evaluation of the genre threatened to limit its appeal to mass audiences, a real concern for film studios in the early '50s.

Space Opera and Superheroes: SF Media and the Juvenile Market

Given the widespread interest in popular science and technology, the UFO sighting phenomenon, and the gradual mainstreaming of SF literature, the genre appeared to be ripe for exploitation by film studios. Yet there were dangers involved, particularly for studios investing in more expensive SF films. Although the audience for SF was expanding rapidly, studios still had to contend with the genre's deeply entrenched reputation as having only a niche appeal, to either adult fans or children. On one hand, the more reputable SF magazines like Campbell's *Astounding* attracted educated readers, generally young men, with sophisticated, smart, and relatively well-written stories by authors such as Isaac Asimov and Robert A. Heinlein. However, in the late 1940s and early '50s, adult SF fans had considerably less cultural capital than they do today and were commonly depicted by the popular press as a small, insular group of obsessives. In 1949 the *New Republic* declared: "They seem to be infected with a virus. They read, reread, and analyze stories with the zeal of a scholar . . . they correspond with other sufferers, sometimes in letters running to twelve pages."[37]

Ironically, one of the points of distinction for the best SF of the period, attention to scientific accuracy, became a handicap in the general market, as the heavy use of technical jargon and fixation on scientific theories could alienate the average reader and limit the genre's audience. This led to a tension within fandom, highlighted in the *New Orleans Times-Picayune*'s coverage of the 9th World Science Fiction Convention in 1951, in which some fans argued that SF "with more fiction and less science would have a wider reader appeal," while others "called for more accuracy in science details."[38] Trapped in the middle were publishers and editors, looking to expand their audience without alienating existing readers. At the same 1951 convention, pulp editor Hans Stefan Santesson argued, "Attempts to make science fiction more readable are not concessions to scientific illiterates. We need novels that don't require the use of a scientific dictionary to read."[39] As we shall see, film studios venturing into the realm of SF would have to toe a thin line between exploiting the novelty of scientific innovation and letting technology overwhelm the narrative's human interest.

While the insularity of adult SF fandom was surely a concern to film studios looking to produce SF for mass audiences, perhaps the biggest threat to their efforts was the proliferation of more juvenile forms of the genre, which marked SF as frivolous and intended primarily for young consumers. In the pulp magazines, this took the form of "space opera," which was the dominant narrative mode of SF literature until approximately the mid-1940s. While the term itself did not become common parlance until the 1950s, and its meaning has shifted over time, what is known today as space opera can be traced back to the late 1920s with influential pulp stories like E. E. "Doc" Smith's *The Skylark of Space* (serialized in *Amazing Stories*, 1928).[40] In short, space opera was the type of SF John W. Campbell sought to avoid in *Astounding* (although, ironically, Campbell's own early stories are pure space opera). It consists of action-based, romantic adventure stories that typically involve interstellar exploration and combat with monstrous aliens. In *The Skylark of Space*, for instance, an Earth scientist invents faster-than-light travel, builds his own spaceship, and becomes embroiled in a war on a distant planet.

Despite its popularity, by the 1940s space opera was being harshly criticized by a contingent of readers who considered it unsophisticated — the term itself was originally derogatory, coined in 1941 by fan Wilson Tucker to refer to "the hacking, grinding, stinking, outworn space-ship yarn."[41] Critics took issue with space opera's lack of interest in scientific accuracy, its shameless use of convenient pseudoscience (like the mysterious "metal x" that allows space travel in *The Skylark of Space*), and its emphasis on action over philosophical argumentation, political commentary, or informed technological speculation. By using the phrase "space opera," Tucker explicitly linked the stories to the formulaic narratives of westerns ("horse operas") and radio melodramas ("soap operas"), two genres considered unsophisticated by the middle-class male readers of SF. The maturing of pulp SF led by Campbell gradually shifted attention away from the space opera, although it was still a popular form in the late 1940s and early '50s, particularly in magazines targeting younger readers. More importantly, space opera had expanded out of the narrow world of the pulp magazines, to media with a much wider reach, such as radio and comics.

Based on Philip Francis Nolan's novella "Armageddon 2914 A.D.," which appeared in *Amazing Stories* in August 1928, *Buck Rogers in the 25th Century A.D.* was the first dramatic SF comic strip. Premiering in January 1929, the strip told the story of a man trapped in a mining accident only to be held in suspended animation by a mysterious (and inexplicable) gas for five hundred years. In the twenty-fifth century, Rogers joins a small group of American freedom fighters rebelling against the "Mongol Reds" who have conquered the earth. Widely successful, *Buck Rogers* was followed by a number of competing strips, most notably *Flash Gordon*, which debuted in 1934. Rather than traveling through time like Buck, Flash Gordon travels through space to the planet Mongo, which, reflecting the "Yellow Peril" tropes of the day, is somehow also under the control of sinister Chinese despots — in this case, Ming the Merciless.[42] *Gordon* was distinguished by its strong emphasis on action and the brilliant, almost photorealistic art of Alex Raymond, which is arguably the visual high water mark of early space opera. These nationally syndicated comic strips helped to introduce the tropes of space opera to a wider audience, much to the chagrin of later SF writers who would struggle for respectability. In 1951 Ray Bradbury griped to the *New York Times* that SF "has a bad name because of the space operas. You say 'science fiction' and people think of Buck Rogers and Flash Gordon."[43]

In the early 1930s, publishers began to collect newspaper comic strips into magazines, and by the middle of the decade comic books containing new material had become popular. Genres included "funny animal" stories featuring characters like Mickey Mouse, and adventure comics reminiscent of the male action narratives from the pulps. The comic book industry did not come into its own, however, until the rise of superhero comics in the late '30s. Ever since, the American comic book has been synonymous with the superhero genre. But the prominence of the superhero in American culture did not benefit efforts to legitimate the SF genre. Mike Ashley argues that superhero comics "gave science fiction the juvenile image from which it has never escaped."[44] While their stories are usually more earthbound, superhero comics of the 1940s through the 1960s resemble space opera in their simple, action-oriented plots, Manichean good vs. evil morality, and reliance on pseudoscientific concepts. (For instance, the Flash was a student who gained super-speed after inhaling experimental "hard water" fumes.) As pulp SF grew more complex and sophisticated in the 1940s, a number of popular but outmoded writers like Edmond Hamilton, who specialized in space opera, transitioned to writing superhero comics instead.

Superman, the prototype for the modern superhero, famously debuted as the lead story in *Action Comics* #1, released in April 1938. Superman differed from pulp characters like Doc Savage and the Spider in that his origin was explicitly science fictional; originally, Superman was the sole survivor of a planet of highly evolved humanoids gifted with enormous strength, speed, and other powers, which he used to fight crime.[45] The character was an instant hit for publisher National Comics (later called DC Comics), and soon a host of superheroes in the Superman mold flooded the market. In 1946 DC sold over twenty-six million comics in the first quarter alone, and mid-1940s market research suggested that seventy million Americans read comics. The bulk of the audience was understood to be children between the ages of six and seventeen, with readership trailing off as readers grew older.[46] Although the superhero genre briefly fell into decline after World War II in favor of crime and humor comics, superhero stories remained among the most visible exemplars of SF in '50s American popular culture.

Alongside the more popular superhero titles, a number of space opera comic books were published in the 1950s, such as DC's *Mystery in Space* (1951–1966) and *Strange Adventures* (1950–1973). These books showcased heroes in the Buck Rogers/Flash Gordon mode like Adam Strange and Captain Comet, all the while reproducing the blend of action, horror, and pseudoscience found in the early pulps. The SF books (such as *Weird Science* and *Weird Fantasy*) released by notorious horror comics publisher EC Comics from 1950 to 1956 were, ironically, usually much more sophisticated in their storytelling, themes, and artwork. As superhero comics grew increasingly silly (if still imaginative) in the 1950s, EC published intelligent, faithful adaptations of lyrical Bradbury stories like "A Sound of Thunder," and "There Will Come Soft Rains" from *The Martian Chronicles*.[47] Although still making use of many of the tropes of pulp SF, EC's writers often dealt seriously with issues such as intolerance, racism, and atomic disaster. While EC's stories tended to be rather heavy-handed, the willingness of publisher William Gaines to incorporate more complex themes into his comics separated them from their competitors in the superhero genre. For instance, while Superman was teaming up with Tharka, the "superwoman from space," in 1953, EC was publishing an allegorical SF story in which an African American astronaut visits and criticizes a segregated civilization in which blue robots are oppressed by orange robots.[48] Despite the generally higher quality of EC's SF comics, circulation numbers attest to the dominance of the more juvenile superhero format. EC's SF titles sold approximately 550,000 copies in total per month, a pittance compared to the millions of Superman comics sold monthly by DC.[49]

Characters like Superman and Flash Gordon remained so visible in popular culture not only because of the wide circulation of their comics, but because they had been licensed to a number of different media. As today's film studios are well aware, by converting comic characters into transmedia franchises, rights holders can increase their property's market exposure and generate new revenue. A Buck Rogers radio show premiered in 1932, followed by a Flash Gordon show in 1935. Universal released three Flash Gordon film serials: *Flash Gordon* (1936), *Flash Gordon's Trip to Mars* (1938), and *Flash Gordon Conquers the Universe* (1940), and one Buck Rogers serial in 1940. Similarly, Superman was nearly ubiquitous in the '40s, with three comic book series supplemented by a radio show, a newspaper strip, a series of cartoon shorts released by Paramount, and two serials by Columbia, in 1948 and 1950. A popular syndicated Superman television program starring George Reeves also ran from 1952 to 1958.

The proliferation of these comic book characters throughout the mass media only served to further perpetuate the common perception of SF as a children's genre, as their appearances in film and radio were, like comic books, clearly aimed at younger audiences. For instance, the Buck Rogers radio program premiered at 7:15 p.m. in 1932, but was quickly moved to the late afternoon to accommodate children returning home from school.[50] The show was also sponsored for several years by the powdered drink Cocomalt, advertised as "providing almost double the health-building elements so essential to the growing child."[51] The sponsor ran a promotion in which children could submit a proof-of-purchase from a can of Cocomalt and receive a cardboard Buck Rogers ray gun and helmet.[52]

Likewise, the serial films of the 1930s and '40s were children's fare.

Rafael A. Vela has studied the transition from the adult serial of the silent period to the children's sound serial. He argues that the rise of vertical integration in the late teens led to the banishment of adult serials from the screens of first-run theaters. As serial-producing studios like Universal and Pathé did not own theaters, their serials were limited to smaller, less lucrative subsequent-run theaters. In response, budgets for serial films plummeted, and when reformers intensified their protests of movie violence in the early '30s, the serial format was reformulated to be more oriented toward children.[53] After the success of the initial *Flash Gordon* serial in 1936, juvenile superhero-type plots began to dominate the serial format, with presold comic and radio characters like Dick Tracy and the Phantom receiving their own "chapterplays."

The original *Flash Gordon* serial was unique in that Universal was aiming for more than a children's matinee audience. The studio did not neglect children; for example, it licensed a great deal of *Flash Gordon*–themed merchandise, such as costumes, ray guns, and spaceship models. But with *Flash Gordon*, Universal was hoping to attract the larger "mixed audience" of both children and adults that watched serials in the teens and 1920s.[54] The thirteen-chapter film was accorded a $350,000 budget, nearly three times the cost of the average Universal serial at the time.[55] *Flash Gordon* was heavily advertised in local newspapers and earned a (favorable) review in *Variety*, which rarely reviewed serials in the sound era. The trade paper praised *Flash Gordon* as a throwback to "the old serial days when story and action, as well as authentic background, were depended upon to sustain their vigorous popularity." *Variety* also recognized that *Flash Gordon* was intended to transcend the low-budget serial format, noting "*feature production standard* has been maintained as to cast, direction, writing, and background" [my emphasis].[56]

Although *Flash Gordon* performed well for Universal, subsequent sound serials would eschew its ambition and aim primarily at youths. The second Flash Gordon serial, *Flash Gordon's Trip to Mars*, cost half as much as the original and was a more slapdash, albeit still entertaining, effort.[57] *Variety* remarked that the serial was "prime plucking for nabes [neighborhood theaters] which have kid audiences avid for this sort of fare. . . . In view of the fact kids today favor pseudo-scientific thriller-givers, this far-fetched stuff is right in the groove."[58] By the late 1940s the

AUTHOR'S COLLECTION

Universal's 1936 *Flash Gordon* serial was expensive for its time and well-received but also contributed to the dominance of the juvenile pulp SF paradigm, to the exclusion of other forms of the genre.

serial format was in decline, with only Columbia and Republic producing serials for weekend matinee screenings at subsequent-run neighborhood theaters. Budgets continued to shrink, and the quality of the films plummeted. Serial historian Gary Johnson writes: "The scenarios [were] becoming increasingly silly and lazy with each week. Serials such as *The Purple Monster Strikes* (1945) even recycled the exact same camera shots for key scenes week after week."[59]

The rise of television put the serial format out of its misery in the early '50s, as children could watch similar programs like *The Lone Ranger* (ABC, 1949–1957) in the comfort of their homes. Of all the mass media, it was television that most solidified SF's reputation as cheap and childish in the 1950s. Early television continued many of the same production strategies of radio, serials, and B films, and SF television was no exception. At first, a more sophisticated approach to the genre was attempted. Several short-lived SF anthology dramas were broadcast in the early '50s; for instance, *Out There* (1951–1952), described by CBS as "geared for an adult audience with great appeal for children," adapted Heinlein, Bradbury, and other SF luminaries but lasted only twelve episodes before being canceled.[60] It was succeeded by ABC's *Tales of Tomorrow* (1951–1953), which broadcast versions of prestigious works by H. G. Wells, Jules Verne, and Mary Shelley alongside contemporary stories about flying saucers and new technological inventions. Both shows used reputable Hollywood personnel and were examples of outstanding craftsmanship (within the limitations of early live television) and thoughtful storytelling that would influence later, more successful anthology series like *The Twilight Zone* (CBS, 1959–1964). Despite the quality of these programs, they were both short-lived and utterly overwhelmed by the large number of juvenile SF shows that illuminated American television screens in the early-to-mid-1950s—none more popular than *Captain Video* (DuMont, 1949–1955).

Captain Video featured the interstellar exploits of the title character, a heroic inventor and two-fisted man of action who battled evil scientists, aliens, and robots. The stories were pure comic book pulp, full of the kind of explicit moralizing unique to children's television, and the show's production values were practically nonexistent. David Weinstein writes, "*Captain Video* was notorious for its low budgets, cheesy costumes, and set design that was schlocky even by early television standards."[61] Owing to its evening time slot, the show attracted its share of adult viewers, but children were clearly its target audience. Critics were baffled by the program's curious fetishization of technology and pseudo-scientific jargon, as well as its fragmented, convoluted narratives, a product of the show's daily production schedule. Like the cheapest B films, *Captain Video* had neither the time nor the money to develop balanced, classical story lines. Instead its episodes were full of dead spots, blown lines, and strange budget-saving digressions, including the frequent and extended inclusion of stock footage from old westerns and serials. Children, of course, were less disturbed by the show's violations of classical narrative traditions. They were more concerned with devotedly following the Captain's daily adventures and buying the cornucopia of merchandise associated with the show, which reportedly netted sponsor DuMont $50 million in 1951.[62]

By 1952 *Captain Video* had grown marginally more sophisticated, with script contributions by respected SF writers like Jack Vance and James Blish. But its formula did not change significantly, and the show would never be confused with an adult anthology drama like *Out There*. Although children's watchdog groups criticized *Captain Video*'s violence, the show's pulpy action and pseudoscience, indebted to the comic book tradition of Superman and Buck Rogers, would help define the SF genre in this period for a great many Americans.[63] *Captain Video* was extremely successful during its six-year run, attracting an audience of as many as 3.5 million and spawning a host of equally popular imitators like *Tom Corbett, Space Cadet* and *Space Patrol* (both 1950–1955).[64] Columbia producer Sam Katzman also released a *Captain Video* film serial in 1951.

SF's prominence in American popular culture in the early '50s made it an attractive genre for a film industry struggling to retain its audience. But this cultural prominence was not unproblematic, as SF was known to mass audiences primarily through the juvenile pulp paradigm of superheroes and space opera. This type of SF had a strong following with younger viewers, but at the time the film industry was not yet adequately structured to best exploit this audience. Children were understood as a niche group, catered to primarily via the cartoons, serials, and B movies of Saturday afternoon matinees. The evening first-run screenings that drove the economic engine of the industry were still aimed at adults.

The youngsters who tuned into *Captain Video* and read Superman comics were an insufficient audience to justify the cost of an A-level motion picture. Therefore, it was incumbent upon film studios to not only produce SF films that appealed to an adult audience, but also to assure adult moviegoers through marketing and promotion that the films were tailored to their tastes rather than children's. These were the challenges faced by the independent studio that initiated the SF boom of the 1950s.

Liftoff: Eagle-Lion and *Destination Moon*

The 1948 Supreme Court decision that outlawed the major studios' vertical integration was intended to stimulate competition and level the playing field for the independents that had long been the victims of monopolistic practices. Divestiture of the majors' exhibition arms would theoretically eliminate the first-run theaters' bias toward major studio product and open their screens to the independents, who could now compete directly with the companies that had previously stifled their expansion. Because the majors had cut production in response to the box office slump, there was more room on American screens for independent films in the postwar period. For a brief period, the major studios' hegemony seemed in jeopardy. The late 1940s saw a surge in the number of independent production companies, all seeking to capitalize on this perceived weakness. Yet "independent" was a relative term; most big-budget independent producers were still affiliated with a particular studio, which provided studio space, financing, and distribution in return for a percentage of the profits.[65]

Eagle-Lion Films was a much bolder proposition than the average independent company; it was an attempt to directly compete with the major studios. Instead of distributing through one of the majors or limiting itself to only low-budget product, Eagle-Lion intended to make relatively expensive A pictures and release them to first-run theaters through its own distribution network—in essence establishing itself as a new major.[66] Republic and Allied Artists (formerly Monogram) were the only other studios that attempted to break into the first-run market in this fashion during the late '40s and the 1950s. These independent distributors were poised to transform the industry in a way the major studios were not; the complex infrastructure and rationalized mode of production that helped the majors maintain a dominant oligopoly throughout the classical studio era also left them resistant to large-scale change. In contrast, the peripheral industrial status of the independents necessitated bold new tactics, particularly in terms of production and marketing. While the majors endured several lean years in the late '40s before they began to actively adapt to the new film market, independent producers and distributors had no such luxury — a single bad season could be disastrous.

Because they lacked the majors' distribution networks, access to stars, and advertising resources, the independents relied on the novelty of their films to attract audiences. This often meant the production of exploitation films as defined above — films based on a novel, easily marketable concept. In rare cases, the popularity of a certain film would contribute to the creation of a new genre cycle. This was the case with Eagle-Lion's 1950 release *Destination Moon*. The film's box office success attracted the attention of the majors, which would soon begin producing their own even more spectacular productions. Ultimately, the industrial barriers to entry that prevented outsiders from encroaching on the majors' terrain thwarted Eagle-Lion's ambition. The influence of *Destination Moon* would be felt for decades, however. By appropriating successful independent experiments like *Destination Moon*, the majors were able to maintain control of the industry through this tumultuous period.

Destination Moon's mix of exploitation appeals and A-movie gloss is a function of its distributor's liminal status within the studio hierarchy. A brief history of Eagle-Lion is necessary, therefore, to better understand the studio's tenuous position between industrial categories, as neither a major studio nor a Poverty Row independent. Eagle-Lion Films was the brainchild of J. Arthur Rank, the powerful English film magnate who had a stranglehold on the UK industry, owning over five hundred theaters as well as a distribution network and studio space. However, the oligopoly of the Hollywood majors initially prevented Rank from making substantial inroads in the American market. Rebuffed by the majors who refused to share screens with foreign distributors, Rank formed Eagle-Lion with businessman Robert Young in 1947. Young owned Poverty Row studio Producers Releasing Corporation, which had its own nationwide system of distribution exchanges. For his part, Young hoped the association with

Rank would bring a prestige to the studio that was absent from PRC, notorious for its extremely inexpensive B films.[67]

Eagle-Lion got off to an auspicious start. Not only would the studio distribute Rank's British films in America; it would also produce its own features and distribute them through PRC's exchanges.[68] In 1947, Eagle-Lion announced the production of "twelve major films," including four with budgets exceeding $2 million, a far cry from the cheap product of PRC.[69] Despite Eagle-Lion's efforts to distance itself from its sister corporation, its true intentions were revealed by its hiring of Bryan Foy as head of production, as Foy had spent the previous decade in charge of the B-film production unit at Warner Bros.[70] Eagle-Lion's production slate for its first two years was considerably more conservative than its initial press releases claimed, with cheaper fare outnumbering the million-dollar productions.[71] But even this tentative approach failed, as the box office performances of the costlier projects failed to justify their expense. Eagle-Lion and PRC suffered a combined loss of $2.2 million in 1947.[72]

The early A pictures were expected to help Young recover his $12 million investment in Eagle-Lion. When they failed, the studio turned to a form of independent production beginning in late 1947 in which Eagle-Lion would partly finance films in exchange for a distribution fee and a share of the profits.[73] The new strategy was intended to prevent the enormous losses of the first year, but with reduced risk came reduced profits. Eagle-Lion was now required to share the film rentals with the independent producer.[74] For example, the influential crime film *T-Men* (1947) made $1.25 million against a cost of $466,000, but Eagle-Lion retained only one-third of the profits after prints and advertising deductions, the rest going to producer Aubrey Schenck.[75] By late 1948 the studio was no closer to recovering its reported $11 million debt to the First National Bank of Boston.[76] Mimicking the United Artists model, Eagle-Lion declared itself solely a distribution company in late 1949.[77]

As the new decade opened, Eagle-Lion faced tremendous challenges. Even after a series of successful film noirs, the studio remained approximately $3 million in debt.[78] It could not achieve profitability unless its films were booked according to a percentage basis, like a conventional A film, rather than the smaller flat fees offered by subsequent-run houses for B product. Consistent top-of-the-bill access to first-run theaters in the downtown areas of major cities was crucial. Although only about 25 percent of the theaters in the United States were considered first-run, their high ticket prices ensured that they were responsible for nearly half of the country's annual box office revenue.[79] But first-run theaters generally showed only the highest-profile, most expensive films — the type of films that Eagle-Lion could no longer afford to make.

One solution was what historian Brian Taves calls the "programmer," an intermediate-budgeted film that existed between the A and B categories.[80] Programmers did not have the high production values or top stars of A films, but could be sold as A films if they were made to look sufficiently attractive to exhibitors. This was typically accomplished via a unique promotional angle. While Eagle-Lion was acutely concerned to keep its films out of the unprofitable B market, the studio had developed a reputation for peddling low-budget, low-grossing product. Big-budget A films like Walter Wanger's oil industry drama *Tulsa* (1949) were the exception to the rule; of the 195 films distributed by Eagle-Lion from September 1946 to September 1950, only 18 grossed more than $500,000.[81] In 1949 independent producer George Pal pitched an SF film to Eagle-Lion; as discussed earlier, space travel was precisely the kind of topic that, with the proper treatment and a strong marketing push, had the potential to secure top-of-the-bill bookings from major theater chains.

Although the Hungarian immigrant Pal would soon become arguably the single most important figure in SF filmmaking of the 1950s, at the time he was best known for his "Puppetoons," animated children's films featuring vivid wooden models. Pal produced forty-one of the short films for Paramount between 1941 and 1947; seven were nominated for Academy Awards, and in 1944 the Academy awarded Pal a plaque honoring his films' "special methods and techniques."[82] In 1949 Pal began shopping feature film ideas, including *Operation Moon*, a space exploration screenplay penned by Robert A. Heinlein and screenwriter Rip Van Ronkel. In the script, a rocket scientist, a military general, and a prominent aircraft manufacturer combine resources to finance and coordinate the world's first lunar landing. The rocket blasts off despite the U.S. government's fearful and shortsighted attempts to scuttle the mission. The astronauts overcome a number of technological breakdowns and eventually land on the moon and manage to return to Earth safely. The script was a combination of elements of Heinlein's 1947 juvenile novel *Rocketship Galileo* and his 1949 novella "The Man Who Sold the Moon," about the privatization of the moon by a business tycoon.

Pal ended up at Eagle-Lion owing primarily to Peter Rathvon, who had previously heard Pal's pitches while president of RKO.[83] In 1949 Rathvon was responsible for allocating bank financing to Eagle-Lion's independent producers.[84] Pal was signed to a two-picture deal; he funded the films in part through a loan from the financing company Motion Picture Capital Corporation, run by Rathvon. In return, MPCC received a large portion of the films' profits (78 percent for *Destination Moon*) — if indeed the films were profitable.[85] The deal got off to an inauspicious start when Pal's first film, *The Great Rupert* (1950), featuring Jimmy Durante acting opposite an animated Puppetoon squirrel, disappointed at the box office with earnings of only $400,000 against a budget of about $500,000.[86] As the films were cross-collateralized, Pal needed his second film, the newly retitled *Destination Moon*, to be a hit.[87] Fortunately for both Pal and Eagle-Lion, they were the first to recognize the potential of SF cinema in the '50s.

Destination Moon's final budget was $587,000, which positioned it squarely as a programmer: too cheap to be a conventional A film, too expensive to be a B film.[88] If the film were sold to theaters for a low flat rate, like a typical B film, Eagle-Lion and Pal would never recoup their investment. For *Destination Moon* to be a hit, Eagle-Lion would have to persuade theaters to share a percentage of the box office take. Three obstacles stood in the studio's way: first, Eagle-Lion had already developed a reputation as the purveyor of B-level product. None of its films featured top stars, and its only notable successes had been either British imports from Rank like *The Red Shoes* (1948), or overachieving low-budget noirs like *T-Men*. Eagle-Lion's close association with PRC, which it absorbed in 1947, did its industrial status no favors. Second, *Destination Moon* lacked well-known performers. Hollywood's most prominent stars were either under contract to a major studio, or were independent producers themselves. And Eagle-Lion learned in its first year that the marquee value of aged stars like Paul Lukas or George Brent was not worth the extra expense. The association of SF with niche audiences, discussed earlier, was a final problem faced by Eagle-Lion as it attempted to market *Destination Moon* to a general, first-run audience.

Eagle-Lion had two primary strategies for establishing *Destination Moon* as an A-level feature and avoiding the B stigma. First, it packed the film with elaborate special effects and colorful imagery that made it appear more expensive than it was. Its cast of unknowns and Poverty Row regulars freed up money for Technicolor cinematography, at the time an indulgence utterly alien to B films.[89] Although the bleak lunar landscape would seem to limit opportunities to showcase the Technicolor process, each of the astronauts' spacesuits was given a different color, to brighten the mise-en-scène and aid in character differentiation. *Destination Moon*'s special effects were also sophisticated and costly for their time, especially for an independent film. A 150-foot-tall model of the rocket ship's tail was constructed in the Mojave Desert for location shooting, a $35,000 network of gimbals was erected around the control room to facilitate shots of "weightlessness," and some two thousand Oldsmobile headlights were hung on seventy thousand feet of wire to simulate a star field.[90]

While spectacle was the film's main selling point, Eagle-Lion needed to frame it within a particular context. Specifically, a strong emphasis on scientific realism, both within the film itself and the marketing discourse surrounding the film, helped to disassociate *Destination Moon* from the pulp SF tradition of Flash Gordon and Buck Rogers. The swashbuckling bombast and pseudoscience of space opera were replaced with a commitment to strict scientific accuracy, which marked the film as socially topical rather than mere escapism. Robert A. Heinlein, determined to make the first utterly plausible SF film, was key to the film's discourse of realism. On set as technical adviser, he wrote an essay titled "Shooting *Destination Moon*" that ran in the July 1950 issue of *Astounding Science-Fiction*. Appealing to that magazine's educated readership, Heinlein spent the article highlighting the elaborate efforts made by the production crew to ensure that the film was scientifically correct: "The entire company . . . became imbued with enthusiasm for producing a picture which would be scientifically acceptable as well as a box office success." Heinlein described the "deluge" of rocket scientists and other technical personnel who visited the set, and detailed the painstaking creation of the film's special effects.[91]

Technical details that would be lost upon nearly every moviegoer were as authentic as possible in *Destination Moon*, including the calculation of

Famed astronomical artist Chesley Bonestell painted the lunar backdrop used in *Destination Moon* (Eagle-Lion, 1950). The sharp peaks of the lunar mountains were considered scientifically accurate at the time.

the rocket's thrust and trajectory. Famed astronomical artist Chesley Bonestell, a notorious stickler for authenticity, was enlisted to paint the lunar landscape onto an expansive sound stage backdrop. Most importantly, the film's script was devoid of any element of pulp fantasy, structuring itself around technology-based obstacles like a defective radar antenna rather than alien invasions or killer robots. The climax centers on a lack of sufficient fuel to return home; when the crew can no longer lighten their load any further, one of the crewmen valiantly offers to sacrifice himself so the others may survive. Fortunately the resourceful Dr. Cargraves (Warner Anderson) finds a way to jettison the crewman's spacesuit and radio equipment while also saving the man's life.

The rhetoric of realism surrounding the production of *Destination Moon* carried into the film's marketing. Eagle-Lion conducted a far-reaching saturation exploitation campaign, which cost a reported $500,000, or nearly as much as the film's production budget.[92] Of course, the subject matter lent itself to colorful promotions, typically coordinated by the individual theaters. For instance, exhibitors rented spacesuit costumes from Eagle-Lion and positioned "astronauts" in the theater lobby, or even around town in the days leading up to the film's premiere.[93]

But *Destination Moon* could not rely simply on gimmicks; it also needed a classier, more traditional campaign to draw a general adult audience. This was accomplished primarily through a number of feature articles in mainstream publications. Its theatrical trailer announced that *Destination Moon* was "the picture you've been reading about in every important national magazine and newspaper, among them *Life, This Week, The New York Times, Popular Science, Seein' Stars, Popular Mechanics, Parade, The New*

York Daily News." These articles exploited the current national interest in popular science and technology by linking *Destination Moon* to the latest scientific research and stressing the extent to which it represented a believable and accurate depiction of the first lunar mission. For instance, in April 1950 the *Los Angeles Times* declared, "The amazing thing about *Destination Moon* . . . is not its fantasy but its adherence to known facts and reasonable conjecture."[94] Likewise, the May 1950 article in *Popular Mechanics* assessed the film's plausibility in light of current research at Cal Tech's jet-propulsion center.[95] The marketing campaign was also careful to explicitly differentiate the film from pulp SF. Pal assured the *Los Angeles Times* that *Destination Moon* would contain "no Buck Rogers comic-strip stuff at all."[96] A promotional "fact book" distributed to exhibitors proclaimed, "There is no hokum, no comic-book sensationalism, no pulp magazine fantasy about DESTINATION MOON. Here is FACT."[97]

While the promotion for *Destination Moon* was rooted in a realism-based discourse, Eagle-Lion was also mindful that overemphasizing science and technology could alienate the average moviegoer. Studio publicity director Leon Brandt recommended, "All promotion . . . should be angled from the point of view that this is the greatest exploitation special ever, rather than a scientific treatise. In this way we shall guarantee ourselves mass appeal."[98] The more frivolous exploitation strategies, like the spacesuit costumes, added a sense of fun to the campaign. Two comic adaptations, from Fawcett and DC Comics (including the cover to the first issue of DC's long-running *Strange Adventures*) helped built interest among children.[99] Special effort was also made to attract women, for whom the film would be an especially tough sell; other than a brief farewell scene between the astronauts and their wives, the film is bereft of women. Working with what they had, the marketing team emphasized this lone scene in print advertisements aimed at women. One reads: "Would you let Your Man take the first flight to the Moon? Will you have to say woman's most heart-breaking good-bye?"[100] The top of the ad features a line drawing of a man and woman embracing. This particular appeal may not have been especially effective: *Washington Post* critic Sonia Stein reported that her screening was "almost 90 percent male . . . and I suspect it will largely stay that way."[101]

Overall, Eagle-Lion's aggressive promotion paid off; *Destination Moon*

Eagle-Lion promoted *Destination Moon* heavily in the popular press, including this cover story in the May 1950 issue of *Popular Mechanics*.

was booked into a number of first-run sites, including the Mayfair in New York. Looking to make a splash on Broadway, Eagle-Lion painted an enormous rocket ship on the façade of the Mayfair; this image would figure prominently in newspaper ads for the film.[102] Early reports indicated that *Destination Moon* would do quite well, with *Variety* reporting "long lines for tee off" at the Mayfair.[103] Exhibitor response also affirmed Eagle-Lion's A-level aspirations: one theater owner described *Destination Moon* as "a show well worth showing, even on percentage," suggesting that the film could sustain an A booking.[104] The film also received excellent reviews, with the *Hollywood Reporter* calling it a "triumph of imagination over formula. The film is nearly everything that its advance reports had it—beautiful to look at, fascinating in the details of its unique story, and utterly compelling in its dramatic motivation."[105] The *New York Times*'s Bosley Crowther listed *Destination Moon* among his ten best films of the year, and in 1951 the film was awarded an Oscar for Best Special Effects.[106] Subsequent SF films would become better known, but it was *Destination Moon* that first put the genre on the map in the '50s.

By the end of 1950, *Destination Moon* had earned $1.3 million in film rentals, its studio's most successful film of the year.[107] However, the film's performance was damaged by Eagle-Lion's lack of access to certain first-run theaters, especially those in New York City. After a successful run at the Mayfair, *Destination Moon* was primed for a lucrative jaunt through the neighborhood theaters of the New York metropolitan area, owned by RKO and Loew's. But *Destination Moon* was shut out of the "prior-run nabes" of New York and found itself in the cheaper subsequent-run theaters. Claiming that their overall grosses were hurt by as much as 14 percent by these distribution restrictions, Eagle-Lion sued the eight major distributors and the Loew's and RKO theater chains, charging them with antitrust violations for conspiring to keep independent films from directly competing with their own.[108] According to *Variety*, the "boiling point" that initiated the lawsuit was *Destination Moon*'s inability to secure a run in the nabes despite its success on Broadway.[109]

In 1956 the U.S. District Court for the Southern District of New York dismissed the case, arguing that Eagle-Lion's attorneys had failed to prove the studio was the victim of a conspiracy to exclude its product. Writing the opinion, Judge Archie O. Dawson noted that the theater chain defendants prescreened as many as 129 of the 195 films released by Eagle-Lion from September 1946 to September 1950 and booked 85 of them. The films left unbooked were low-budget westerns, reissues, or foreign films, types of films that rarely played in neighborhood theaters. Dawson noted that of the eighty-five Eagle-Lion films booked by RKO and Loew's, only eight of them played at the top half of the double bill. This, along with the weak financial status of Eagle-Lion, suggested to the court that Eagle-Lion's films were simply inferior in quality. Furthermore, Eagle-Lion failed to call any witnesses, such as sales agents, who could testify that Eagle-Lion's films were treated unfairly.[110]

In 1957 the U.S. Court of Appeals sided with the original decision on a 2–1 vote; however, Chief Justice Charles Edward Clark offered a dissenting opinion that stated, in part, "To hold that this gigantic and complete monopoly does not reach the independent distributors, but leaves them free to compete with the big companies, does not make sense."[111] Today, of course, it is common knowledge among film historians that the majors and their associated theater chains did indeed conspire to favor their own product over those of independents. The fact that *Destination Moon* was not booked into the New York nabes despite a successful Broadway run, positive critical notices, and an elaborate nationwide marketing campaign suggests strongly that the RKO and Loew's chains were indeed discriminating against the independent distributor. At the same time, Eagle-Lion was a fledgling studio whose films were largely low budget and not comparable in production quality to those of the majors. *Destination Moon*, the highlight of Eagle-Lion's 1950 schedule, was a mere programmer. Putting aside distribution inequalities, Eagle-Lion simply did not have the capital to compete with the major studios in a marketplace that was shifting toward bigger-budgeted films. In 1951, Eagle-Lion president William C. MacMillen Jr. admitted that "middle-grade and lower-grade product just isn't doing the business."[112] Also, most of the films' box office rentals were still retained by the producer, rather than Eagle-Lion. For instance, the studio took a 26 percent distribution fee from *Destination Moon*'s earnings, which amounted to only $393,000.[113] Considering Eagle-Lion's sizable prints and advertising investment, it likely earned little or nothing from the film.

In April 1951 Robert Young shocked the industry by abruptly selling

Eagle-Lion to United Artists, which was looking for a quick influx of product while its own distribution schedule stabilized.[114] Despite its efforts to establish itself as a legitimate, A-level organization, Eagle-Lion was treated by exhibitors as little more than a glorified Poverty Row studio. Ironically, if the studio would have been content to produce cheap exploitation films for the subsequent-run market, it might have survived longer, as this market grew more lucrative as the decade progressed. Despite Eagle-Lion's ultimate fate, its efforts to carve out a place for itself in the marketplace led to one of the most iconic film cycles of the 1950s. Taking notice of *Destination Moon*'s success, Paramount signed George Pal to a producing deal in October 1950.[115] And the strategies employed by Eagle-Lion to legitimate *Destination Moon* and attract a general audience to an SF film would be quickly appropriated and adapted by other studios.

Realism and the Semidocumentary Mode in 1950s SF

Destination Moon's attention to scientific accuracy, crucial to its success, was part of a larger trend in Hollywood toward heightened authenticity. Drew Casper argues that the influence of "documentary realism" is a key characteristic of postwar American cinema, stretching across genres from adventure films like *King Solomon's Mines* (1950) to westerns such as *High Noon* (1950). For Casper, the turn toward realism encompassed everything from long-take, deep-focus cinematography to the use of more naturalistic makeup.[116] When publicizing *Destination Moon*, George Pal described his film as a "documentary" or "semi-documentary."[117] At the time, the "semidocumentary" label was applied by the industry to a wide variety of films. It could refer to a specific stylistic mode inspired by documentary filmmaking, or simply to a film with content that was considered more realistic than typical Hollywood glamour and artifice. *Destination Moon* falls into the latter category, as a film that is semidocumentary in content more than style; visually, the Technicolor, studio-bound film has little in common with the documentary filmmaking of the period. Ironically, as the SF genre moved away from the scientific realism of *Destination Moon* and toward the more outlandish SF/horror of the exploitation film, films would employ the semidocumentary-inspired visual style as a shorthand for authenticity.

The postwar semidocumentary style was anticipated by social-problem films of the 1930s and other antecedents but most directly reflects the mix of startling immediacy and didacticism of wartime newsreels and other documentaries. Its general characteristics, according to Thomas Schatz, include "objective voiceover narration, location shooting, use of non-actors, and little or no musical scoring."[118] Location shooting was facilitated by lightweight, portable equipment developed during the war, as well as high-speed lenses and film stock that enabled low-light shooting. Documentarian Louis de Rochemont, who worked on Fox's Movietone News as well as the *March of Time* newsreels, innovated the Hollywood semidocumentary with *The House on 92nd Street* (1945), an espionage film produced by de Rochemont for Twentieth Century-Fox. Typically, postwar semidocumentaries were procedurals that detailed each step of a criminal investigation. An authoritative, dispassionate voiceover (colloquially known as "the voice of God") provides exposition, lending an air of journalistic authenticity. The voiceover narration, use of real locations, and "torn from the headlines" scenarios function as "authenticating discourses" that differentiate semidocumentaries from typical Hollywood films.[119] These discourses foreground the heightened realism of the narrative and mark the semidocumentary form as "quality" filmmaking. Casper cites the increasingly sophisticated taste of movie audiences as a factor in the popularity of this new stylistic and narrative approach; after being exposed to war (or war coverage) for five years, audiences were less tolerant of the artificiality of sound stages and the typical glossy escapism of Hollywood product.[120]

Along with the aesthetic and cultural factors behind the semidocumentary movement were important economic determinants. William Lafferty argues that the semidocumentary mode was partly a response to increasingly limited studio space due to the rise of independent production, as well as rising labor and set construction costs in the postwar period.[121] Location shooting also allowed producers to avoid expensive studio overhead. While the original de Rochemont semidocumentaries were A films — *13 Rue Madeleine* (1946) cost $2 million, for instance — all the potential for cost cutting associated with semidocumentary shooting made the style especially attractive for low-budget filmmakers.[122] Location shooting was a way to avoid the cheap, claustrophobic look of a B film shot on sound stages; '50s exploitation film producer Arnold Laven notes that "the richest, most visual, effective sequences, production-wise, were those that were shot outdoors, where even a low budget film is in a sense on equal standing with the most high-budgeted pictures."[123] By appropriating an effective filmmaking mode from the majors and adapting it to their needs, low-budget filmmakers could give their films a sense of realism and legitimacy while keeping costs down.

The first SF film made fully within the semidocumentary style was *The Magnetic Monster*, a low-budget independent production released by United Artists in early 1953. The film was unusual for '50s SF in that it aimed for documentary realism in both style and content. At a time when SF was moving toward the pulp fantasy of alien invasions and rampaging monsters, producer Ivan Tors insisted on a realistic, adult tone rooted in contemporary scientific research. Like George Pal, Tors was a Hungarian immigrant; he worked as a staff writer at MGM from 1940 to 1945 before venturing into independent film production.[124] In the fall of 1952 Tors teamed up with actor Richard Carlson and screenwriter Curt Siodmak to form "A-Men Productions," which signed a three-film partial financing and distribution deal with United Artists.[125] The men planned to make a series of SF films centered on the "Atom-Men" of the "Office of Scientific Investigations" (OSI), a fictional government agency organized to combat the dangers of a postatomic world.

The Magnetic Monster places an SF concept within the semidocumentary police procedural format popularized by *Dragnet*, which premiered on the radio in 1949 and television in 1951. Richard Carlson does his best Jack Webb impression at the beginning of *The Magnetic Monster*, establishing the routinized, procedural qualities of the narrative with a first-person voiceover: "I reported for work as usual at 8:55 a.m. My name is Stewart, Jeff Stewart—class of '39 M.I.T., Boston, Mass." Carlson's narration also explicitly foregrounds the film's merger of the SF and police procedural genres: "A-Men are detectives with degrees in science. The criminals we seek are sometimes invisible to the human eye, like radiation from outer space or particles held prisoner deep in the heart of the atom." As with *Destination Moon*, the dramatic obstacles in Tors's films are scientific or technological. The "magnetic monster" is not an alien or giant insect, but rather an unstable radioactive element that expands rapidly, threatening to pull Earth off its axis.

Following semidocumentary convention, *The Magnetic Monster's* story line is structured around the investigative procedure of the scientists. In the opening minutes, OSI scientists are called to a hardware store where objects have inexplicably become magnetized; they use Geiger counters to track a dangerous radiation trail to a dying physicist who has been unwisely experimenting with a new element, "serranium." The OSI team takes a sample of the element, analyzes it with spectrographs and analog computers, and in the film's climax uses a giant underground power generator to overload the growing serranium "monster" with nine hundred volts of electricity, destroying it. In Tors's productions, rationality and the scientific method, rather than military force, win the day.

Visually, *The Magnetic Monster* was a typical low-budget effort, employing flat, high-key lighting and conventional camerawork that rarely rises above the functional. Although this look was a sizable departure from the more expressionistic, stylized cinematography of earlier crime semidocumentaries, it became the status quo for SF semidocumentaries, which were usually inexpensive exploitation films. The primary motivation for the prosaic visual style was economic: complicated lighting schemes and camera work were costly and impractical, given the films' minimal resources and limited shooting schedules of only a week or two. As SF film historian Bill Warren notes, "No worry about atmospheric lighting, just light everything more or less the same, and let shadows fall where they will."[126]

However, there were also artistic advantages to the spare look: first, it differentiated the new SF/horror films of the 1950s from the supernatural horror cycles of the past, which were currently out of fashion. Gloomy gothic foreboding, moonlight, and shadows, cliché by the early '50s, were replaced by the stark, indifferent light of rationality and technology, as superstition was supplanted by science. The flat style also communicated a dispassionate, documentary realism that, like the procedural narrative format itself, attempted to link the films with the values of quality and distinction associated with de Rochemont's more prestigious films. Most importantly, the style normalized the fantastic elements of the plot, giving the overall narrative a sense of uncanny plausibility. Vivian Sobchack writes: "What finally adds to our amazement is the camera's eerie and inhuman *lack* of amazement. The incongruence is accepted and contained with the utmost blandness by the camera, the camera which not only rejects the hysteria of motion and the emotionalism of angles but which faces the incongruence with such documentary coolness, such bizarre placidity, that one wonders at the implacability of its stare as much as one wonders at the subject of its gaze."[127]

In spite of its very slim $105,000 budget, *The Magnetic Monster* received generally favorable reviews and even a number of first-run, top-of-the-bill bookings, albeit usually in smaller theaters.[128] The film's serious tone impressed critics; additionally, some of *The Magnetic Monster*'s relative success may be attributed to its skillful incorporation of footage from the 1934 German SF film *Gold*. *Variety* noted that the shots from *Gold* were "blended in well and help give a touch of realism that's badly needed. Budget is an obviously modest one on this release."[129] Film editor Herbert L. Strock claimed that he was ordered to take over direction of *The Magnetic Monster* from screenwriter Curt Siodmak partly because the film was so reliant on stock footage, and therefore needed the guidance of an experienced editor.[130] As the *Variety* review suggests, the material from *Gold*, used to depict the enormous underground power generator featured in the climax, gives *The Magnetic Monster* a visual impact and sense of scale that it could not have otherwise afforded—essentially making a rather cheap film resemble a more expensive one.

Tors completed his OSI trilogy in 1954 with *Riders to the Stars* and *Gog*, and later that same year struck a deal with Ziv Television to produce an "adult-angled science fiction anthology" titled *Science Fiction Theater*. Just like Pal with *Destination Moon*, the creators of the show carefully distanced it from the juvenile pulp paradigm. Ziv president John L. Sinn told *Billboard* that *Science Fiction Theater* would avoid "bug-eyed monsters, men from Mars, and creatures from outer space."[131] And while *Science Fiction Theater* did occasionally dabble in stories about extraterrestrials, the show maintains a fairly sober tone. *Science Fiction Theater* was canceled in 1957, and Tors abandoned the genre, disgusted with what it had become. In 1958 he complained, "Science fiction has become an ugly word. They made it vulgar. They emphasized horror to such a degree that the scientific aspects have become secondary."[132] The intelligence and maturity that made Tors's SF films unique were also arguably their downfall; they could not compete with the more visceral thrills of exploitation films like *Tarantula*

(1955). Tors's films are also ridden with scientific jargon and too often fall into tedious didacticism, as scientists stop to discuss their research at length. Herbert L. Strock elaborates: "Tors had a great intrigue for the *Scientific American* magazine, he became overly talky in what he wanted, and you were stuck with that. . . . He wanted that 'science fact' slammed into the pictures, and that's the way we had to do it."[133] Tors turned his attention from outer space to the ocean, producing famous aquatic television series like *Sea Hunt* (syndicated, 1958–1961) and *Flipper* (NBC, 1964–1968).

As the plots of SF films grew more fantastic, "documentary realism" became even more crucial, serving as a countermeasure that assisted the audience in its suspension of disbelief. This was particularly important for major studio A films, which, like *Destination Moon*, sought to attract a wide general audience. Along with the documentary influence and emphasis on verisimilitude apparent in the films themselves, promotional discourse such as press books and interviews underscore just how important this strategy was to the major studios. A key example is Twentieth Century-Fox's *The Day the Earth Stood Still* (1951), a $995,000 A film in which an alien lands a flying saucer on the National Mall in Washington, D.C., and exhorts Earth's political leaders to cease nuclear proliferation.[134] As a "message film," *The Day the Earth Stood Still* was squarely in the social-problem tradition that Fox had fostered since the end of the war, with titles like *Gentleman's Agreement* (1947).

In order for its political message to be taken seriously, *The Day the Earth Stood Still* had to be set squarely in a plausible facsimile of 1951 America, from its political structure to the limits of its scientific knowledge. In an interview with the *Los Angeles Times*, producer Julius Blaustein asserted, "Everything in the picture will really be an extension of known facts."[135] Considering the film features a scene where a humanoid alien is revived from the dead by a giant robot, Blaustein could reasonably be accused of exaggeration. Yet, working within the constraints of its fantastic story line, *The Day the Earth Stood Still* strives for verisimilitude. During preproduction, Twentieth Century-Fox studio head Darryl F. Zanuck recommended that the opening scenes "be dramatized like the opening of a documentary film" in order to immediately establish a realistic tone.[136] While it does not employ the procedural semidocumentary format of *The Magnetic Monster* or de Rochemont's earlier films for Fox,

The Day the Earth Stood Still does take pains to situate its events within an accurate representation of the real Washington, D.C. The second unit picked up extensive location shots of landmarks like the Lincoln Memorial, and real journalists like Elmer Davis and Drew Pearson appeared in cameos, reporting the landing of the flying saucer near the White House. The casting of well-known media personalities added authenticity and respectability to the project.

George Pal's SF A films for Paramount, discussed more thoroughly in the next chapter, continued the producer's commitment to verisimilitude begun with *Destination Moon*, even as they contained much more sensational narrative elements. Scenes in the apocalyptic *When Worlds Collide* (1951) that occur in the United Nations building were intended, according to director Rudolph Maté, to have "an almost newsreel quality." He continues, "I tried to be as realistic as I could; the story is so incredible that if the audience doesn't believe every word it won't believe anything."[137] Promotional materials affirm this attitude. The press book for *When Worlds Collide* boasts: "IT COULD HAPPEN . . . After special previews for men who know their stars and rockets best, the outstanding scientific authorities praised the film's accuracy and realism."[138] For *The War of the Worlds* (1953), Pal stated that he and his collaborators "decided we should do as much as we could to make the audience feel that they're actually witnessing an attack and that the Martians are really here."[139] Likewise, in a 1951 studio meeting at Paramount, director Byron Haskin described *The War of the Worlds* as "a documentary of Martians landing all around."[140]

As these examples demonstrate, documentary realism was a priority for the major studios as they, like Eagle-Lion, sought to legitimate their big-budget SF films and attract a wide audience. Yet, as with *Destination Moon*, "documentary" was defined more in terms of narrative than style. Although the gritty expressionism of *The Day the Earth Stood Still*, typical of Fox's social-problem films, connotes semidocumentary realism, *When Worlds Collide* and *The War of the Worlds* are shot in the colorful Paramount house style and rely more on a narrative emphasis on governmental and military procedure to add authenticity. Likewise, Warner Bros.' giant-ant film *Them!* (1954) is structured as a police procedural but was originally planned as a 3-D, color spectacular before its budget was slashed just as production began.[141]

As we have seen with *The Magnetic Monster*, it was low-budget SF filmmaking that was, primarily out of economic necessity, motivated to more aggressively exploit the semidocumentary style. However, unlike that film, most low-budget SF efforts used authenticating strategies in a clumsy or cynical fashion. The appeal to authority reaches the point of absurdity in Universal-International's *The Mole People* (1956), which opens with a four-and-a-half-minute on-camera introduction by Dr. Frank C. Baxter, professor of English at the University of Southern California. Standing at a globe, Professor Baxter speaks extemporaneously about the history of the "hollow earth" legend around which the film bases its story line, citing Dante and the epic of Gilgamesh. Baxter retains some semblance of credibility by not trying to claim the film's underground civilization of albinos is literally true; but his ludicrous efforts at legitimating this ridiculous (if entertaining) exploitation film demonstrate how the semidocumentary mode had decayed into travesty by the mid-1950s.

Perhaps the biggest culprit behind the corruption of the semidocumentary was the overuse of stock footage. Reliance on stock footage was a common cost-saving strategy for low-budget cinema of all kinds, including B movies and serials. When used in concert with "voice of God" narration, stock footage could expand the narrative and visual scope of a film, cheaply progress the narrative, and interject a sense of authenticity. The stock footage used in low-budget exploitation SF is often documentary in nature; for example, *The Beast from 20,000 Fathoms* incorporates footage of actual atomic bomb tests into its opening scenes. Here the stock footage functions to draw a connection between external reality and the fantasy of the film's narrative. Patrick Lucanio argues that the documentary footage "serves as the reference point for the real world . . . its repetition throughout the film [makes] it a constant reminder that the film is an extrapolation from the known world."[142] Military stock footage, very common in SF exploitation films of the 1950s, works with the "voice of God" narration to project a sense of military power and efficiency.

Stock footage also served a more utilitarian function: it was a cheap way to pad a low-budget film's running time. In 1955, Universal-International producer William Alland noted that Columbia's SF exploitation films were just as successful as U-I's, even though, at the time, Columbia's were much cheaper. Alland attributed this disparity in budgets partly to Columbia's

The Deadly Mantis (Universal-International, 1957) cut costs by intercutting stock footage of jets firing rockets with model shots of the flying creature.

use of stock footage in films like *It Came from beneath the Sea* (1955).[143] Universal responded by slashing the budgets of its exploitation films and increasing the use of stock footage. Arguably the weakest of Universal's SF films, *The Deadly Mantis* (1957), produced by Alland, manages to fill fifteen and a half minutes of its seventy-eight-minute run time with stock footage. The mantis in question is able to fly from the Arctic Circle to the eastern coast of the United States, an ability that motivates the use of an extraordinary amount of aircraft-related stock footage, some of which is intercut with model shots of the mantis in flight. By expanding the scope of action to involve the U.S. Air Force, *The Deadly Mantis* breaks from the usual insular claustrophobia that often plagues traditional B-pictures. However, the use of stock footage becomes excessive; particular stock shots are repeated several times, diluting their impact, and the film includes a long digression about the Air Force Ground Observer Corps, the military entity that initially spots the mantis. The stock footage also tends to be substantially degraded in quality, in contrast to the rest of the film, which only makes its overuse more obvious. As Blair Davis notes, "The use of stock shots in middle- and low-end Bs is often quite jarring because of their failure to convincingly suture the stock footage into the film."[144]

By the late 1950s, the semidocumentary style had become cliché, visible to some extent in most low-budget SF films. In Ivan Tors's OSI trilogy, the style fit the narrative approach, which was respectful of scientific fact. With the typical exploitation film, rooted in pulp SF and horror, the style is often little more than a feeble effort to rehabilitate an absurd story line by cynically appropriating elements of documentary form or other authenticating discourses. This appropriation is an example of the parasitic dimension of exploitation filmmaking; beginning in the 1930s with B-movie knockoffs of A-level hits, low-budget filmmakers frequently sought to exploit the success of big-budget films through mimicry. However, the relationship between the major studios and smaller independents was complex and symbiotic; *Destination Moon* is one key example of an independent film sparking a trend in which the majors would later participate. And, as the '50s continued and the majors struggled to find a place for SF in the traditional adult market, independent exploitation studios would offer a different, more lucrative path.

2

THE PULP PARADOX

///

SF Film of the 1950s

Destination Moon may have kicked off the 1950s SF film boom, but its approach to the genre was something of a dead end, commercially. Placed within the context of the rest of '50s SF, *Destination Moon* seems almost incomplete in its lack of pulp elements. One might ask, "They go to the moon, and that's it? Where are the aliens?" Such was the easy marketability of pulp SF tropes that it became almost impossible to find films in the 1950s (Ivan Tors aside) that did not employ them. This was the case across all budget categories, although with larger budgets came greater box office expectations and thus a larger target audience. Attracting this larger audience proved to be a challenge for the major studios as they produced expensive SF films for the general first-run market in the early-to-mid-1950s. *Destination Moon* had been a "class" production, tied closely to legitimate scientific speculation. Adding flying saucers and little green men to the equation threatened to mark the films as unworthy of attention by adult moviegoers, even as those same elements aided in exploitation. The majors were unable to resolve this "pulp paradox," as they saw low-budget exploitation films perform just as well or better at the box office. In response, the majors ceased big-budget SF production for a time. Mid-budget programmers were more successful; Universal-

International, lacking the resources of the larger studies, managed to secure a first-run audience for its SF/horror programmers by exploiting new exhibition technologies like 3-D.

Ultimately, however, the low-budget exploitation film was the SF success story of the 1950s. Independent studios working with tiny budgets had no need to cater to the middlebrow tastes of the average moviegoer —they instead appealed to teenagers by exaggerating the lurid aspects of their films. Independent exploitation filmmaking emerged as a kind of alternative sub-industry in the '50s, with its origins at a major studio (Columbia) but brought to its apex by the independent American International Pictures. Exploitation films were parasitic upon the majors, but also hugely influential upon them—not only at the end of the '50s when the majors began distributing their own exploitation films, but in the decades to follow as well.

The Problem of the 1950s SF A Film

The enduring popularity and historical prominence of the SF A films released by the major Hollywood studios from 1951 to 1956 belie their small number. Only six such films were produced in all: Paramount's *When Worlds Collide* (1951), *The War of the Worlds* (1953), and *Conquest of Space* (1955); Twentieth Century-Fox's *The Day the Earth Stood Still* (1951); RKO's *The Thing from Another World* (1951); and MGM's *Forbidden Planet* (1956). As discussed in chapter 1, the SF genre was ideally suited to the majors' production strategies in the '50s, particularly the emphasis on spectacle and topicality. Furthermore, SF represented serious profit potential; *Destination Moon* had grossed nearly three times its production cost. With the majors' greater resources and access to first-run theaters, their own SF films stood to do even better.

Although the six movies listed above are sometimes described by critics and scholars as "B films," this is incorrect if one is using an industrial definition. Their budgets of between $1 million and $2 million place them firmly within the price range of the typical A feature of the period.[1] As they were about twice as expensive as *Destination Moon*, it was even more crucial for these films to separate themselves from the juvenile SF paradigm and attract a general audience. *Destination Moon*'s $1.3 million in rentals was very good for a relatively inexpensive film but would be much less impressive for a studio A picture. To that end, the majors both reproduced and elaborated upon the strategies used by Eagle-Lion to position *Destination Moon* as a major mainstream release, such as the emphasis on scientific realism, discussed earlier, and colorful spectacle.

Differentiation from the niche, pulp SF model was an especially pressing concern when the majors entered SF film production in 1951, because Poverty Row studios had already begun to release their own attempts at the genre. Aside from *The Flying Saucer* (1950), an espionage film that was only marginally SF, the first low-budget SF film of the decade was *Rocketship X-M* (1950), a $94,000 quickie that independent producer-distributor Robert Lippert rushed into production after Eagle-Lion announced *Destination Moon.*[2] Despite Eagle-Lion's head start, the eleven-day shooting schedule of *X-M* allowed it to reach theaters first, undercutting the novelty of George Pal's more expensive production. A piqued Eagle-Lion issued a press release titled "A Slight Case of Mistaken Identity" that reiterated the difference in budget, attention to scientific accuracy, and overall prestige between the two films, making clear that "DESTINATION MOON was the FIRST picture to be made on the exciting subject of planetary exploration."[3]

It is impossible to judge precisely the extent to which *Rocketship X-M* damaged *Destination Moon*'s box office performance, but Lippert's film was extraordinarily successful for its budget category, earning nearly $650,000 in the domestic market.[4] Poverty Row studio Monogram followed *X-M* with the similar *Flight to Mars* (1951), an early Walter Mirisch production that used the inexpensive two-strip Cinecolor process to add production value to a very low-budget effort. Although these films were put into production to capitalize on *Destination Moon*, they are more firmly in the pulp SF tradition and less in the realistic style of the Eagle-Lion film. While the first half of *Rocketship X-M* is very similar in scenario to *Destination Moon* and contains the same lengthy scientific exposition, it diverges sharply from Pal's film when the titular lunar spacecraft (*X-pedition Moon*) is thrown off-course to Mars, where the crew is attacked by the troglodytic survivors of a Martian nuclear war. *Flight to Mars* is even more indebted to the pulps; its Mars is not a postatomic wasteland, but home to a vast underground civilization. The human

Martians with their Greco-Roman tunics and pseudoscientific technologies recall the outlandish space fantasy of *Flash Gordon* rather than *Destination Moon*. Just like early television shows such as *Captain Video*, these films threatened to permanently link SF with low-budget, juvenile fantasy and harm SF's wider potential as an A genre. Therefore, it was crucial for the majors to clearly distinguish their SF films from those produced by Monogram and similar studios.

To stake a claim for SF as a viable A genre, the major studios needed to exploit the fundamental difference between A and B filmmaking—which was, of course, budget. If, as I argued in the previous chapter, SF filmmaking is acutely concerned with establishing a sense of verisimilitude, A films are much better positioned to achieve this than low-budget films, forced as they were to rely on cost-cutting measures like the use of stock footage. The creation of expansive, believable science fictional environments was tied to the SF A film's primary strategy of differentiation: the showcasing of extraordinary spectacle that neither Poverty Row nor television could hope to replicate. One key strategy employed by George Pal for his first two films at Paramount was the foregrounding of immense, global disaster. Stephen Keane contends that the SF disaster film of the 1950s represents a new, more potent and visceral approach to spectacle when compared to the detached splendor of contemporary epics like *Quo Vadis* (1951).[5] Rather than simply gazing at the magnificence of the ancient world, the SF disaster film invites the spectator to become immersed in the destruction.

The first SF disaster film of the decade was *When Worlds Collide*, Pal's follow-up to *Destination Moon*, directed by Rudolph Maté. In 1949 Pal had purchased the rights to the 1933 source novel from Paramount, which had wanted Cecil B. DeMille to shoot an adaptation in the mid-1930s.[6] The plot concerns the efforts of scientists to escape into space before Earth is destroyed by a collision with a wayward star. At first Pal struggled to raise interest in the property, but after the success of *Destination Moon* he was signed to a producing contract with Paramount, which put him in the position of selling the studio's own *When Worlds Collide* property back to them for a profit.[7] Major studio filmmaking suited Pal for several reasons. First and foremost, a major like Paramount could provide far greater financing than an independent, and had unimpeded access to first-run theaters. Not

Paramount special effects artist Gordon Jennings used miniatures and composite photography to create the flooding of New York City in *When Worlds Collide* (Paramount, 1951).

only could Pal's films be more expensive, but they could also be potentially much more profitable. Despite *Destination Moon*'s success, Pal did not make money on the film, partly because his financial interests were cross-collateralized against the failed *Great Rupert*.[8] With his Paramount deal, Pal was ensured a steady salary — although he did not receive profit participation in his productions, which were fully financed by the studio.[9]

Importantly, Pal also had access to Paramount's special effects unit. Lee Zavitz's effects work on *Destination Moon*, although ingenious, was limited by budget and had to be created from scratch. Paramount had an existing infrastructure and an experienced crew led by Oscar-winner Gordon Jennings, in his third decade at Paramount and responsible for the effects in DeMille's *Samson and Delilah* (1949), among dozens of other films. The scenario of *When Worlds Collide* provided ample opportunity for elaborate scenes of destruction; the key effects sequence was the flooding of downtown New York City, convincingly accomplished with miniatures, superimposition, and matte paintings.[10] Paramount was somewhat cautious with the film's budget; at $875,000, it was on the low side for the studio's A features.[11] But this is apparent only intermittently, as when the destruction of Earth is reduced to a quick flash seen through a rocket ship's viewing screen. *When Worlds Collide* was a solid performer for Paramount, its $1.6 million in rentals slightly surpassing those of *Destination Moon*.[12] After the release of *When Worlds Collide*, Paramount renewed Pal's option for another year.[13] The short length of the contract suggests skepticism on the part of the studio as to the long-term viability of Pal's kind of project, despite the producer's promising track record.

Pal's next film, an adaptation of H. G. Wells's 1898 novel *The War of the Worlds*, is the pinnacle of 1950s SF disaster filmmaking. This was Pal's highest-profile property yet; not only was Wells widely read, but the story had achieved international notoriety as a result of Orson Welles's infamous Halloween 1938 broadcast, which fooled some listeners into believing that a real Martian invasion was imminent.[14] Once again, decades earlier Paramount had secured the rights to the novel as a potential project for DeMille, and Sergei Eisenstein had also expressed interest in adapting the novel during his short-lived tenure with Paramount in 1930.[15] By 1952 the novel's combination of SF and global disaster made it an obvious choice to be Pal's second film for Paramount. Although the studio refused to let the producer shoot the final reel in 3-D (likely owing to budget overruns), the film, directed by Byron Haskin, remains one of the most visually stunning SF pictures of the decade.[16] Because *The War of the Worlds* was produced at twice the budget of *When Worlds Collide*, its special effects were far more elaborate.[17] For instance, its models and miniatures were built to a larger scale and with greater detail than in Pal's earlier films. The final result was widely praised in the trade press, and Gordon Jennings won an Academy Award for his effects work.[18]

As with Pal's previous efforts, the Technicolor cinematography was another key selling point. *The War of the Worlds* was shot by famed cinematographer George Barnes, who had won an Oscar for Hitchcock's atmospheric, black-and-white *Rebecca* (1940) but who also specialized in colorful Paramount epics like *Samson and Delilah* and *The Greatest Show on Earth* (1952). The film immediately foregrounds its color cinematography in its title sequence, which begins with black-and-white newsreel footage, only for bright red title credits to suddenly spring onto the screen.

The opening scenes use a more restrained, naturalistic color scheme, but the otherworldly nature of the alien invaders allow the filmmakers to eventually depart from this and indulge in more unusual, vivid colors. By the movie's conclusion, when the aliens have reduced Los Angeles to rubble, the screen is flush with the reds of bonfires and the bright greens of the Martians' destructive rays. In a climactic scene, pink light pours from the Martian ship as a pulsating green alien hand reaches out, flailing in its death throes. *The War of the Worlds* ended up costing $1.7 million, but brought in $2 million in domestic rentals, making it Pal's biggest hit yet.[19]

Opulent special effects were one key strategy of legitimation; the majors also differentiated their SF films through the relative intelligence and sophistication of their narratives when compared to low-budget pulp SF. Because the studios needed adult moviegoers to take SF just as seriously as any other dramatic genre, each film needed to exude a sense of maturity and class. Literary adaptations like *The War of the Worlds* were desirable; H. G. Wells was a respected author and political figure. Even better was William Shakespeare, whose play *The Tempest* provided a basic plot outline for 1956's *Forbidden Planet*.[20] Instead of the sorcerer Prospero and his virgin daughter Miranda exiled on a deserted island, the scientist Dr. Morbius and his virgin daughter Altaira are stranded on the deserted planet Altair IV, where a rescue team disturbs their strange, hermetic existence. Alongside the Shakespearean analogues, pop-Freudianism runs through the film; Morbius's use of ancient alien technology inadvertently creates a violent "monster from the id," a manifestation of his repressed jealousy and rage over the rescue team's romantic interest in Altaira. MGM, the Tiffany's of the major studios, had long avoided the SF genre. But Irving Block and Allen Alder's script must have been sufficiently erudite to appeal to studio head Dore Schary, who claimed that "up until that time, I had seen virtually nothing even close to what we thought could be the studio's first science fiction entry."[21] The intellectual pretensions of *Forbidden Planet* allowed it to transcend the average SF picture and better fit MGM's long tradition of middlebrow classicism.

A final literary source was the Bible, obviously the ultimate in prestige and respectability in 1950s America. George Pal's films in particular are full of Christian meaning, assuring audiences that God holds dominion over the entire universe. In case *When Worlds Collide*'s parallels to the biblical Noah story were too subtle, the film opens with a manuscript page quoting the book of Genesis: "And God said unto Noah, The end of all flesh is come before me; for the Earth is filled with violence through them; and behold, I will destroy them with the Earth." Through the character of the selfish industrialist Stanton, who dies as the worlds collide, the film suggests that humankind is again being punished for its base egoism. *When Worlds Collide* ends with the sounds of a heavenly choir as the young, earnest romantic leads, representing the new Adam and Eve, journey down the landing ramp to their new planet. The nondiegetic choir would recur in *The War of the Worlds*, an even more overtly religious film than its predecessor. The story retains Wells's original ending, in which the Martians are felled by bacteria harmless to humans, but departs from Wells by attributing this conclusion to divine intervention. In the film the survivors of the Martian attack on Los Angeles have retreated to a nearby cathedral for sanctuary. As they pray, the alien warships fall from the sky. The sounds of the choir swell over the film's final shot . . . of a cathedral, still standing amid the debris. While the film's desire to foreground the deity can be considered a betrayal of the original novel's antipathy toward organized religion, inclusion of religious themes adds gravitas to the fantastic narrative, as well as reaffirming the dominant American ideology for its mainstream audiences.

The major-studio SF film could also communicate its refinement by directly (as opposed to allegorically) engaging with sociopolitical issues. The best example of this strategy is *The Day the Earth Stood Still*, described by the *Motion Picture Herald* as "graduat[ing] that type of screen entertainment out of the pulp magazine field and into the slick paper class."[22] The film depicts America as xenophobic, bellicose, and paranoid, as the visiting alien Klaatu is met with hostility at nearly ever turn. *The Day the Earth Stood Still* concludes with Klaatu chiding world leaders for their immature and shortsighted militarism. The film's pacifist message appealed to Darryl Zanuck, who had over the course of his long career cultivated a reputation as a producer of social-problem films like *The Grapes of Wrath* (1940) and *Gentleman's Agreement* (1947). However, this type of direct engagement with important political issues was largely abandoned as part of a wider industrial trend away from films with explicitly liberal themes. By 1951, anticommunist fervor was in full force; in March the House

Committee on Un-American Activities had resumed its interrogation of Hollywood employees, begun in 1947. The film industry faced strong government pressure to avoid themes and topics that could be construed as "anti-American," and creative personnel faced blacklisting if they were even slightly implicated in radical activity. For its part, *The Day the Earth Stood Still* was cited as a subversive text by HUAC.[23] Klaatu's call for a single, unified ruling body was interpreted as implicit support for a strong United Nations, the legitimacy and value of which were currently being challenged by right-wing politicos.

After *The Day the Earth Stood Still*, explicitly political SF was largely absent from American screens in the 1950s unless it was clearly anticommunist — as in *Red Planet Mars* (1952), in which God sends messages to Earth from the Red Planet, eventually leading to the embrace of Christianity in the Soviet Union. More common was political allegory — a form particularly suited to SF, which could safely couch political commentary in the guise of escapist futuristic fantasy. In many instances, however, the political message is not clear-cut. For instance, screenwriter Ben Hecht contributed to Howard Hawks's *The Thing from Another World*, using the film as "an effective allegorical vehicle with which to poke fun at growing Cold War paranoia about Communism."[24] However, the film was typically understood by contemporary critics as an example of anticommunist fervor, with the violent, relentless, amoral Thing as a surrogate for Soviet troops, and the film's last line — "Watch the skies!" — advocating American vigilance against Communist attack.[25] Likewise, in his study of *Invasion of the Body Snatchers*, scholar Al LaValley has shown how the collaborative process among creative personnel with different political stances can lead to texts that lend themselves to multiple, sometimes contradictory interpretations.[26] *Body Snatchers* can be read as an anticommunist allegory that warns Americans to beware of the infiltration of emotionless, collectivist "pod people," or conversely, as a critique of McCarthyist conformity.[27] Regardless of the different meanings derived from these films, it is clear that some filmmakers understood SF allegory as a productive way to deal with contemporary issues without attracting unwanted scrutiny. It would not be until the late 1960s that the clandestine politics of allegory would be replaced by more overt sociopolitical content.

Another characteristic that separates the SF A films from other SF films of the period is the greater attention paid to developing characters and their relationships. Even *Destination Moon*, the progenitor of the SF A-film cycle, is fairly indifferent to characterization. Aside from Dick Wesson's comic-relief mechanic, the script makes little effort to distinguish among the lead characters. The drama that propels the narrative is based not on character relationships or arcs, but rather the solving of technological problems. Only the film's climax contains a touch of interpersonal conflict, as the men must decide who stays behind so the damaged rocket ship can return to Earth — but even here, the conflict is essentially a technical one that is solved using scientific ingenuity (one of the astronaut's spacesuits is ditched).

The lack of attention paid to character is partly a result of the semi-documentary, procedural nature of the narrative. In *Dragnet*, Joe Friday serves as the dispassionate embodiment of law enforcement, and his personal life and feelings are irrelevant to the cases he investigates. Likewise, *Destination Moon*'s Jim Barnes, Dr. Charles Cargraves, and General Thayer are not intended to be complex characters but rather simple representatives of American industry, science, and the military, respectively. At the same time, *Destination Moon* reflects a B film's usual emphasis on action over character. Interpersonal relationships and character arcs are present in most B films; they simply tend to be perfunctory, formulaic, and strongly subordinated to the primary, action-oriented plotline. Romance plots appear regularly, as though obligatory, but are rarely given the attention necessary to ensure their emotional effectiveness. The SF exploitation film *Attack of the Crab Monsters* (1957), directed by Roger Corman, is representative. While trapped on a remote island populated with giant telepathic crabs, engineer Hank flirts with biologist Martha, who is currently dating her work partner Dale. This love triangle is far from an integral part of the narrative; the first flirtation occurs at the forty-eight-minute mark in a sixty-three-minute film and seems introduced only to add some last-minute emotional weight to the film's conclusion, when Hank sacrifices himself to destroy the crabs.

In contrast, the love triangle between pilot Dave Randall, Joyce Hendron, and her boyfriend Tony Drake in *When Worlds Collide* is introduced early in the plot and is a key story line throughout. Upon Pal's moving to Paramount, his productions immediately exhibited a much stronger emphasis on characterization. Far from being a straightforward exercise in spectacle or a cold scientific tract, *When Worlds Collide* addresses the human cost of Armageddon. As she faces the end of the world, Joyce's interest in the staid Tony wanes and she begins to prefer the more spontaneous, exciting Dave. A number of scenes develop this conflict: a drunken Dave flirts with Joyce just as Tony proposes to her; Joyce confesses her mixed emotions to her father; and a jealous Tony nearly abandons Dave in the middle of a disaster zone. Eventually, Tony selflessly arranges it so that Joyce and Dave can be together on the rocket ship that flees Earth. Aside from its apocalyptic particulars, the film's love-triangle plotline is not blindingly original, yet it is considerably more developed and substantial than the throwaway romances of the typical "exploitation market" B film. Critics noticed, with the *Hollywood Reporter* pointing out that the film "goes a step further than its predecessor [*Destination Moon*] in that Pal has gone to considerable lengths to achieve a real, believable personal story line that unfolds dramatically against the fascinating background of a world whose very existence is threatened by an impending collision with another planet."[28]

Other critics, however, actually criticized *When Worlds Collide*'s emphasis on romance. *Variety* claimed that the "love story digression detracts instead of adds to film's overall audience impact."[29] Likewise, the *New York Times* took Pal to task for allowing "a considerable amount of romance to have extravagant play."[30] These critics imply an incompatibility between the SF and romantic story lines, that despite its relatively skillful integration into the larger narrative, the love triangle of *When Worlds Collide* was ultimately unnecessary and feeble compared to the epic disaster story. This mixed feedback illustrates the conflicting expectations for the SF A film of the 1950s and a tension between SF genre conventions and the existing storytelling norms of Hollywood A films. On one hand, romantic story lines were believed to broaden the appeal of an SF film beyond the usual genre crowd; in 1956 the *Los Angeles Times* noted that the romantic plot in *Forbidden Planet* was "presented partially as a concession to 'human' interest and box office."[31] Here, while romance is seen as an advantage at the box office, it is also an aesthetic liability. The implication is that the overemphasis on character relationships is a distraction from the film's primary appeal of SF spectacle.

George Pal in particular seemed to chafe against what he considered to be the obligatory inclusion of romantic plots. According to Pal, Paramount VP of production Don Hartman, best known for writing several of the Hope and Crosby "Road" pictures, felt that a greater emphasis on romance would ensure a larger box office take for *The War of the Worlds*.[32] In 1953 an apologetic Pal defended himself to SF fans in *Astounding Science Fiction*: "In the film business you have to be practical. No one is less interested in doing routine boy meets girl stories than I. But a boy-and-girl theme is necessary . . . audiences want it."[33] The problems with the studio continued with Pal's *The Naked Jungle* (1954), ostensibly a "killer ant" action picture that became under the auspices of Paramount a turgid mail-order-bride melodrama.[34] Pal's final film for Paramount, *Conquest of Space* (1955), is in some respects the opposite of *Destination Moon*, in that the space exploration plotline becomes bogged down by a subplot concerning a dysfunctional father-son relationship. The father, the commander of a mission to Mars, gradually goes insane with religious fervor and becomes convinced that travel to other planets is against God's law. Eventually he is accidentally shot after attempting to sabotage the mission. *Variety* panned the film for its "talky" and "stodgily developed" script.[35]

By emphasizing character development and conflict, studios like Paramount were attempting to expand the audience for their SF films and differentiate them from low-budget SF films and television, whose simple, archetypal characters were often little more than ciphers moving through the plot. However, the largely negative reaction to this focus on characterization among filmmakers, fans, and critics suggests that it was considered little more than a gratuitous diversion from the film's "true" purpose, its genre appeal. This attitude was reinforced by the SF A films' avoidance of top stars, who would presumably be showcased via character-driven story lines. As film reviewers rarely failed to point out, the special effects were the stars, not the actors.[36] In 1954 George Pal explained, "That's why none of my pictures has a big name star. Special effects and color are my stars."[37] The use of inexpensive unknowns freed up money that could be spent on effects — for instance, the entire cast of *The War of the Worlds* cost Paramount only about $76,000,[38] at a time when single stars demanded $100,000 or more.[39] Because the SF genre was defined at the time by spectacle and the novelty of its concepts, Paramount clearly believed that adding a major star would only increase a film's budget needlessly without guaranteeing a larger audience. It did not help that major actors were reluctant to sign onto an SF picture because of the genre's poor reputation. Even minor ingénues such as Universal's Julie Adams were unhappy to be cast in films like 1954's *Creature from the Black Lagoon*.[40]

Another key decision faced by the majors as they dabbled in SF A production was the extent to which they would employ pulp SF tropes in their marketing materials and in the films themselves. *Destination Moon*'s success in the mainstream market was predicated to a large extent on its strict adherence to realism and its avoidance of typical SF iconography like aliens, robots, and flying saucers. But these qualities also rendered the film somewhat dull and dramatically inert when compared to the pulpier SF films to follow. Even *Rocketship X-M*, with its postapocalyptic Martians, is a much livelier film than Pal's stolid production. The success of *Destination Moon* was rooted in its spectacle and sheer novelty more than the quality of its threadbare drama. That novelty would not exist for subsequent films. In order to liven up the *Destination Moon* model, the majors integrated into their SF films pulp elements that surely would have appalled Robert A. Heinlein. For instance, despite the sophistication of their scripts, both *The Day the Earth Stood Still* and *Forbidden Planet* are rooted in space opera tropes like flying saucers and robots. Even George Pal quickly rejected the realistic approach of his first SF film for the alien heat rays and little green men of *The War of the Worlds*.

Ironically, the highest-grossing of the six SF A films of the period was the one that unabashedly embraced the genre's most lurid qualities: *The Thing from Another World* (1951), produced by Howard Hawks. *The Thing* was part of a three-picture deal between Hawks and RKO, wherein Hawks would direct two of the films and produce a third, cheaper film. For the final film Hawks bought the rights to John W. Campbell's 1938 pulp story "Who Goes There?," in which a group of Arctic scientists and military personnel battle a shape-shifting alien menace. Hawks selected editor Christian Nyby to direct, although accounts from the cast and crew suggest that Hawks himself was in firm control of the film's production.[41] By giving Nyby credit, Hawks was able to dabble in a genre not usually associated with directors of his stature.

As opposed to someone like George Pal, Hawks seems to have had little interest in making anything other than a straightforward horror film in the exploitation tradition, albeit a rather expensive one at $1.26 million.[42] The earnest scientific speculation, realism, and optimism of *Destination Moon* are replaced in *The Thing* by a horror plot that takes a fearful, suspicious attitude toward the possibility of extraterrestrial life. The alien visitor of Hawks's film is not the reasonable, enlightened intellectual of *The Day the Earth Stood Still*, released the same year; instead, "the thing" is an unremittingly hostile aggressor that must be met with deadly force, rather than a meeting of the minds. Unlike Pal's films, which seem more expensive than their relatively small budgets, *The Thing* manages to look cheaper than it actually was. There are no star performers, the special effects are limited, and the story necessitated only a handful of modest sets and props. Nevertheless, *The Thing* was the second-highest-grossing film of May 1951 and eventually earned about $2 million in domestic rentals.[43]

The success of *The Thing* contributed to a shift in the genre's development in the 1950s, particularly in the low-budget realm. Dozens, if not hundreds, of low-budget SF films would bear the influence of *The Thing*'s blend of SF and horror. Previous SF/horror films were usually mad scientist tales, whereas *The Thing* derives its terror from the threat of alien attack. Compared to an invasion film like *The War of the Worlds*, *The Thing* is more indebted to the conventions of classical horror, which elicits fear by setting its narrative in shadowy, confined spaces. Low-budget filmmakers could more easily reproduce *The Thing*'s small-scale shocks than the epic spectacle of Pal's productions. Some saw the widespread influence of Hawks's production as detrimental to the SF genre. In 1959 critic Richard Hodgens referred to *The Thing* as "the great villain" that moved SF cinema away from intelligent speculation and toward the primitive, irrational intolerance of the horror film.[44]

The use of pulp tropes in films like *The Thing* facilitated exploitation, as attention-grabbing SF iconography could be used in advertising materials. The sensational qualities of SF A films were often exaggerated in their promotional campaigns; the posters for both *The Day the Earth Stood Still* and *Forbidden Planet* feature a menacing robot clutching a beautiful woman in its arms, an image that hardly gives an accurate sense of the somber, adult tone of either film. The brief scene in *The Day the Earth*

AUTHOR'S COLLECTION

The sensational pulp iconography of this promotional poster for *Forbidden Planet* (MGM, 1956), using imagery that was not in the film, was meant to attract audiences but may have discouraged adults from attending.

Stood Still in which Gort carries actress Patricia Neal lacks the violent, horrific connotation of the poster. And *Forbidden Planet* does not even contain a scene where (the relatively innocuous) Robby the Robot holds an unconscious Altaira (Anne Francis). One exhibitor complained in *Boxoffice* about *Forbidden Planet*: "Misleading advertising, as usual."[45]

Yet there were also disadvantages to playing up the more sensational aspects of the genre. The majors faced the pulp paradox: while pulp iconography might be effective in attracting spectators looking for SF/horror thrills, the activation of these tropes also signaled to general audiences that the film was just another cheap exploitation film for kids. The majors, caught between trying to sell their SF A films and trying to represent them as sophisticated adult entertainment, were left with films that contain a mixture of competing appeals. Ultimately the SF A films were short-lived in the 1950s because, on the whole, they performed no better at the box office than the much cheaper SF exploitation films. For instance, in 1953 *The War of the Worlds* was slightly outgrossed by Warner Bros.' exploitation film *The Beast from 20,000 Fathoms* (1953), which was made for approximately one-tenth the budget of Pal's film.[46]

The fact that major studio films with sizable budgets, Technicolor cinematography, and state-of-the-art special effects failed to attract a larger audience than cheap, black-and-white exploitation films suggests two things. First, that audiences for SF films did not especially privilege the higher production values of the A films. Second, that SF A films did not successfully appeal to a general audience, as the studios had hoped. Despite the numerous production and promotional strategies undertaken by the majors to establish SF as a legitimate category of A filmmaking, they were unable to overcome the genre's reputation as childish and cheap. While the SF A films of the early-to-mid-1950s were modest successes, most failed to justify their substantial production costs. Even apparent hits like *The Thing from Another World* and *The War of the Worlds*, which each earned $2 million domestically, were considered disappointments because of their large budgets.[47] According to RKO's financial records, *The Thing* just barely broke even.[48] In 1954, Twentieth Century-Fox was considering producing a major SF film titled *Saber Tooth*, budgeted in the $2.5 to $3 million range. The project was eventually shelved, in part on the advice of an executive at Paramount, Jack Karp, who warned Fox that *The War of the Worlds*, by all accounts a box office success, was barely profitable. When told about *Saber Tooth*, Karp responded that Fox "must be nuts to even consider such a thing."[49] In 1955 George Pal was dropped by Paramount after *Conquest of Space* returned only $1 million against a budget of $1.65 million.[50] The following year, *Forbidden Planet*, the most expensive SF film of the era at nearly $2 million, and arguably the best, earned only $1.6 million in domestic rentals.[51]

Regardless of their budget, SF films released by the majors in the early-to-mid-1950s tended to generate between $1 million and $2 million in rentals. Additionally, although the films were usually quite successful in their initial weeks of release, their box office numbers quickly trailed off in subsequent weeks.[52] This pattern and the consistency in the films' final grosses suggest that they appealed to a relatively small but fervent audience of children and SF fans but, despite the studios' best efforts, largely failed to cross over to a more general adult audience. Reviews and exhibitor reports in the trade and popular presses support this claim. The *Chicago Tribune* wrote that "small boys probably will enjoy" *Conquest of Space*, which it described as a "highly improbable" film.[53] One theater owner reported about *The War of the Worlds*: "This is one of the best of the fantastic pictures but mostly students and kids turned out for it, and some of those twice! The oldsters here think these are silly, so refuse to come."[54] Reviewing the performance of *Forbidden Planet*, another exhibitor wrote: "Even if they dress these space pictures up in CinemaScope, color, and with top stars, the public still says 'no go.' It's kids' stuff."[55] Yet another remarked about the same film: "Adults missed a good one by dropping the kids off for this one."[56]

Ultimately, it appears as though the major studios were unable to successfully challenge the dominant SF paradigm, rooted in the juvenile fantasy of pulp SF. One can see the genre's devalued status represented in dismissive reviews of the films. Reviewing *The Day the Earth Stood Still*, the *New York Times*'s Bosley Crowther argued that "in a fable of such absurd assumptions as this one amusingly presents, cold chills might be more appropriate than lukewarm philosophy. One expects more — or less — than a preachment on political morality from a man from Mars."[57] The film's major studio pedigree and ambitious political themes were insufficient to overcome Crowther's preconceptions of the genre. In fact, for

Crowther the elements of the film meant to appeal to adults were unwelcome. Rather, SF is suited best for "cold chills" and is not an appropriate vehicle for political rhetoric.[58] Because of its ubiquity in television, radio, pulp magazines, and comic books, the juvenile pulp paradigm was inescapable for the majors. Even *Variety* referred to *Forbidden Planet* as "*Space Patrol* for adults."[59] The majors tried to have it both ways. As effective as pulp iconography might be in attracting a particular audience, the pulp paradox, or the contradictory position of simultaneously embracing and rejecting the tropes of pulp SF, helped ensure the failure of big-budget SF in the 1950s.

Upgrading the Classical B Film: Universal-International's SF Programmers

Although *The War of the Worlds* outearned *Destination Moon* by $700,000, the latter was more profitable because of its considerably smaller budget. The SF success stories of the early-to-mid-1950s were not big-budget films like *War of the Worlds*, but rather low-budget exploitation films and mid-budget programmers. Keeping costs down was essential, as the SF A films had demonstrated the genre's inability to attract a large general audience. Instead, cheaper films could do quite well by rejecting the crossover ambitions of films like *Forbidden Planet* and simply targeting a niche audience of children and SF fans. *Destination Moon* was a programmer, a mid-budget film that could be sold as either an A or B film to exhibitors. As we saw in chapter 1, Eagle-Lion worked feverishly to market *Destination Moon* in an effort to get skeptical theater owners to book it for a percentage of the box office. The strategy worked for *Destination Moon*, but as Eagle-Lion discovered, complete reliance on programmers was not a sustainable business practice, as there was too much risk involved. Pal's film was a "shaky A," a relatively cheap film trying to pass as a major, big-budget feature.[60] Other programmers are best understood as nothing more than upgraded B films. The difference lies in the approach to genre; *Destination Moon* carefully avoided anything that resembled the taint of horror or space opera. Other subsequent SF programmers, some of them more successful than *Destination Moon*, were much less skittish.

Programmers are a key production strategy in this period, one that has been largely ignored by previous histories. Even Blair Davis's excellent history of low-budget cinema in the 1950s fails to identify them as a separate production category. In general, Davis's book is keenly attuned to budget distinctions, arguing quite rightly that "B-movies of this decade have seemingly become a homogenized product in the minds of many, despite the fact that the films had a wide range of budgets."[61] Davis separates low-budget films of the period into three categories: high-end, middle-end, or low-end. For Davis, a high-end B movie is something like Universal's *The Deadly Mantis*, which cost approximately $450,000. I argue below, however, that films like *The Deadly Mantis* actually represent a substantial decline in budget from Universal's earlier SF efforts like *It Came from Outer Space*, which cost $700,000. Davis's book conflates all the Universal SF films of the period, which obscures important distinctions between low-budget exploitation films and programmers.

With the lone exception of Warner Bros.' *Them!*, the SF programmer of the 1950s was a production strategy of one studio, Universal-International. The programmer was a crucial part of U-I's production schedule in the 1950s, rooted in the studio's aspirations to improve its industrial status. The postwar move away from the classical B film and toward the programmer was crucial for a "minor" (as opposed to major) studio like Universal, which was heavily reliant on low-budget product. Along with United Artists and Columbia, Universal is referred to as a "Little Three" studio, as opposed to the "Big Five" of Paramount, MGM, Twentieth Century-Fox, Warner Bros., and RKO. In general, during the classical era of the 1930s and '40s, a studio's profits were proportional to the number and quality of theaters it owned. As they did not own theaters, Universal, Columbia, and United Artists operated in the shadow of the five vertically integrated majors.[62] Without revenue from first-run exhibition, the Little Three could never hope to match the larger firms. The peak year of 1946 provides an especially vivid example of the majors' dominance. Paramount, which at the time owned a stake in over fifteen hundred theaters, made $193.5 million in revenue, $39.2 million of it profit. In comparison, Universal made $53.9 million, with only about $4 million reported as profit.[63]

The relationship between the major and minor studios was mutually beneficial. The minors could rent their films to independent theaters, but relied on the majors' screens for most of their income. And with most theaters showing double features and often changing their program as many as three times a week, the majors relied on the low-budget films of the minor studios to fill out the dual bills in their theaters. In the classical studio period, Universal released relatively few films that could be considered A material. There were exceptions, such as Lewis Milestone's *All Quiet on the Western Front* (1930), but in general the studio's releases were low-budget affairs, often B-level musicals, mysteries, and westerns. In 1939 the average length of Universal's forty-nine films was 69.7 minutes, a typical length for a B picture.[64] In contrast, MGM's average length for the year was 84.4 minutes, suggesting the extent to which its schedule was dominated by A product.[65] Because they released far fewer A pictures, to stay solvent the smaller studios needed some of their low-budget features to perform beyond expectations. For instance, Deanna Durbin's relatively inexpensive (about $600,000 per film) musicals were huge hits, helping keep Universal afloat during the lean years of the mid-1930s.[66]

Emboldened by the wartime industry boom in the mid-1940s, Universal began to focus more on A features, including several by independent producers like Walter Wanger (*Scarlet Street*, 1945) and Mark Hellinger (*The Killers*, 1946). The Paramount decision only reinforced this strategy; without the collusion that characterized studio distribution and exhibition in the classical studio era, all studios directly competed with one another for screens. More than ever before, smaller studios could gain access to first-run bookings. Studios like Universal needed prestigious product featuring major talent in order to compete with the Big Five, which had begun to focus their attentions on a small number of expensive films per year. Universal was especially well poised to improve its status in the postwar marketplace, as in 1946 it had merged with Leo Spitz and William Goetz's International Pictures. Spitz and Goetz, both veteran studio executives (Goetz was Louis B. Mayer's son-in-law), specialized in respectable, star-driven fare like *Along Came Jones* (1945) with Gary Cooper and *Tomorrow Is Forever* (1946) with Orson Welles and Claudette Colbert. As studio heads, they planned to bring the same level of prestige to the new Universal-International. Major films budgeted at between $1 million and $1.5 million, like George Cukor's *A Double Life* (1948), were newly emphasized. Spitz and Goetz also eliminated serial film production and dramatically curtailed the production of B films. This was part of their campaign to make Universal more respectable; B pictures were an embarrassing eyesore at a time when the film industry was desperate to retain its audience. Former Fox president Joseph Schenck complained in 1949: "People come and see a stinker and they go away panning all Hollywood. Sometimes they're so annoyed with a mediocre B that they don't even wait for the top A picture."[67]

U-I's de-emphasis of low-budget programming also reflected the decline of the B film in the first-run market, a trend that would continue through the 1950s. Because B films could no longer be packaged with As in distribution contracts after the Paramount decision, major studios struggled to find sufficient bookings to make B production worthwhile. In 1952 an anonymous studio executive remarked to *Variety* that "the Bs for a long time have not stood on their economic feet. . . . The point may well come when it is more profitable to leave stages empty and chewing up costs than it is to make pictures we can't liquidate."[68] Moviegoers had become more discriminating; whereas in the '30s and '40s they were happy to sit through a several-hour program that included newsreels, shorts, and two features, the postwar population shift to the suburbs and the rise in entertainment options made their leisure time more valuable. Television in particular was understood as contributing to the obsolescence of B pictures; as Jack Warner said in 1953, "The public can see mediocre pictures on television for free."[69] The double bill remained popular through the early 1950s, but mostly in smaller neighborhood houses that were financially irrelevant to the majors when compared to first-run theaters in large cities.[70] Davis notes that "most major studios removed B-movies from their release schedules by the end of 1951."[71]

U-I's focus on expensive product in the late 1940s turned out to be disastrous, as Spitz and Goetz's prestige pictures fared poorly at the box office. U-I lost $4.3 million between 1948 and 1949, a catastrophe that necessitated the short-term closure of the studio in 1950.[72] Ironically, it was the success of the few remaining low-budget films on the schedule that helped to mitigate the failures of films like *Another Part of the Forest* (1948), an adaption of Lillian Hellman's play. For instance, the rural comedy *Ma and Pa Kettle* (a spin-off of 1947's *The Egg and I*) earned $2.3 million against a cost of only $200,000 and led to a series of nine films.[73] In 1952 Spitz and Goetz sold their interest in Universal-International to Decca Records, which was already the studio's largest shareholder.[74] Longtime Universal executive Edward L. Muhl became the new head of production. Learning from the mistakes of the previous administration, Muhl took a more conservative approach to running the studio by supplementing A films like Douglas Sirk's *Magnificent Obsession* (1954) and Anthony Mann's *The Glenn Miller Story* (1954) with a wide variety of cheaper films.

Most of Universal's low-budget films in the 1950s were destined for the bottom of the bill, but some found unlikely success in the first-run market. Particularly profitable were black-and-white comedies like the Francis the Talking Mule series, and the continuing adventures of Ma and Pa Kettle. Despite their small budgets, these films consistently earned over a million dollars each for Universal, and the early entries in the series were among the studio's highest grossing of the year. These films were exceptions, however; generally you had to spend money to make money in the new postwar marketplace. To this end Universal turned to programmers costing approximately $500,000 to $700,000—an intermediary budget, between the $150,000 to $300,000 generally spent on studio Bs, and the typical studio A film, which cost $1 million and up.[75] The most popular programmer genres at the time were westerns and "easterns," or Middle Eastern period adventure films in the *Thief of Baghdad* vein that featured colorful sets, swashbuckling action, and skimpy costumes.

To have a chance in the first-run market, programmers needed to resemble big-budget A films as closely as possible. As with *Destination Moon*, color cinematography was key. The introduction in 1950 of the one-strip "tripack" format from Eastmancolor made color shooting much more cost-effective.[76] By the mid-1950s, half of Hollywood films were color, including many programmers.[77] The new, simpler color process also facilitated location shooting, as cameramen no longer needed to move the bulky three-strip Technicolor cameras. Western programmers took advantage of this new mobility, as they began to more closely resemble A films in their use of scenic outdoor locations rather than studio back lots. Expanded budgets also allowed a number of '50s programmers to feature better-known talent than the average B film. They may have been past their prime, but stars like Maureen O'Hara, Paul Henreid, and Teresa Wright retained enough marquee appeal to give films like *California*

Conquest (1952) a chance at top-of-the-bill bookings.[78] Smaller majors like Universal and Columbia were particularly reliant on programmers, but studios like Warner Bros. released these upgraded B films as well. The success of these intermediary films contributed to the weakening of the A/B distinction.

Some of Universal's most successful programmers were SF/horror films, which offered unique exploitation appeals that westerns and costume pictures could not. The studio had famously achieved first-run success in the 1930s with a cycle of horror films, but by the mid-1940s Universal's horror films were cheap B fare like *Pillow of Death* (1945) and *The Spider Woman Strikes Back* (1946). The potency of the classic monsters had been diluted through innumerable sequels, and the atmosphere and menace of the earlier films had decayed into parody, best represented by 1948's *Abbott and Costello Meet Frankenstein.* Universal-International avoided the horror genre during the Spitz and Goetz regime, but when Muhl took over in 1952 and reestablished the studio's commitment to cheaper filmmaking, he looked to initiate a new horror cycle. The gothic iconography of the classic horror film had become cliché, so Universal adapted its horror formula to fit the current *genre du jour*, SF. The crucial element of the monster was retained, but supernatural origins were replaced by pseudoscientific rationalizations, with vampires and werewolves supplanted by aliens and atomic mutations.

The ambivalence toward pulp SF evidenced by the SF A films of the 1950s is largely absent from the programmers of the period. With smaller budgets, there was less pressure to appeal to sophisticated viewers. Additionally, despite its dabbling in prestige films in the late '40s, Universal was by reputation a smaller studio that relied on genre films as its bread and butter, and therefore was less likely to be cautious with pulp SF than Paramount or MGM. The studio of Dracula and Frankenstein instead embraced the more sensational aspects of the genre in all aspects of its SF/horror productions, from the formal properties of the films to their marketing. With its scaled-back production style, effective mix of SF concepts and horror conventions, and box office success, *The Thing from Another World* was an ideal model for Universal as it reapproached the horror genre. By reproducing *The Thing*'s black-and-white, low-key photography and monster-based narrative, Universal could exploit the new vogue in

SF while simultaneously producing films that fit its already-established horror tradition.[79] *Creature from the Black Lagoon* in particular appears to be an effort to introduce a new horror character that could be marketed in the same way that Dracula, the Wolf Man, and the like were marketed in the classical period; *Creature* would be the only Universal SF film of the fifties to inspire sequels, a fact that highlights its particular affinity to the previous horror cycles.

Unlike Universal's horror films of the mid-1940s, its 1950s SF programmers were fully intended for distribution at the top of the bill in major markets. An emphasis on spectacle was necessary to enhance the films' market value, but instead of upgrading the SF pictures with color cinematography, as it did with its western and adventure programmers, Universal-International initially attempted to attract first-run audiences by experimenting with the newly popular technologies of widescreen and 3-D. These techniques were intended to heighten the visceral quality of the films' horror plots. They also served to differentiate the films from other studio programmers, such as westerns like *Gunsmoke* (1953) with Audie Murphy, which featured more conventional, often star-based, appeals rather than sensational exploitation qualities.

Universal's first SF picture of the 1950s was *It Came from Outer Space*. Based on a detailed story treatment by Ray Bradbury, it was the tale of an amateur astronomer's encounter with an alien vessel that has crashed in the middle of the Arizona desert. The film features a number of chilling moments, including eerie sequences in which aliens assume the guise of humans, and a few glimpses of the aliens' true form — a grotesque floating eyeball covered in stringy hair. Overall, however, in its attitude toward the unknown the film resembles *The Day the Earth Stood Still* more than *The Thing*, in that Bradbury's aliens are simply looking to return home and are fearful of humans.[80] *It Came from Outer Space* was only the second fiction feature directed by Jack Arnold, whose relatively subtle, effective work would go largely unnoticed by critics at the time, but who years later would be praised in fan circles as the quintessential SF auteur of the 1950s.

It Came from Outer Space was exhibited in widescreen, with the full frame matted to a 1.85:1 ratio. Masking the top and bottom of the screen was an easy and inexpensive way for studios and theaters to offer a wide

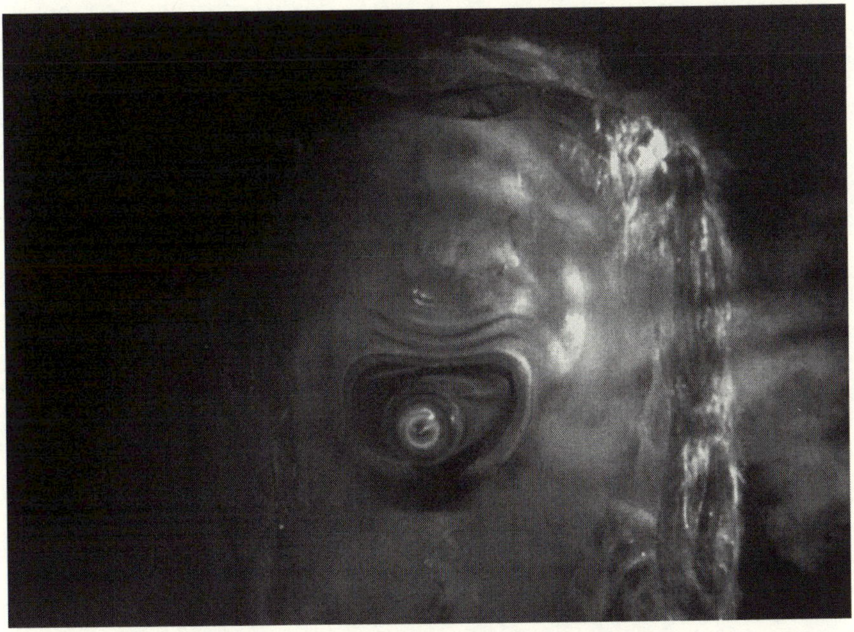

It Came from Outer Space (Universal-International, 1953) includes a number of shots that foreground its 3-D cinematography, such as this image of an alien approaching the camera.

image, as yet another means of differentiation from television. *It Came* is notable as the first widescreen film to be exhibited in 3-D. Since the 1950s, 3-D projection has recurred as a potential savior to bail out the industry in times of lowered attendance. Kevin Heffernan positions the initial 3-D boom as an attempt on the part of distributors to sell costly new projection equipment to exhibitors and to justify increasingly steep rental fees.[81] Apart from these motives, 3-D was the key technology used by studios to place exploitation-type programmers into the A market. The cycle of 3-D genre films from 1952 to 1955 represents one of the first extended introductions of exploitation narrative and stylistic norms into mainstream cinema.

The first 3-D film was *Bwana Devil*, a jungle adventure that cost only about $325,000 but became a phenomenon in the winter of 1952–1953.[82] The film itself was no better than the typical adventure programmer, but its 3-D effects (including a spear that appeared to be tossed at the spectator) were, at the time, startling and exhilarating. After the film's successful independent run, United Artists picked it up for $1.75 million and released it to first-run theaters.[83] *Bwana Devil* ended up earning $2.7 million in rentals, an astounding sum for such an inexpensive film.[84] Hoping that the new technology would pull the industry out of its prolonged slump, the major studios followed *Bwana Devil* with a number of 3-D films. Traditional B genres like horror, SF, and thrillers were emphasized, ostensibly because their story lines provided more frequent opportunities to showcase the 3-D technology. Heffernan notes that the more upscale 3-D films like Columbia's *Miss Sadie Thompson* (1953) gravitated toward a "less intrusive" use of the technology; however, this approach was less frequent than the more aggressive tack taken by exploitation films, which involved gimmicks like tossing items directly at the camera.[85]

The budgets of the majors' 3-D genre films were much larger than that of *Bwana Devil*, though, at less than a million dollars, still within programmer range. The lower the budget, the greater the profit potential, and the novelty of the three-dimensionality would hopefully compensate for any budget deficiencies. Warner Bros.' colorful horror hit *House of Wax* (1953), starring Vincent Price, cost about $650,000 but returned an astonishing $5.5 million.[86] *Wax* had the advantage of being the first 3-D film produced by a major studio; *It Came from Outer Space* followed about six weeks later. Universal's first 3-D film received good reviews for a film of its kind, with *Variety* noting that the "stereo process is not used as just an excuse to pelt the audience with flying objects" — a quote that demonstrates the extent to which 3-D was already inescapably linked to exploitation-type shock effects.[87] The *Los Angeles Times*'s Philip K. Scheuer did note that, once the effect of the 3-D had worn off, he realized "what we succumbed to was little more than the pretension of a glorified 'B.'"[88]

It Came from Outer Space did extraordinarily well in its opening week in first-run theaters. In Los Angeles it was the top film of the Memorial Day weekend, earning approximately $70,000 at two locations, where it was the only film on the bill.[89] By the end of its run, however, *It Came* was only a solid performer for Universal, its seventh-highest-grossing film of 1953 (behind the Francis and Kettle installments, among others). The film returned $1.6 million domestically against a budget of approximately $700,000, making it the seventy-sixth-highest-grossing film of the year overall. The modest final box office numbers when compared to the opening weekend grosses suggest that, as with the SF A films of the period, interest was frontloaded and limited to SF fans and novelty seekers.

Universal-International followed *It Came from Outer Space* with *Creature from the Black Lagoon*, which featured many of the same key personnel as its predecessor, including director Jack Arnold, producer William Alland, star Richard Carlson, and screenwriter Harry Essex. Another 3-D programmer (with a budget of $600,000),[90] *Creature* was more obviously an SF/horror hybrid, its "Gill Man" creature recalling the somewhat sympathetic monsters of Universal's classic horror films.[91] Like *It Came*, *Creature from the Black Lagoon* received A bookings in major first-run theaters and performed reasonably well, with $1.3 million in domestic rentals.[92] However, the benefits of the 3-D format were quickly fading. In May 1954, two months after *Creature*'s release, *Variety* declared "3-D Looks Dead in United States."[93] There was a litany of problems with 3-D, from uncomfortable glasses, to irritating intermissions during reel changes, to expensive conversion costs for theater owners.[94] It was also a matter of general audiences simply losing interest in a technology that was generally associated with cheap exploitation films. Few major filmmakers worked in 3-D; Alfred Hitchcock's *Dial M for Murder* (1954) for Warner Bros. was an exception that proved the rule. Far more prevalent were dirt-cheap independent films trying to exploit the public's interest in the new gimmick — SF examples include *Cat Women of the Moon* (1953) and *Robot Monster* (1953), made for a reported $16,000.[95] The 3-D format became inescapably linked with the shock effects, thrills, and gimmicks of exploitation; once the novelty had worn off, little remained to attract general audiences.

Because of their intermediate budgets, genre programmers like *Creature from the Black Lagoon* suffered the most as a result of 3-D's inability to catch on. Three-dimensionality offered a way for studios to book less expensive products as A films in first-run situations. Without it, films like *It Came from Outer Space* and *Creature* were too obviously, as Philip K. Scheuer put it, glorified B films, but also too expensive to recoup their costs in the subsequent-run market. Universal was reluctant to give up on 3-D; in 1955 it released *Revenge of the Creature*, a sequel that was the last major film to be released in 3-D in the '50s. For *This Island Earth*, another U-I programmer from 1955, 3-D was dropped in favor of color and widescreen, which aligned the film more closely with A productions than exploitation. The upgrade in production values, particularly the outstanding special effects by Cleo Baker, were frequently cited in the rave reviews received by *This Island Earth*.[96] Despite its high quality, the film performed no better than the earlier programmers. "Too bad," wrote one critic about *This Island Earth*, "that science-fiction films seem to be going out of fashion at the box office just as Hollywood's mechanical whizzes are getting so expert at making them."[97]

Like the Big Five, U-I learned that larger budgets did not boost the box office performance of an SF film. With $1.7 million in rentals, *This Island Earth* earned as much as Columbia's giant octopus rampage film *It Came from beneath the Sea* (1955), which cost only $150,000.[98] Universal responded by slashing the budgets of its SF films, primarily by cutting their production schedules in half from one month to two weeks.[99] For instance, 1957's *The Deadly Mantis*, budgeted at $450,000, was shot in thirteen days, compared to *It Came from Outer Space*'s twenty-eight days (plus six second-unit production days). Of course, the quality of the films suffered. The long-term damage done to the genre's reputation was subordinated to the short-term profitability of low-budget exploitation cinema, a form that came to define SF in America by decade's end.

Delirium at the Drive-Ins: SF and '50s Low-Budget Exploitation

While most of the enduring classics of 1950s SF were costlier films like *The War of the Worlds* and *Forbidden Planet*, from an economic standpoint these films were failures in their initial theatrical runs compared to low-budget fare like *It Came from beneath the Sea* and *I Was a Teenage Werewolf* (1957). By 1957 the majors had largely relinquished the SF genre to low-budget exploitation producers. The appeal of exploitation films was rooted in their ability to generate a disproportionately large amount of revenue from their tiny budgets. They accomplished this through saturation booking, a distribution method by which a film was booked into multiple theaters in a particular area — for instance, a large city or a section of a state — in order to heighten its visibility in that market. Saturation releases were supported by aggressive advertising that emphasized the film's more sensational aspects. The combination of saturation distribution and marketing enabled exploitation films to maximize their box office potential; audiences would be lured in by the intense promotion, and the film could make its money quickly and move on to the next town before the marketing buzz subsided and audiences realized they had just seen (in most cases) a run-of-the-mill cheapie. As Richard Maltby notes, the saturation booking method was best suited for "movies unlikely to build a reputation through word-of-mouth"; in this way it was antithetical to traditional studio distribution tactics, which were based on a slow rollout over several months.[100] By using marketing to create a hype that was incommensurate with the film's actual quality, studios added another definition of "exploitation" to the exploitation film.

Rocketship X-M was the first SF exploitation hit in 1950, but the genre did not really begin to flourish in the low-budget realm until three years later. The key event was not the release of a new film, but rather the rediscovery of a classic. RKO's 1952 reissue of Merian C. Cooper and Ernest B. Schoedsack's *King Kong* (1933) would shape the trajectory of the SF exploitation film in several ways. First, at the generic level *King Kong* provided a narrative template for many subsequent SF/horror films. Historian Bill Warren argues that "without *Kong*'s influence, the SF movies of the 1950s probably would have gone in a different, perhaps short-lived direction."[101] Pointing to the dearth of SF films in 1952, Warren claims that the resurgence of the genre in 1953 was a response to *Kong*'s success. This is something of an overstatement; for instance, *The War of the Worlds* had been in the works at Paramount since 1951, and it seems inconceivable that Universal, with its history of genre production, would have failed to pursue SF/horror in the '50s, whether *King Kong* had been reissued or not. However, *Kong*'s monster-on-the-loose plot would inspire dozens, if not hundreds of films. Even more importantly, the success of the reissue's saturation release would establish a precedent for future exploitation films.

In 1952 RKO was nearing the end of its existence. Eccentric millionaire Howard Hughes had purchased the studio in 1948 and immediately crippled his new enterprise by cutting personnel by 75 percent. Hughes also badly damaged the studio's efficiency through obsessive micromanagement.[102] Production was slashed to a bare minimum; most of the studio's releases in the early '50s were independent productions, which were less lucrative for the distributor. In 1952 the studio would lose over

$10 million.[103] That year a desperate RKO rereleased two of its most successful films, *Snow White and the Seven Dwarfs* (1937) and *King Kong*. As the beleaguered studio had no other major releases for the year, the two classics received A-level promotional treatments. *Kong* (with Val Lewton's 1943 *The Leopard Man* at the bottom of the bill) first opened in a regional saturation pattern in about four hundred theaters across the Pittsburgh, Cincinnati, Cleveland, Detroit, and Indianapolis regions.[104] The rerelease was supported by what *Boxoffice* described as "the first big-scale test of television for picture-selling."[105] Twelve television stations in the five regions mentioned regularly broadcast a one-minute advertisement for *Kong* that featured clips from the film and listed the nearby theaters where it was playing. The midwestern campaign was so successful, RKO repeated the strategy with saturation releases across the East and West Coasts.[106] The innovative distribution pattern and use of television advertising helped propel *King Kong* to more than $2 million in rentals, a remarkable achievement for a rerelease.[107] *Variety* attributed most of this success to the effectiveness of RKO's ad campaign, facilitated by the film's easy exploitability, which "appealed to a completely new generation for whom the [film was] completely novel."[108]

The *King Kong* reissue was a clear influence on Warner Bros.' treatment of *The Beast from 20,000 Fathoms* (1953), one of the most profitable and influential SF films of the decade. *Beast* was an independent production from Mutual Pictures, a consortium of former Monogram producers who had previously specialized in East Side Kids films and the Joe Palooka boxing series. The screenplay was essentially *King Kong* with an atomic twist: a dinosaur is released from frozen hibernation by an Arctic nuclear test and eventually embarks upon a Kong-esque rampage through New York City until it is eventually dispatched in spectacular fashion, stumbling through the flaming wreckage of a Coney Island roller coaster. Costing only $210,000, *Beast* was B-level fare, although it did feature sophisticated special effects by stop-motion animator Ray Harryhausen, a protégé of *King Kong* animator Willis O'Brien.[109] Also, midway through shooting, the producers purchased the rights to a Ray Bradbury story from the *Saturday Evening Post* for $2,000 and added a brief scene from the story in which the monster happens upon a lighthouse.[110] Minor touches of prestige such as this could aid when selling a film to distributors.

Mutual sold *The Beast from 20,000 Fathoms* outright to Warner Bros. for $550,000 — a solid profit for the producers, although they surely regretted the deal after seeing the film's final box office numbers.[111] With *Beast* Warners was clearly trying to capitalize on the first-run success of *King Kong* the prior year. By the early '50s the studio was no longer producing films specifically for the bottom of the bill; its cheapest films were programmers with A potential, like *I Was a Communist for the F.B.I.* (1951), produced by former Eagle-Lion head of production Bryan Foy. For *Beast*, Warners replicated RKO's saturation booking strategy for *King Kong* but took it to a new level, releasing the film in 1,560 theaters in the summer of 1953.[112] With all major cities receiving the film within three weeks of its premiere, *Beast*'s release was, according to the studio, "the quickest payoff in key and secondary runs ever demonstrated under modern releasing conditions."[113] The nationwide marketing campaign, which included intensive use of television and radio, cost more than the film itself at an estimated $250,000.[114] The expensive campaign was well worth it, as it elevated the film's status tremendously in the marketplace. *Variety* reported in 1954 that exploitation films like *Beast*, "as a result of forceful ballyhoo, have taken on the aura of 'A' pix and have obtained bookings in key situations as the main feature."[115] As a result of its wide distribution in first-run theaters, *Beast* earned a remarkable $2.25 million in rentals, making it Warner Bros.' seventh-highest-grossing film of 1953. *Beast* equaled the grosses of epics like Fox's *Titanic* (1953) and outperforming much costlier movies like MGM's *The Prisoner of Zenda* (1953).[116]

A year after the release of *The Beast from 20,000 Fathoms*, the saturation distribution method had become common among low- and mid-budget films with a unique exploitation angle. In mid-June 1954 Warner Bros. produced six hundred prints of the programmer *Them!*, its follow-up to *Beast*, and booked it in two thousand theaters in the span of only a month.[117] The studio also used the strategy with the 3-D horror film *Phantom of the Rue Morgue* (1954), as it had with *House of Wax* the year prior.[118] Independent studios also got in on the action: Allied Artists gave its prison reform film *Riot in Cell Block 11* (1954) a saturation release and a $350,000 ad campaign. The film, which cost about $300,000, went on to earn over $1.5 million.[119] A successful saturation release involved an expensive promotional campaign, but considering the relatively low production budgets of these films, this was not a serious financial risk. Low-budget SF films like *It Came from beneath the Sea*, *Earth vs. the Flying Saucers*, and *Invasion of the Body Snatchers* would all receive top-of-the-bill, first-run bookings in the '50s. The saturation release strategy would, of course, only grow wider and more elaborate as the decades passed, becoming industry standard for nearly all major studio releases by the late 1970s.

While a relatively small number of 1950s exploitation films broke into the first-run marketplace compared to the number produced, the minimal risk involved in their production made them a worthwhile venture. As *Variety* noted in 1954, "If the pic doesn't get off the ground as expected, it can still recoup most of its cost via normal double bill dates."[120] Even though the major studios' interest in producing B films had declined, the double-feature market remained strong throughout the 1950s and into the early '60s. As Heffernan has discussed, the majors' production cutbacks fueled a boom in low-budget genre films made by Poverty Row studios and other independents. Neighborhood and small-town theaters relied on these films in order to survive during fallow periods in the majors' release schedule.[121] Drive-in theaters were also key venues, springing up quickly in the postwar period following the population shift to the suburbs. In 1945 there were only twenty-five drive-ins in the United States; five years later there were over two thousand, built on inexpensive land on the outskirts of towns and cities.[122] Drive-ins were subsequent-run venues; distributors considered them second-rate and would usually only allow them to book A films that had completed their initial runs.[123] Therefore, like the smaller "hard-top" neighborhood theaters, drive-ins also needed a steady stream of new, low-budget films to add novelty to the marquee and combat the majors' production shortages.

Studios like United Artists, Republic, and Allied Artists specialized in producing cheap films for these subsequent-run exhibitors; some of the movies, including SF pictures such as *Phantom from Space* (UA, 1953) and *Target Earth* (AA, 1954), had exploitation appeal, while others, particularly in the early '50s, were run-of-the-mill, black-and-white westerns and thrillers indistinguishable from classical B films. The profits from these films supported the studios in their more expensive endeavors. UA's A features were especially successful, although Republic (*The Quiet Man*, 1952) and AA (*Love in the Afternoon*, 1957) also tested the first-run market with a number of big-budget films.[124] Perhaps the most prolific purveyor of B product in the period was Columbia producer Sam Katzman, whose production strategies would set the standard for the independent exploitation filmmakers to come.

Katzman began churning out low-budget films for Poverty Row studios in the mid-1930s. In 1946, after six years at Monogram, Katzman moved to Columbia, where he became an in-house independent producer with his own studio space near the Columbia back lot. Using a variety of different names, such as "Esskay Pictures" and "Clover Productions," Katzman produced more than one hundred low-budget feature films and serials for Columbia from 1947 to 1962. The studio approved and financed each of Katzman's projects, with the producer taking a 25 percent share of the profits.[125] Katzman produced films in a variety of genres, including westerns, "easterns," film noir, horror, and "Jungle Jim" films starring Johnny "Tarzan" Weissmuller. Katzman boasted to *Time* in 1952 that he never spent more than $500,000 on a film, and that none of his pictures lost money.[126] Aside from the occasional breakout success like *The Miami Story* (1954) or *Rock around the Clock* (1956), which exploited current interest in organized crime and rock and roll, respectively, Katzman's films were confined to the bottom of the bill in dual houses, including many first-run venues. In 1955, however, Columbia employed the saturation release strategy with Katzman's production *It Came from beneath the Sea*, another "monster rampage film," which, like *The Beast from 20,000 Fathoms*, featured special effects by Ray Harryhausen. Supported by Katzman's *Creature with the Atom Brain* (1955), *It Came* hit twenty-two hundred theaters in the summer of 1955, including thirty-seven in the Los Angeles area alone.[127] As mentioned earlier, *It Came from beneath the Sea* was one of the most profitable SF films of the decade, generating $1.7 million in domestic rentals against a production budget of only $150,000.[128]

Katzman's films were valuable in that they provided consistent revenue that supported Columbia's more ambitious efforts. Like Universal, Columbia looked to improve its industrial status in light of the Paramount decision. By the early 1950s, Columbia head Harry Cohn had signed prestigious independent producers like Sam Spiegel (*On the Waterfront*, 1954) and Stanley Kramer (*The Caine Mutiny*, 1954); it also released a number of in-house productions that were critical and commercial successes, such as *From Here to Eternity* (1953), which grossed $18 million worldwide and won eight Oscars.[129] But *From Here to Eternity* was hardly representative of Columbia's output in 1953: of the thirty-four films released by the studio that year, fully half were programmers or B films with running times under eighty minutes — and thirteen of them were produced by Sam Katzman.[130] In 1964 Katzman left Columbia for MGM, where he produced Elvis Presley programmers like *Kissin' Cousins* (1964).

Sam Katzman provided a model of efficient, profitable low-budget filmmaking that influenced the independent studio that would have the most impact on the exploitation film market in the 1950s: American International Pictures. While Columbia and Universal continued to produce low-budget films as a necessary evil to support their rise to major studio status, AIP relied entirely on profits from low-budget films, a situation that would lead it to revolutionize independent exploitation filmmaking, distribution, and marketing, elaborating upon preexisting strategies like saturation booking. As Blair Davis notes in his history of the studio, AIP "was successful not only in forging a new way of creating B-films, but more importantly in devising a radically new business model. . . . AIP's entry into the market in 1954 was a deciding factor in the industry-wide rebirth of the B-movie in the latter half of the decade."[131]

The studio was founded in 1954 by James Nicholson and Samuel Z. Arkoff under the name American Releasing Corporation. Several of its earliest films were conventional B westerns like *Five Guns West* (1955) and *Apache Woman* (1955), both directed by twenty-nine-year-old Roger Corman. The company first exhibited a tendency toward exploitation topics with its third release, *The Beast with 1,000,000 Eyes* (1955), an SF/horror film that Corman shot for under $30,000.[132] Independent producers like ARC were able to keep budgets so low because they often used nonunion labor and did not add overhead charges, which could add as much as 33 percent to the final cost of a major studio film. Also, of course, the films lacked the production values of even the cheapest Katzman films — the monster costume from *The Beast with 1,000,000 Eyes* cost $200, including labor.[133]

Nicholson and Arkoff quickly grew dissatisfied with the paltry flat-fee rentals they were receiving for their films, which invariably played at the bottom of the bill in subsequent-run dual houses and drive-ins. In order to receive a cut of the box office take, they began to package two films together and sell them for a lower percentage than what a major studio would charge for a single A film.[134] For their first attempt, Nicholson and Arkoff selected the easily exploitable SF genre: *The Day the World Ended* (1955), a postapocalyptic survival film directed by Corman, was paired with *The Phantom from 10,000 Leagues* (1955), a sea monster film independently produced by B movie veterans Dan and Jack Milner. At $96,000, *The Day the World Ended* cost approximately $20,000 more than its counterpart, owing in part to its use of SuperScope, a low-rent widescreen process that squeezed the image anamorphically during printing rather than shooting.[135] Initially exhibitors would only book the films as Bs, but in December 1955 ARC managed to book the dual bill into a large downtown theater in Detroit; at the time the majors were withholding their films from Detroit theaters because of a newspaper strike that eliminated their primary advertising medium. ARC aggressively marketed the combination, putting men in monster suits on flatbed trucks and driving them through the streets of Detroit.[136] The stunt generated television and radio coverage, and the two films were a success, leading to bookings in large cities throughout the country, including Los Angeles, New York, and Boston. After two months in release the films had generated $400,000 for ARC.[137] Renaming itself American International Pictures in March 1956, the studio continued to release exploitation double features, including *The She Creature/It Conquered the World* (both 1956) and *Hot Rod Girl/Girls in Prison* (both 1956).

Sam Katzman's exploitation dual bills were an obvious influence on AIP; as historian Mark McGee notes, "Katzman often led the way while Arkoff (and Nicholson) merely had the sense to follow."[138] However, Katzman made clear which film was the main feature and which was the support. AIP's approach to the double feature was unusual in that it did not differentiate between the top and bottom of the bill; the two films were equals in the eyes of the distributor. There are some antecedents here: during the classic studio era, smaller theaters that could not afford to book an A film every week frequently paired two low-budget films. For instance, in September 1936 the College Theater in New Haven, Connecticut, showed *Meet Nero Wolfe* (1936) and *The Mine with the Iron Door* (1936), two B films from Columbia.[139] Theatrical reissues were another example;

two popular films were often rereleased with no distinction made between A and B. For example, in 1952 Warner Bros. reissued two Humphrey Bogart films, *High Sierra* (1941) and *To Have and Have Not* (1944), as a preconstituted double bill. As with exploitation double features, one film was not obviously more appealing than the other; some theaters placed *High Sierra* at the top of the bill, while others privileged the later film.[140] Particularly influential on AIP were independent distributor Realart's rereleases of the Universal catalog, which included horror combinations like *Dracula/Frankenstein* (both 1931) and *Bride of Frankenstein* (1935) with *Son of Frankenstein* (1939).[141] AIP cofounder James Nicholson was responsible for packaging these double bills in the early '50s, an experience that would prove valuable in the years to come.[142]

The exploitation double bill was a game-changer for independent exploitation studios, an innovative way to induce exhibitors to pay a percentage of the box office take. First-run bookings would remain elusive for AIP for most of the decade, however. Unlike Katzman, who received access to first-run houses via his distribution agreement with Columbia, Arkoff and Nicholson were almost entirely reliant on smaller neighborhood theaters and drive-ins, many of which were still refusing to pay a percentage fee for AIP's double features.[143] Fortunately for AIP, American drive-ins had proliferated to over four thousand by 1956, so a studio could still make substantial profits even if it was denied percentage deals at some venues.[144] By 1958 AIP was securing five thousand bookings per double feature.[145] Each dual bill would open with saturation releases in key markets and then proceed to smaller and smaller exhibition outlets. Arkoff estimated that it took between one and two years for a film to complete the distribution circuit—and even then, each print would continue to run until it was too worn to project.[146]

The success of the exploitation double bill was due in large part to the studio's exploitation of the burgeoning teenage audience; research at the time indicated that over half of all moviegoers were ages fifteen to twenty-nine.[147] Thomas Doherty has detailed how the industry gradually, almost reluctantly, came to understand that young people were responsible for the bulk of its revenue. He writes, "Prior to 1956, there was no industry-wide consensus on the vital importance of the teenage market, much less an earnest assault on it."[148] Major studios initiated this assault in 1955 with teen-oriented "problem films" like *Blackboard Jungle* (1955) and *Rebel without a Cause* (1955). However, as major studio A productions (from MGM and Warner Bros., respectively), these films were produced for the traditional first-run adult market. The low-budget exploitation teenpics to follow would target the teenage drive-in audience more specifically. Ahead of the curve, Sam Katzman had already produced the "Teen Agers" series for Monogram in the late forties. In 1956 he scored the first big teenpic hit by tapping into the new rock-and-roll craze with *Rock around the Clock*. AIP responded later in the year with *Shake, Rattle, and Rock*, starring Fats Domino. Drive-in double features appealed to teens in particular, presumably because they gave them an excuse to spend the entire night away from their parents and with their friends or a date.[149]

Davis writes, "AIP's approach to audiences went against prevailing industry notions at the time, whereby the major studios made blockbuster films in the hopes of attracting a wider range of viewers."[150] Importantly, this directed targeting of teen audiences was not only a departure from A film strategy, but from exploitation marketing as well. While Doherty argues that a teenage audience is a necessary condition of the "1950s exploitation formula," it was not until the middle of the decade that teens were singled out specifically for attention.[151] Earlier films like *Beast from 20,000 Fathoms* and *It Came from Outer Space* were marketed to general audiences. But these were first-run films; the expansion of the drive-in market enabled studios like AIP to focus on the teen demographic in a way that would not have been possible in the early '50s. While SF exploitation films had always been rooted in a pulp tradition commonly understood as juvenile, it was not until 1957 that the films exhibited specific appeals to younger audiences, such as the teen protagonists of *The Blob* (1958), *Teenage Caveman* (1958), and AIP's *I Was a Teenage Werewolf* (1957), which, accompanied by *Invasion of the Saucer Men* (1957), grossed a spectacular $2 million.[152]

Because its films were so cheap and had little chance at securing first-run bookings, AIP was not under the same pressure as the majors to "class up" its genre films for general audiences. On the contrary: in the eyes of its target audience, the more lurid, the better. AIP's SF films were firmly horror hybrids, emphasizing monsters not just in their story lines but in their titles as well (*I Was a Teenage Frankenstein, How to Make a Monster*).

The plotlines were typical horror fare but with a science fictional twist: in *I Was a Teenage Werewolf*, the titular monster is not the result of a gypsy curse but rather a serum developed by a mad psychiatrist.

And while the films were rarely as explicit as the marketing would suggest, they still generated controversy among moral crusaders, politicians, and film industry representatives. This negative reaction was predictable, as the delinquency of minors was a crucial political issue in the mid-1950s. In 1954 the United States Senate Subcommittee on Juvenile Delinquency held hearings focusing specifically on horror and crime comics, leading the comic industry to ban those genres via a new self-regulatory agency, the Comics Code Authority. In 1958, U.S. Senator Paul H. Douglas of Illinois sent telegrams to Washington, D.C., jurisdictions asking whether anything could be done to prevent the screening of horror films: "In view of the terrible outbursts of juvenile crime, movies such as these are advertised as being would seem to be pandering to and a stimulant of the sadistic impulses of impressionable boys and girls."[153] James Nicholson defended his studio's releases in the *New York Times*: "Our stories are pure fantasy, with no attempt at realism. Because of this, it is difficult to see how anyone could take our pictures so seriously that psychological damage could occur. . . . [Teenagers] laugh at the caricatures we represent, rather than shrink in terror."[154] Regardless of whether or not exploitation films were actually leading to juvenile delinquency, their high profile and sheer number contributed to a sense of the SF genre as disreputable.

By 1958 the exploitation market was in flux, as AIP faced competition on a number of fronts. Most importantly, the major studios had begun to embrace low-budget exploitation filmmaking. As we have seen, the majors' interest in these low-risk/high-profit-potential films tends to occur during times of economic crisis. In 1958 theatrical receipts dropped below $1 billion for the first time since 1941.[155] One strategy to cope with the downturn was to target the subsequent-run market the majors had previously neglected. By the late '50s it had become impossible to ignore the success of independent studios like AIP and the low-budget exploitation hits of Columbia and Universal-International; the films were simply too profitable. For instance, Allied Artists had a hit with Roger Corman's SF double feature of *Attack of the Crab Monsters* (1957) and *Not of This Earth*

(1957), which cost about $170,000 in total and grossed $800,000 domestically.[156] In late 1957 *Variety* reported: "The 'Little' man in exhibition, and the lowbudget [*sic*] pictures he needs, are again drawing the sympathetic attention of the major companies. Attitude represents a drastic reversal in the business view of the film companies which, over the past couple of years, have drifted toward fewer releases and a concentration on keycity firstruns. . . . The way the companies reason is that they can only gain, not lose, by keeping the smalltown theaters alive."[157]

Twentieth Century-Fox was the first to reappraise the value of low-budget filmmaking when in 1956 it signed independent producer Robert Lippert (producer of *Rocketship X-M*) to a deal wherein he would produce for the program market six black-and-white CinemaScope films with budgets of only $100,000 each.[158] Lisa Dombrowski notes that the net receipts for Lippert's films were split evenly between Fox and Lippert's company, Regal Films.[159] Also, "Fox reserved the right to approve story and cast and requested the films be shot in Fox studio property, using some studio equipment."[160] In these respects, Lippert served much the same purpose as Sam Katzman at Columbia. Regal peaked in 1957 with twenty-two films —nearly half of Fox's output for the year. Westerns, crime films, and SF/horror were popular; budgets ranged from $100,000 to about $400,000, with most films relegated to the bottom of the bill.[161]

Regal's SF films included Kurt Neumann's *Kronos* (1957) and Edward Bernds's *Space Master X-7* (1958). But its most famous SF production would be the one that got away: *The Fly* (1958), directed by Neumann and starring *House of Wax*'s Vincent Price. Based on a 1957 short story in *Playboy*, *The Fly* is a fairly typical SF/horror story of a scientist who is punished for arrogant, reckless experimentation when his body is accidentally merged with that of a housefly. The film was in preproduction at Regal in November 1957 when Fox production executive Sid Rogell contacted studio head Buddy Adler via memo: "Lippert must have an outstanding property in 'The Fly.' . . . Is it ridiculous to assume that we might in some way acquire this for one of our pictures if it is as good as everyone says it is?"[162] By February 1958 Rogell had his way; Fox reimbursed Regal the $14,000 it had already spent on *The Fly* and purchased the distribution rights for $25,000.[163] Regal also retained a 25 percent share in the film's profits, which would be substantial. Shot in eighteen days for $501,000,

The Fly would earn $1.7 million in domestic rentals upon its release (with *Space Master X-7*) in the summer of 1958, making it the most successful SF exploitation film since *It Came from beneath the Sea* in 1955.[164]

The Fly was successful in part because it shed the low-budget Regal banner; as a color programmer distributed by Fox, the film was able to secure first-run bookings. Surprisingly, although it was its studio's most profitable film of 1958, Fox did not follow *The Fly* with another similarly upgraded exploitation film. Instead, it relinquished all exploitation product to Lippert, including *Return of the Fly* (1959), which in contrast to its predecessor was a cheap, black-and-white effort. Under the Associated Producers name, Lippert continued his relationship with Fox until the mid-1960s, releasing low-budget westerns and exploitation films like *The Cabinet of Caligari* (1962) and *The Day Mars Invaded Earth* (1963).

Of all the Big Four studios (RKO halted production and distribution in early 1957), Fox was the most committed to low-budget filmmaking in the late '50s and early '60s. Yet other majors similarly reassessed their earlier dismissal of exploitation films and the subsequent-run market. After jettisoning George Pal in 1955 in the wake of the failure of *Conquest of Space*, Paramount returned to SF filmmaking in 1957 by signing producer William Alland.[165] Alland had just left Universal-International, where he had been a contracted employee for seven years, producing most of the studio's classic SF programmers. Universal's financial difficulties in the late '50s, its fading commitment to quality SF filmmaking, and the opportunity to earn a percentage of the profits persuaded Alland to make the move.[166] Unfortunately for the producer, none of his five films for Paramount, including two SF projects, performed well, and by the mid-1960s he had left the industry. Paramount had much more success with *The Blob* (1958), a teen-oriented monster flick that it purchased from independent producer Jack H. Harris for $300,000.[167] The studio spent an additional $300,000 on marketing, which helped drive *The Blob* to a $1.5 million domestic gross.[168]

By 1958 all the major studios were distributing low-budget exploitation films. SF, still the preeminent exploitation genre, received a boost in late 1957 when American papers filled with reports of the launch of the Soviet satellite *Sputnik*.[169] That year, Warner Bros., which had abandoned SF after *Them!*, distributed *The Black Scorpion* (1957), a similar if cheaper giant-bug film. By the end of the decade Warners was funding and distributing rather disreputable exploitation films like producer Albert J. Cohen's *Island of Lost Women* (1959), which cost only $200,000.[170] Even MGM was willing to lower itself to take advantage of the burgeoning exploitation market. It distributed and sometimes funded SF/horror projects from British exploitation producer Richard Gordon like *Fiend without a Face* (1958) and *The First Man into Space* (1959), as well as the low-budget success *Children of the Damned* (1960), shot in Britain and starring George Sanders.

The aggregate effect of the Big Four's newfound interest in low-budget filmmaking was the reclamation of much of the exploitation market from the independents, as the majors had much more clout with exhibitors than even successful exploitation companies. But the majors were not the most immediate threat to studios like AIP; it was other low-budget producers and distributors who threatened to irrevocably harm the exploitation market. By the end of the 1950s, theaters were flooded with cheap SF/horror films from small independent producers, who would typically distribute via state's rights to drive-ins and smaller nabes. Several of these production companies were formed by the owners of theater chains who decided to be proactive in their fight against chronic product shortages. Their films would play exclusively in their theaters before receiving wider distribution in the exploitation market. For example, an SF/horror double feature of *Beginning of the End* (1957) and *The Unearthly* was released by AB-PT (American Broadcast–Paramount Theaters) in June 1957, and Howco Productions, part of the southeastern Consolidated Theaters chain, released films like *Mesa of Lost Women* (1956) and *Brain from Planet Arous* (1958).[171] These movies, as well as those from distributors like Allied Artists, DCA (Distributors Corporation of America), and Astor, can be described as "Z films," to differentiate them from more expensive exploitation product. Z films typically cost about half the average AIP budget of $150,000 — *The Brain from Planet Arous*, for example, was budgeted at only $58,000.[172]

Nicholson criticized Z film producers in a 1958 *Variety* article: "Many other companies do it for $50,000, and the difference shows. When a moviegoer sees one, he's not anxious to go back to see another exploitation picture."[173] Putting aside issues of quality, the bigger problem with Z films was that they were driving down rental prices for exploitation films. SF/horror films were now a dime a dozen, and AIP could not sustain itself on the meager terms offered by exhibitors. In 1959 the studio announced that it was cutting back on production "due to low-budget horror and science fiction product having lost its potency in a flooded market. . . . Company is currently unable to secure sufficient playing time for cheap, run-of-mill exploitation pix."[174]

AIP's solution was to upgrade its product; majors had ventured into its territory, and now AIP would return the favor. As Arkoff explains in his autobiography, "Our first decision was to produce more expensive pictures, and make them in color. 'We can take the money that we would have otherwise spent on two movies and channel those funds into just one,' I said."[175] These films were still relatively cheap — between $200,000 and $300,000, according to director Roger Corman — but looked more expensive, similar to major studio programmers.[176] And like programmers, they were reaching for a general audience in first-run situations. Davis notes that AIP "began to branch out beyond the teenage demographic that had defined the company since its inception."[177] The models for the new-look AIP were the gothic horror films of England's Hammer Studios. Films like *The Curse of Frankenstein* (1957) and *Horror of Dracula* (1958) replaced the flat visual style and playful teenage irony of exploitation SF/horror with colorful cinematography and ornate sets and costumes, as well as a controversial emphasis on gore and sexuality. *The Curse of Frankenstein*, distributed by Columbia in the United States, grossed over $2 million against a $400,000 budget.[178] AIP responded with a series of Edgar Allan Poe adaptations starring Vincent Prince and directed by Corman. Critics noticed that the films represented a new approach from AIP, with the *Los Angeles Examiner* calling the first entry, *House of Usher* (1960), "a film that kids will love that never once insults adult intelligence."[179] Playing in first-run houses nationwide, *House of Usher* was AIP's most successful film to that point, with an estimated $1.45 million in domestic rentals.[180]

The ascent of an independent exploitation studio to the rank of major first-run distributor was the ultimate blow to the A/B binary that was a vital component of the industry's structure in the classical period. Films like *The Beast from 20,000 Fathoms* and *It Came from beneath the Sea* proved that certain highly exploitable genres like SF did not need the budget upgrades that the major studios were applying to their traditional B product; a novel concept, a saturation release, and a large advertising budget were all that was necessary to propel a low-budget film to first-run status. AIP was able to succeed for several years while being ignored by the first-run market entirely, forcing the major studios to rethink their neglect of secondary venues like drive-ins and subsequent-run theaters, as well as their distaste of low-budget exploitation films. By the late 1950s it was clear that low-budget filmmaking was the only economically sensible approach for genres like SF. As always, when the industry seizes upon a profitable production strategy, it continues along those lines until the market is saturated. The exploitation films that glutted the marketplace in the late 1950s would not only define the genre for decades, but would also greatly harm SF's cultural and industrial status. It would take a radical shift in direction for SF film to enter the mainstream.

3

FROM PARODY TO PROFUNDITY

///

2001: *A Space Odyssey* and the Critical Legitimation of SF Film

When a genre becomes represented primarily by $70,000 films like *Attack of the Giant Leeches* (1959), it is a good sign a production cycle is coming to a close.[1] With the SF/horror exploitation market shrinking in the early 1960s, the SF genre splintered and combined with other existing genres to create new story types. Comedies and parodies were the most popular — rather than desperately trying to legitimate pulp tropes, films like *The Three Stooges in Orbit* (1962) simply played them for laughs. In terms of drama, the majors returned to the SF A film by approaching the genre obliquely through historical adventure films that took place in the nineteenth century, thus avoiding the futuristic SF plots and iconography that had become toxic in the first-run market. Espionage films were another way to incorporate SF plot elements without fully committing to the genre. Traditional forms of SF could be found primarily in the exploitation imports and coproductions that took advantage of foreign government subsidies and cheap labor.

SF production continued along these lines through the mid-1960s, with the genre largely irrelevant from a commercial and cultural standpoint, until the release of Stanley Kubrick's blockbuster *2001: A Space Odyssey* (1968). One of the most widely discussed and debated films of the 1960s, *2001* legitimated SF cinema more than any other single film in history, proving that the genre could be much more than just exploitation. The mountain of critical discourse on Kubrick's film, exploring its philosophical implications, symbolism, and aesthetic merit, led to a broader critical reassessment of SF film. A new generation of critics who grew up watching '50s SF films began to explore their subtextual meanings, making a case for them as intriguing cultural artifacts, if not always great art. Writing for alternative outlets such as academic journals, specialized film magazines, and fanzines, these critics also paid much closer attention to the new influx of auteur SF films than did the mainstream press. By establishing a critical tradition that took SF film seriously and offered extensive thematic and formal analysis, this discourse provided the foundation of contemporary SF film studies.

Generic Exhaustion and Cycles of Hybridity, 1958–1968

The SF film wave of the 1950s, which began in earnest in 1953, peaked in 1958 with the theatrical release of thirty-nine films. Aside from one programmer (*From the Earth to the Moon*), all were low-budget exploitation product, and only two of them — Fox's *The Fly* and Paramount's *The Blob* — earned over $1 million at the box office. Only a year later, *Variety* expressed skepticism that "there remain[ed] much of a market for the science fiction-fantasy exploitation film."[2] SF film production continued through the early '60s, but at a slower rate. In 1962 only twenty-two SF films were released to theaters, with two comedies (Disney's *Moon Pilot* and Columbia's *The Three Stooges Meet Hercules*) the only entries to make more than $1 million. Bill Warren ends his history of the American SF film of the 1950s in 1962, after which "1950s-style SF movies were rare."[3] Warren is referring to the plots and iconography of the '50s-era films — space travel, alien invasion, giant bugs, and the like. These conventions had proliferated so quickly throughout American culture that by the early '60s they had already calcified into cliché. In a sense, SF cinema had become a victim of its own rapid success.

SF's inescapable association with hackneyed monster-on-the-loose story lines and shoddy Z-film production values kept the genre trapped in the exploitation ghetto. But even there it was suffering. Other genres, such as horror and the Italian sword-and-sandal epic (or peplum), emerged to poach the audience for exploitation SF. Traditional horror underwent a major revival beginning in the late '50s with the success of Hammer Studios and American International's Poe series. While the early-to-mid-1950s were nearly bereft of traditional horror films, by the early '60s dozens of such films, many of them British and Italian imports, filled screens in the exploitation market. The horror genre also reached mainstream audiences through the surprise success of Alfred Hitchcock's *Psycho*, the third-highest-grossing film of 1960.[4] Hitchcock was inspired to pursue a lower-budget, black-and-white horror project based on the tremendous profitability of exploitation films like *The Curse of Frankenstein* (1957) and William Castle's *Macabre* (1958).[5] *Psycho*'s success spurred further production of low-budget psychological thrillers (including several by Castle), as well as A-budget thrillers like *Whatever Happened to Baby Jane?* (1962) and *Cape Fear* (1962).

Shocking audiences with its violent murders, transvestism, and suggestions of necrophilia, *Psycho* was a key step in the assimilation of exploitation tropes into the mainstream. In the words of Drew Casper, "*Psycho* dropped the major studio film smack dab into the exploitational arena where it has since burrowed in."[6] However, as a horror film released by a major studio, featuring a top director and established stars, *Psycho* was well positioned to reach a mainstream audience. Perhaps the more impressive achievement was the unlikely success of the Italian import *Hercules* (1958), which grossed over $4 million in the United States. The distribution rights to *Hercules* were purchased for $125,000 by Joseph Levine, an American independent producer and distributor who specialized in exploitation product.[7] Levine spent an extraordinary $1.2 million on publicity for the film, which received a saturation release from Warner Bros. in the summer of 1959.[8] The stunning box office performance of *Hercules* (it was the twelfth-highest-grossing film of 1959) led, inevitably, to a cycle of sword-and-sandal Italian imports, released by independent and major studios alike.

The typical SF exploitation film of the late '50s was ill-equipped to compete with the color cinematography and relatively lavish production values of the new horror and peplum films. No longer could filmmakers pass off the semidocumentary style as anything more than shameless cost-cutting. In order to adapt to the new, more discriminating exploitation market, studios began to both purchase the distribution rights to foreign films and coproduce with foreign companies. Coproductions allowed American studios to bypass restrictive quotas and apply for subsidies and other financial incentives provided by European governments. This, combined with cheap foreign labor costs, enabled American studios to release "features with production values far beyond what could be made for the same amount of money in Hollywood."[9] For instance, the cinematography and mise-en-scène of films like the Japanese *Matango* (released as *Attack of the Mushroom People* by AIP in 1963) and the Italian *Planet of the Vampires* (released by AIP in 1965) were substantially more colorful and complex than the typical American SF film of the period. Despite these films' ornate sets and extravagant visuals, budgets remained low, owing to cheap labor and traditional cost-saving strategies such as the inclusion of footage from other films. *Journey to the Seventh Planet* (1962), a U.S.-Danish coproduction made for only about $75,000, includes several effects shots from AIP's *Earth vs. the Spider* (1958).[10] Imports and the occasional American exploitation film like *The Time Travelers* (1964) kept SF at what Richard Nowell calls "base level production" through the '60s. Nowell observes that genres never truly disappear once they have been introduced to the marketplace; rather, production continues at a low pace even while a particular genre is considered dormant.[11]

In contrast to the declining fortunes of SF cinema in the early-to-mid-1960s, the genre achieved a new prominence on television. While most SF programs of the period were short-lived, canceled because of poor ratings or rising costs (especially when compared to cheaper genres like the western), many attracted a fervent cult following and lent themselves to merchandising, qualities that would become increasingly important in the decades to come. The longest-running and most critically acclaimed SF show of the '60s was *The Twilight Zone* (CBS, 1959–1964), an anthology drama featuring fantasy and SF story lines that was aimed at an adult audience. The reputation of the show's creator and head writer Rod Serling, best known for the Peabody-winning "Requiem for a Heavyweight" episode of *Playhouse 90* (CBS, 1956), lent *The Twilight Zone* a sense of seriousness and prestige that elevated it above typical SF of the period. Serling was nominated for three Emmys for writing *The Twilight Zone*, winning two, and the show itself was nominated for "Outstanding Program Achievement in the Field of Drama" for its second season. *The Twilight Zone* was even mentioned as an example of quality television ("dramatic and moving") by FCC chair Newton Minow in his famous 1961 "Vast Wasteland" jeremiad to the National Association of Broadcasters.

The other most prominent SF television show of the 1960s, critically and commercially, was *Star Trek* (NBC, 1966–1969), producer Gene Roddenberry's space drama that offered a utopian perspective of Earth's future. The show, chronicling the voyages of the USS *Enterprise*, occasionally featured scripts by respected SF writers like Theodore Sturgeon, Richard Matheson, and Harlan Ellison. *Star Trek* was nominated twice for "Outstanding Drama Series" by the Academy, and breakout star Leonard Nimoy was nominated three times for his performance as the alien Mr. Spock. The show lasted three seasons, thanks in large part to intense letter-writing campaigns organized by dedicated fans, including high-profile SF writers like Isaac Asimov and Frank Herbert.[12]

At a time when SF films would never have been considered among the most outstanding examples of their medium, *The Twilight Zone* and *Star Trek* made a strong case for SF's potential as intelligent, adult entertainment. Crucial was the shows' willingness to tackle social and political issues, much as EC Comics had attempted in the '50s. For instance, the 1960 *Twilight Zone* episode "The Monsters Are Due on Maple Street" critiques McCarthyism, as neighbors are subtly encouraged by alien visitors to turn on one another in paranoiac violence. Producer Dick Berg remarked that Serling "had much on his mind politically and in terms of social condition, and science fiction — and *Twilight Zone* specifically — gave him as much flexibility in developing those themes as he might have had anywhere else at that time."[13] For its part, *Star Trek* was known for its (often heavy-handed) allegories: for instance, "A Private Little War" mirrors the Vietnam conflict, as Captain Kirk struggles with a decision to arm a tribe of technologically primitive aliens whose enemies have already been armed by the evil Klingons. The sociopolitical weight of this kind of content served to justify both shows' use of pulp SF tropes like spaceships and aliens. Unlike exploitation films, these conventions were not merely used for their intrinsic pleasures, which were culturally coded as juvenile, but as avatars for the delivery of Serling and Roddenberry's political themes.

For other shows, the market's demand for traditional iconography generated important creative constraints. *The Outer Limits* (1963–1965), an adult-oriented SF anthology series in the *Twilight Zone* mold, provides one example. ABC executives demanded that producers include a monster "early and often" throughout each episode of the show's second season, as their research indicated that ratings surged whenever a monster appeared. Producer Ben Brady complained that these episodes were "artificially constructed" to showcase the monster costumes of Wah Chang and others, and were artistically compromised as a result.[14] Caught between the producers' desire to create intellectually sophisticated and provocative SF, and the network's desire for the show to fulfill generic expectations, *The Outer Limits* lasted only one and a half seasons, despite producing some of the most intelligent filmed SF of the decade.

The Twilight Zone, Star Trek, and *The Outer Limits* were exceptional in their sophistication, however; more common were SF programs aimed at younger viewers. Producer Irwin Allen was responsible for four such shows: *Voyage to the Bottom of the Sea* (ABC, 1964–1968), based on Allen's feature film; *Lost in Space* (CBS, 1965–1968); *The Time Tunnel* (ABC, 1966–1967); and *Land of the Giants* (ABC, 1968–1970). If Serling and Roddenberry were the visionary auteurs of '60s SF television, Irwin Allen was more closely aligned with exploitation producers like Sam Katzman, concerned with nothing more than churning out simple, cheap entertainment. *The Encyclopedia of Science Fiction* notes Allen's "Poverty-Row worldview," embodied by his shows' use of exploitation tropes, stock footage, and other cost-cutting measures, and overall juvenile tone.[15] Critical reviews reflected this: in a 1967 review of *Voyage to the Bottom of the Sea, Variety* wonders "how Richard Basehart and the other feature players have managed to keep a straight face for three seasons." It goes on to compare the show to the "old Saturday matinee serials" and define its audience as "tots and apparently tot-minded adults."[16] Whereas *The Twilight Zone* and *Star Trek* sought to complicate the usual SF conventions, Allen's shows reproduced them simply and unabashedly, appealing to a younger or less sophisticated audience.

While SF television in the '60s was unafraid to embrace pulp tropes, the decline of the SF exploitation film made it necessary for the genre to take other forms on the big screen. Rick Altman writes, "When a genre reaches the saturation point, studios must either abandon it, restrict it to 'B' productions, or handle it in a new way."[17] The "'50s-style" SF/horror film would be restricted to the low-budget realm throughout the 1960s, largely in the form of foreign imports like the *Godzilla* films. To be viable in mainstream theaters, SF needed to mutate. It adapted to the new demands of the market by merging with existing popular genres, specifically the period adventure film, the espionage film, and the comedy. Raphaëlle Moine argues that genres like SF "lend themselves particularly well to hybridization" because they are defined by their semes, such as iconography, rather than syntax, or structures of meaning.[18] In other words, the images, characters, and scenarios that help define SF can be easily placed into the syntactic structures of other genres; Altman argues that SF most commonly uses the syntax of the horror film or the western.[19]

The SF historical adventure film is one prominent variation that flourished briefly in the late 1950s and early '60s. The historical adventure genre, a perennial favorite in Hollywood, received new emphasis in the postwar era owing to its use of colorful costumes, sets, and action sequences. Classic adventure fiction, from *King of the Khyber Rifles* (novel 1916, film 1953) to *Moonfleet* (novel 1898, film 1955), received lavish cinematic treatment. By the mid-1950s, studios had turned to canonical SF books from the nineteenth and early twentieth centuries from writers like Jules Verne and H. G. Wells. The first SF historical adventure film of the period was Walt Disney's *20,000 Leagues under the Sea* (1954), a relatively faithful adaptation of Verne's classic novel. Featuring stars James Mason and Kirk Douglas and the outstanding production values associated with a $5 million budget, *20,000 Leagues under the Sea* was the fourth-highest-grossing film of the year and the highest-grossing SF film of the decade, earning a massive $8 million in rentals.[20] The film also won two Academy Awards, for Special Effects and Art Direction.

A big-budget version of Verne's *Around the World in 80 Days* was released in 1956, but it was not until 1958 that another SF adaptation was attempted: *From the Earth to the Moon*, produced by RKO and featuring aging stars Joseph Cotton and George Sanders. RKO was in the midst of bankruptcy, and the film evinces all the signs of its studio's death rattle, with

Journey to the Center of the Earth (Twentieth Century-Fox, 1959), which appealed to a wide demographic via stars Pat Boone and James Mason (second and third from the left, respectively) led to a cycle of SF historical adventure films in the early 1960s.

woeful special effects, a slow, awkward pace, and, unforgivably, the lack of any scenes on the moon itself. As a result of RKO's demise, *From the Earth to the Moon* was released by Warner Bros., and promptly flopped. The film that truly ignited the surge in historical SF adventure film production was 1959's *Journey to the Center of the Earth*, released by Twentieth Century-Fox and starring *20,000 Leagues* star James Mason. The picture was a bright spot for Fox in 1959, grossing a huge $8 million worldwide against a production cost of $3.4 million.[21] *Journey* and *20,000 Leagues* established a formula that would be closely followed by later films. Set in the nineteenth century, SF historical adventure films were literary adaptations centered on the exploration of a science fictional environment (such as a "lost world" of dinosaurs or other creatures) by a diverse group of characters intended to attract different audience demographics. For instance, *Journey to the Center of the Earth*'s James Mason appealed to adults, while Pat Boone brought in teen girls, and younger children could delight to Gertrud the pet duck (at least until she is cooked and eaten by the film's villain).

Subsequent SF historical adventure films included Fox's *The Lost World* (1960), MGM's *The Time Machine* (1960), AIP's *Master of the World* (1961), and Columbia's *Mysterious Island* (1961) and *First Men in the Moon* (1964).[22]

These were more modestly budgeted productions, in the $1 million range, and lacked the top stars and stellar production values of *20,000 Leagues* or *Journey*. As such, they performed only moderately well at the box office, similar to previous SF A films of the '50s like *The War of the Worlds* — which is to say, not well enough to warrant a lengthy cycle. The SF historical adventure film had largely run its course by 1964 and ended the next year when AIP's *War Gods of the Deep* (1965) sank without a trace at the box office.

Considering that the majors had ceased production of SF A films after *Forbidden Planet* in 1956, the logic of this brief return to the genre might seem elusive. However, in their period settings and general eschewal of SF pulp tropes, the SF historical adventures deliberately avoided direct comparisons with the typical SF A films, and should thus be considered a distinct cycle. First, alien invasion and space travel plots (aside from *First Men in the Moon*) were banished in favor of the more grounded exploration story line discussed earlier. And instead of commenting upon contemporary technological progress or speculating about the future, as other SF films did, the SF historical adventure films depict an alternate, "steampunk" past in which fictional technologies like time machines and proto-nuclear submarines exist. The urgent timeliness that was crucial to the earlier SF A-film cycle is replaced by a sense of timeless, historical fantasy. While some of the films, like George Pal's *The Time Machine*, would go on to develop strong cult followings, the immediate influence of the SF adventure film upon the genre was negligible.

Another genre to receive an injection of SF elements was the espionage film. The 1960s secret agent movie updated the traditional World War II spy plot with postwar technologies, many of them science fictional, and was set within a romantic, fictionalized Cold War milieu. The cycle was inaugurated by the success of *Dr. No* (1962), the first film based on Ian Fleming's James Bond novels. The Bond films were British/American coproductions between distributor United Artists and independent producers Albert Broccoli and Harry Saltzman. *Dr. No* was produced for $1.2 million and grossed approximately $6 million worldwide.[23] The series was a legitimate cultural phenomenon by the release of the third film, *Goldfinger* (1963), which earned an extraordinary $46 million worldwide in its initial release, against a budget of only about $3 million.[24]

The '60s spy film makes use of SF plots and devices while remaining faithful to the conventions of the espionage genre. This allows films like *Dr. No* to take advantage of SF's novel concepts and iconography, which lend it a cutting-edge flavor, while escaping the then-unattractive SF label. From the beginning, James Bond's persona as a sophisticated purveyor of experimental military technology and other gadgets made him something of a futuristic figure. Promotional materials emphasized the character's "science fiction image," and even the plots of the early, grittier films featured SF concepts.[25] For instance, the villainous Dr. No's evil scheme involves throwing U.S. rockets off course during launch in order to cripple the American space program. Yet to the industry, spy films remained clearly distinct from the SF genre; *Variety* never describes the Bond films as SF, for instance. This reveals the extent to which the SF genre had become associated exclusively with the conventions of pulp fantasy like aliens and speculative futures. Despite their SF elements, spy films remained grounded in a kind of Cold War realism, albeit an extremely exaggerated one. Even when secret agents ventured into outer space, as in *You Only Live Twice* (1967) or *The Ambushers* (1967), the plots are tied to the contemporary space race and do not include extraterrestrials or other more fantastic narrative elements.

The most common form of SF hybridity in this period was the SF comedy, which would typically send up the tropes of '50s SF. Amanda Ann Klein notes that "the appearance of a parody acknowledges that a particular film cycle's themes and images have lost their ability to communicate with the audience as they once did."[26] As suggested earlier, the extremely low-budget "Z films" of the late 1950s and early '60s played an important role in the dilution of the SF genre's efficacy. The ragged monster costumes, risible dialogue, and plywood sets of anti-masterpieces like the $34,000 *Beast of Yucca Flats* (1961) did no favors for the credibility of a genre whose fantastic iconography and story lines already demanded a great deal of credulity. Audiences could demonstrate their superiority over the material by laughing at the ineptness; for instance, critic Bill Warren remembers the "howling, contemptuous teenagers" with whom he watched *Teenagers from Outer Space* (1959) during its original theatrical run.[27] In 1967 the *Motion Picture Herald* predicted that the American/Italian coproduction *Wild, Wild Planet* (1967) would be popular among "those

AUTHOR'S COLLECTION

The proliferation of SF comedies like *Have Rocket, Will Travel* (Columbia Pictures, 1959) demonstrates the extent to which SF was exhausted as a dramatic genre by the late '50s.

devotees who, grown sophisticated and blasé, have come full circle and would like to laugh where once they gaped in horror."[28]

In light of this response, and in recognition of the genre's obvious exhaustion in American popular culture at the time, studios began to release SF films that were deliberately comic. The space race, beginning with the launching of *Sputnik* in 1957, was the catalyst for many of these films, such as Columbia's *Have Rocket, Will Travel* (1959), in which the aging Three Stooges, experiencing a career revival due to television reruns, are accidentally launched into space and end up on Venus. By abandoning any efforts to legitimate the genre as serious adult entertainment, and embracing its more absurd aspects, studios ironically achieved much greater success with SF than they had with the big-budget SF dramas of the mid-1950s. The biggest hit was Walt Disney's *The Absent-Minded Professor*, the fourth-highest-grossing film of 1961 with over $9 million in domestic rentals, making it by far the most successful SF film, comedy or drama, ever to that point.[29] Jerry Lewis also did very well with SF comedies, including *Visit to a Small Planet* (1960) and *The Nutty Professor* (1963), both of which earned about $3 million domestically.[30]

The SF espionage film, grim and violent at its inception, also quickly slipped into parody. By *Goldfinger* the Bond series had begun to embrace a smirking, self-referential attitude that would come to define it for the next twenty years. With this lighter tone came a greater emphasis on the more convoluted, impractical gadgets used by Bond to elude his enemies. The kind of scientific accuracy sought by '50s filmmakers like George Pal or Ivan Tors was discarded in favor of a juvenile delight in inexplicable pseudoscience. Technology is not foregrounded within the narrative as it was in most SF films of the 1950s; instead it becomes a throwaway gag or a gimmick used to provide a modern flavor to traditional action narratives. Bond's trademark reliance on gadgets was an obvious target for spy parodies like *Our Man Flint* (1966), in which secret agent Derek Flint is equipped with a lighter that has eighty-two separate functions, "eighty-three if you wish to light a cigar."

Outright spoofs like *Our Man Flint* attempted to outdo the Bond series by offering more implausible action sequences, more sex appeal, and a broader sense of humor. In 1964 Bond screenwriter Richard Maibaum may have wondered "How does one make a parody of a parody?"

but audiences responded to the goofy hijinks of Flint, and to Matt Helm, played by Dean Martin in a four-film series.[31] In 1966, three of the top ten films at the U.S. box office were spy films, with *Thunderball* firmly in first place, and two parodies (*The Silencers* and *Our Man Flint*) in seventh and ninth place, respectively.[32] The SF elements were still present: for instance, *The Ambushers* (1967) features Matt Helm attempting to recover a stolen flying saucer built by the U.S. military. The comic approach to SF continued throughout the mid-1960s, reinforced by the success of Irwin Allen's campy television shows and SF sitcoms like *My Favorite Martian* (CBS, 1963–1966). But by 1966 the SF comedy had lost much of its luster, as indicated by the underperformance of Jerry Lewis's NASA sex farce *Way . . . Way Out*. Aside from the Bond films, the espionage cycle was also largely kaput by the end of the decade.

The emphasis on hybridization and parody that defines American SF cinema of the early 1960s gives the impression of a genre already fallen into decay after a brief period of classicism. Thomas Schatz has argued that genres inevitably grow more self-conscious as time passes.[33] He applies art historian Henri Focillon's experimental-classic-refinement-baroque pattern to Hollywood genre films, suggesting that eventually the conventions of the genre itself become the primary focus of the filmic discourse, rather than any veridical relationship to reality.[34] According to this model, by the early 1960s, SF had already reached the baroque stage, as the majority of SF films demonstrate a clear awareness of the genre conventions that solidified in the mid-1950s—either by carefully avoiding them or parodying them.

This "evolutionary" model of genre development, to use Altman's term, has been frequently challenged.[35] Steve Neale writes that Schatz's account minimizes industrial and social factors behind genre development and reduces a genre's trajectory to a "smooth, organic development" rather than, more accurately, a "process of contestation and change."[36] Others complain that evolutionary models offer a false view of early genre filmmakers as prelapsarian, unaware of filmic conventions and naively rooting their work in "reality." On the contrary, historical evidence indicates that generic conventions usually solidify relatively early in a genre's history. Tag Gallagher contends that a closer look at the discourse surrounding early westerns reveals considerable controversy about parody and worn-out conventions as early as 1907, when the western genre was saturating American popular culture. Gallagher further suggests that teleological developmental models are often based on inadequate and unrepresentative samplings of the genre in question, focusing largely on established masterpieces by prominent directors or particularly successful films.[37] These critiques ring true for SF film as well. For instance, the question of an initial "experimental" stage is particularly difficult to place: the genre may have solidified in the early 1950s, but examples of SF cinema stretch back to the origins of the medium. Also, parodies like *Abbott and Costello Go to Mars* (1953) and *The Atomic Kid* (1954) existed at the height of the genre's classical period, indicating that the conventions were already well known. Much like the western, the conventions of SF film originated in literature and were extensively developed long before their use by '50s filmmakers.

As I discussed in the introduction, I believe that cycle studies offers the historian an especially useful way of understanding the development of the SF cinema. This is particularly true in the late 1950s and early '60s, when the genre was especially fragmented. Instead of a single baroque unit, SF film in this period can be understood as a complex interweaving of cycles, some of which perpetuate existing norms, others that revise them. This approach avoids the totalizing nature of the evolutionary model by depicting the genre's development as an ebb and flow, along the lines of Neale's conception. For instance, to use Richard Nowell's terminology, *20,000 Leagues under the Sea* was the "Trailblazing Hit" that led to the SF historical adventure film, while *Dr. No* initiated the '60s espionage cycle. Some films of the 1960s, like *Robinson Crusoe on Mars* (1964), can be considered remnants of fading cycles that began in the '50s.

The cycle studies approach allows us to see SF of the late 1950s and early '60s as not simply a collective rejection of '50s SF tropes, but rather as a mixture of new cycles, emerging in response to the decline of previous cycles, which still exist in diminished form. This is a particularly messy, transitional period for the genre; fortunately for the historian, the SF cycles that begin in the late '60s are comparatively easier to chart, as the trailblazing hits are quite obvious. Scholars tend to avoid a "masterpiece approach" to film history, as it can place undue emphasis on a small group of canonical texts to the exclusion of other potentially relevant works. Yet in the history of SF filmmaking in America, a handful of movies have been profoundly influential on the ultimate course of the genre, both aesthetically and economically. Stanley Kubrick's *2001: A Space Odyssey* (1968) would firmly establish SF as a legitimate avatar for innovative, sophisticated filmmaking.

Road-Show Transcendence: *2001: A Space Odyssey*

It took the resources and clout of a major filmmaker to rescue SF from irrelevance and low-budget oblivion. By the mid-1960s, Stanley Kubrick was considered one of the finest young filmmakers in the industry. His previous film, the Cold War satire *Dr. Strangelove or: How I Learned to Stop Worrying and Love the Bomb* (1964), was Columbia's third-biggest hit of the year, earning $4.75 million in domestic rentals and four Oscar nominations, including three for Kubrick (Screenplay, Producer, Director). In April 1964 Kubrick began developing a project with noted SF author Arthur C. Clarke, known at the time primarily for his 1953 novel *Childhood's End*, which chronicles humankind's gradual evolution into a noncorporeal state. Kubrick and Clarke used Clarke's 1951 short story "The Sentinel" as a springboard for a feature-length script. The film opens at the "Dawn of Man," when a group of australopiths discovers a large black alien monolith and quickly learns to use tools and weapons. We then cut to the year 2001, where another monolith has been discovered on the moon and has begun sending a mysterious signal to Jupiter. On the way to Jupiter to investigate, most of the crew of the *Discovery One* spacecraft is killed by the onboard computer HAL, which has malfunctioned. The sole survivor, Dave Bowman, disconnects HAL and is pulled into a "star gate" near Jupiter, after which he is reborn as a giant "star child" that approaches Earth as the film ends. Clarke reworked the manuscript into a proper novel, an early draft of which Kubrick used to pitch the project to MGM.

In February 1965 MGM announced that the film, initially titled *Journey beyond the Stars*, would begin shooting in August for a release in late 1966 or early 1967.[38] This proved to be optimistic. The accolades for *Strangelove* lent Kubrick a level of influence and autonomy that allowed the production schedule and budget for *2001* to extend far beyond their original limits. MGM president Robert H. O'Brien initially allotted a sizable $6 million for production, but by the film's release in April 1968, costs had ballooned to $10.5 million.[39] Much of the delays were due to an extraordinarily long postproduction; Kubrick spent eighteen months working on the film's groundbreaking special effects, which included innovative techniques like the front projection of background elements, as well as perfections of existing processes like traveling matte composite photography.[40] At the time MGM was sufficiently financially stable to take a risk — 1967 had been a record year for the studio, with $227 million in grosses,[41] led by the top hit of the year, *The Dirty Dozen* (1967).[42] Nevertheless, SF had a poor track record as a first-run genre, and MGM had not invested so much in a film since *How the West Was Won*, released five years before *2001*.

MGM's gamble on Kubrick paid off; *2001* earned $8.5 million in 1968 alone, before the film had even entered general release.[43] However, the response to the film was mixed, with younger viewers in particular championing its unconventional style and narration while mainstream critics expressed annoyance. A transitional film caught between the Old and New Hollywood, *2001* was conceived as a traditional adventure blockbuster by MGM but ended up as something quite different. The polarized responses to the film are usually discussed in terms of a generation gap. R. Barton Palmer writes, "For the generation that came of age in the late 1960s, seeing the film (often numerous times) became a *rite de passage* thought to be the source of a special knowledge that distinguished them from their parents and 'square' adults in general."[44] Without denying the important role of *2001* as a marker of subcultural distinction, I wish to explain the disparate responses to the film by studying the stark difference in critical criteria between those who enjoyed the film and those who didn't. By analyzing reviews of *2001: A Space Odyssey*, we can identify the evaluative schemata used by critics. Schemata are preexisting cognitive models or general frameworks that can be applied to specific situations. David Bordwell argues, "In watching a representational film, we draw on schemata derived from our transactions with the everyday world, with other artworks, and with other films. On the basis of these schemata, we make assumptions, erect expectations, and confirm or disconfirm hypotheses."[45] After singling out the different critical schemata, we can identify extratextual factors that helped shape them, such as marketing, distribution strategy, genre, and authorial persona. From this we can better understand the role played by *2001* in challenging conventional notions of SF filmmaking (and Hollywood cinema more generally) and thus broadening the critical schemata for the SF genre.

The road-show distribution method and MGM's initial marketing campaign for *2001* had a clear impact on the earliest reviews of the film. The practice of road-showing had existed since the teens but came into widespread use in the 1950s as a response to the postwar attendance slump. In order to lure audiences back to theaters, a road-show presentation made each screening an elite, "must-see" event. Screenings were limited to luxurious theaters in select major cities and, as John Belton argues, mimicked the traditions of the legitimate theater as a way to redefine moviegoing as a more prestigious, as well as a more spectacular and participatory, experience.[46] Tickets were costly and purchased in advance; ushers provided souvenir programs before escorting audience members to their reserved seats. Road-show features were long, usually between 150 and 180 minutes, including an intermission, and were therefore the only film on the program. Widescreen cinematography (including, often, 70mm projection) and stereo sound were essential components of the road-show experience. Road-show bookings would continue for a lengthy period, sometimes over a year, before the films finally entered general release.[47] Road-showing was highly successful through the mid-1960s, keeping the industry afloat despite competition from television. Epics like *The Ten Commandments* (1956), *Lawrence of Arabia* (1962), and *The Longest Day* (1963) joined the list of the highest-grossing films of all time.

Based largely on the extraordinary success of *Dr. Zhivago* (1965), MGM was heavily invested in the road-show format in the late '60s. In 1967, Mel Maron, the road-show sales manager for MGM, was bullish, claiming that cities with as few as 150,000 people were becoming prime contenders for road-show distribution. Maron reinforced the idea of road-show screenings as sophisticated and classy: "The roadshow offers an evening of real theater — something special . . . and most patrons dress accordingly."[48] Kubrick's space epic premiered first in Washington, D.C., New York, and Los Angeles in the first week of April 1968, and gradually made its way across the country (and the rest of the world) throughout 1968, before entering into general release in early 1969.[49] For its road-show presentations *2001* was exhibited in 70mm Cinerama with six-track stereo sound.

Cinerama was originally a three-camera process that provided a view stretching 146 degrees wide, but the process proved technically problematic and expensive for both studios and exhibitors.[50] By the late 1960s, Cinerama had abandoned the three-camera setup in favor of simply using 70mm gauge film.[51] The Super Panavision 70 format, in which *2001* was shot, gives a 2.21:1 aspect ratio.[52]

On a superficial level *2001* resembles a traditional road-show film, with its spectacular imagery and expansive narrative scope. MGM's initial promotional campaign for the film, which began two years before its release, portrayed it as a conventional space exploration film, in the *Destination Moon* vein. Strongly emphasized were Kubrick and Clarke's commitment to scientific accuracy, and the special effects used to achieve the illusion of realism. Articles published in mass-market tech magazines such as *Popular Mechanics*, *Popular Science*, and *American Cinematographer* previewed technological innovations such as the construction of the giant centrifuge set used to simulate weightlessness in outer space, and the front-projection system used in the opening "Dawn of Man" sequence. *Popular Science* called *2001* "the most realistic science-adventure movie ever filmed" that "uses an astonishing combination of camera tricks and scientific fact to give you the closest thing possible to the actual sensations of space travel."[53]

Popular Mechanics noted that "Kubrick and Clarke insisted that everything in the picture had to be based on known, workable principles. Controls had to be realistically accurate, and many things actually had to work." The same article also highlights the involvement of experts from General Electric, IBM, Honeywell, Bell Labs, and New York University Medical Center, who worked as consultants.[54] Clarke reinforced the predictive quality of the film with a lengthy article in *Vogue*, timed with the film's release, that offered details of his vision of the year 2001, including widespread dehydrated food consumption and aluminum mobile houses carried by "sky cranes."[55] The official program handed out to road-show attendees also insisted on the film's realism: "If computers talk in the film it is because the leading experts in the computer field in the United States and England, where the film was made, assured Kubrick that by the year 2001 computers will talk!"[56]

This emphasis on scientific accuracy was an old tactic, of course, dating

AUTHOR'S COLLECTION

MGM's initial marketing campaign for *2001: A Space Odyssey* (1968) depicted it as a conventional space exploration film.

back to *Destination Moon*. Just like Eagle-Lion, MGM had to establish its blockbuster film as a serious, "epic drama of adventure and exploration," as early posters proclaimed.[57] One such poster depicts a scene in the film in which astronauts explore a lunar landscape, as spacecraft launch from a moon base. By employing this iconography, MGM tied the film to NASA's current Apollo program and distanced it from pulp SF. In 1966 MGM president Robert H. O'Brien vowed to the *New York Times* that *2001* "won't be a Buck Rogers kind of space epic."[58] The failure of *Forbidden Planet* was only a decade old for MGM, and the investment in Kubrick's film was exponentially greater. But MGM was in no real danger of Kubrick and Clarke making a pulp SF adventure film, as neither man had much affection for that narrative tradition. While Clarke felt "that the 'really good' science fiction movie is a great many years overdue," he nevertheless recommended *The Day the Earth Stood Still*, *Forbidden Planet*, *Destination Moon*, and *Things to Come* to Kubrick.[59] The director was unimpressed, telling Clarke after watching *Things to Come* that he would never watch another film recommended by Clarke again.[60]

The departure of *2001: A Space Odyssey* from the conventions of conservative, respectable road-show entertainment was not through pulp escapism, but rather in its rigorous use of art cinema style and narration. The film is arguably the most formally radical big-budget production ever released by a major Hollywood studio. Robert Kolker lists some of *2001*'s most salient experimental qualities: "Denotation is at a minimum and often withheld. The narrative structure refuses to explain itself through conventional means. Actions and events are not immediately motivated, while transitions are startling and spare. There is little dialogue, and much of what exists is deliberately banal. The film has an open structure in which the viewer plays an operative role."[61] Hollywood was stunned by the film's lack of obvious commercial appeal. According to *Variety*, the consensus among industry personnel at the time was, "I feel so sorry for Bob O'Brien being stuck with this $10,000,000 art film."[62]

Most early reviews from major New York critics were strongly negative. Even though *2001* was more closely related to art films like *L'avventura* (1960), these critics, influenced by the prerelease marketing and MGM's distribution strategy, employed typical Hollywood road shows like *Dr. Zhivago* as prototype schemata against which Kubrick's film was compared. When *2001* did not fit that prototype, it was considered an artistic failure. Rather than a deliberate exercise in minimalist narration, some reviewers argued, *2001* was simply dramatically inept. In *The Village Voice*, Andrew Sarris called the film "a thoroughly uninteresting failure and the most damning demonstration yet of Stanley Kubrick's inability to tell a story coherently and with a consistent point of view. . . . *2001* has little writing or acting to speak of, and makes little sense."[63] *Variety* described the film's "star child" ending as "confused," claiming that its ambiguity "smack[s] of indecision or hasty scripting."[64] And Stanley Kauffmann in the *New Republic* wrote, "What is shocking is that Kubrick's sense of narrative is so feeble. . . . The sharp edge, the selective intelligence, the personal mark of his best work seems swamped in Superproduction aimed at hard-ticket theatres."[65]

Along with *2001*'s rejection of conventional narration, the early marketing's emphasis on special effects and production values likely contributed to reviews that criticized the film as a cold, technical exercise. The effects were almost always praised by critics, but frequently in a backhanded fashion. While Judith Crist in *New York* wrote, "It should go without saying that [Kubrick] is an expert craftsman, that he is a master of technical effects, that he is a man of taste," she refers to *2001* overall as "a frequently tedious narrative that provides watered-down adventure."[66] Some reviews suggested that the film was made for a niche audience of SF fans, who would best appreciate the special effects and could more easily understand the story line than the average viewer. The *New York Times*'s Renata Adler griped that *2001* "acknowledged no obligation to validate its conclusion for those, me for example, who are not science fiction buffs." Her most cutting and personal comments are reserved for Kubrick, whom she portrays as a nerdy victim of arrested development: "[The film's] real energy seems to derive from that bespectacled prodigy reading comic books around the block. The whole sensibility is intellectual fifties child."[67] Pauline Kael continues in that vein in her famous 1969 essay "Trash, Art, and the Movies": "Kubrick [has] acted out a kind of super sci-fi nut's fantasy . . . it's the biggest amateur movie of them all."[68]

The attitude of Adler and Kael reflects the typical cultural perception toward SF at the time—that it is a juvenile genre detached from serious, adult concerns. Kael writes, "It's fun to think about Kubrick really doing every dumb thing he wanted to do, building enormous science-fiction sets and equipment, never even bothering to figure out what he was going to do with them."[69] For Kael, Kubrick is a kid in a sandbox, a filmmaker for whom special effects and sets are an end in themselves, and who simply did not bother to fashion a conventional dramatic structure. Some of the negative critical response is also connected to Kubrick's directorial persona. Bordwell writes that the schema of the "personified filmmaker" is common among critics, who understand films as reflections of their director's personality.[70] A filmmaker's authorial persona can be gleaned not just from the films he or she makes, but also from interviews and other public statements. A 1966 *New York Times* profile, for instance, emphasizes Kubrick's meticulousness over small details, as well as his obsessive control of his productions. It ends with a quote from an anonymous friend: "I sometimes get the feeling . . . that Stanley has never quite grown up — that he has remained an immensely gifted child, needing and demanding attention."[71] The idea of Kubrick as an overgrown kid obsessed with gadgets and technology, linked to the low cultural status of SF, seemed to provide an interpretative frame for critics like Adler and Kael as they assessed *2001*.

Other critics acknowledged the art cinema ambiguity of *2001*, but rejected it as indulgent. Russell Baker wrote in the *New York Times* that the film is "obviously designed to titillate us through long evenings of arguing about 'what it really means.' Since you can read it any way you like, the argument is pointless. . . . For the arthouse crowd there is some pretentious (though very pretty) fluff at the very end . . . but it is not to be taken seriously."[72] The *Chicago Tribune*'s Clifford Terry allowed that Kubrick "has every right to be ambiguous, but it's lazy and bad manners to display all sorts of symbolic detours without first providing at least a corner of the roadmap."[73] Ironically, Kubrick did provide a lengthy explanation of the film's concluding scenes to the *New York Times* a few weeks after the film's release: "In the unseen presence of godlike entities who have evolved beyond matter, [Bowman] finds himself in what might be described as a human zoo, created from his own dreams and memories. . . . He dies and is reborn, transfigured; an enhanced being, a starchild. The ascent from ape to angel is complete."[74] Clarke's novel, published nearly three months after the film's release, also eliminates much of the narrative ambiguity.

In general, however, Kubrick was keen to play up the unconventional formal elements of his film, as these qualities were being celebrated by a different set of critics. Publishing in the first week of release, Jim Watters in *Boxoffice* was among the first to recognize that Kubrick was rejecting stylistic and narrative norms: "The old narratives which dominated the film world have given way to themes, techniques and concepts, [that were] once the private property of the avant-garde. . . . Kubrick has delivered a masterpiece."[75] In his review for the *Christian Science Monitor*, John Allen argued that "we are in the habit of approaching film as though it were a book that needed only to be open and read. . . . Passive viewing of [2001] won't do. It is thinking about the film, approaching it intelligently, reaching toward it and beyond it that counts."[76] While other critics struggled to relate one section of the film to another, Penelope Gilliatt in the *New Yorker* offered an insightful analysis, suggesting that the power and freedom of the ape-man swinging the bone weapon had been replaced, by the year 2001, by technology that stifled human imagination and feeling.[77]

Other, more specialized critics approached *2001* as an avant-garde project with the potential to greatly impact the future of cinema. In 1969 New York University professor Annette Michelson wrote a dense, nearly eight-thousand-word theoretical analysis of the film in *Artforum*, discussing it as a "breakthrough" work of reflexivity: "The film as a whole performs the function of a Primary Structure, forcing the spectator back, in a reflexive gesture, upon the analytic rehearsal of his experience. . . . If one were concerned with an 'ontology' of the cinema, this film would be a place in which to look for it." By placing *2001* in an intellectual/aesthetic context that includes Mallarmé, Cézanne, Bergson, Plato, and Piaget, Michelson not only makes a bold claim for its greatness but also, in the words of Greg Taylor, "wrests the film from the clutches of undiscerning middlebrows."[78]

Another early supporter of the avant-garde aspects of Kubrick's film was Gene Youngblood, in 1968 the twenty-five-year-old critic of the *Los Angeles Free Press*, an underground newspaper. Youngblood declared the film a masterpiece upon its release, and later analyzed it in his 1970 book on experimental film, *Expanded Cinema*.[79] Although he disliked *2001*'s concessions to mainstream audiences, namely its "graceless audience manipulation and vulgar expositional devices," Youngblood argued that the film's "contributions to the state of the art and to mass-audience commercial cinema cannot be overlooked or overrated."[80] Youngblood was especially interested in the climactic "star gate" sequence, which recalls the work of avant-garde artists John Whitney Jr. and especially Jordan Belson, whose work in Youngblood's opinion "achieves a sense of cosmic consciousness only hinted at in *2001*."[81] Belson's abstract films, meant to evoke highly subjective metaphysical, spiritual experiences, were influenced in part by the outer space imagery released by NASA in the 1960s. While *2001* is seen to suffer from its commercial taint, for Youngblood it is a crucial link between avant-garde and mainstream cinema.

While Michelson and Youngblood write to niche audiences from a highly specialized vantage point, their appreciation of *2001*'s radical qualities mirrored the appraisal of many ordinary reviewers. Only a few days after *2001*'s premiere, *Variety* published an article suggesting that the harsh opinions of the New York critics were not in tune with audience reactions, which were largely positive. Moviegoers under twenty-five seemed especially enamored, a phenomenon that would receive much media attention and help to define *2001* in the public consciousness. The *Harvard Crimson* published a three-thousand-word review that praised the film's philosophical ambition and technical excellence, referring to it with admiration as "commercial poison . . . a sure-fire audience baffler guaranteed to empty any theater of ten percent of its audience."[82] Likewise, twenty-three-year-old Gary Crowdus published in his new film magazine *Cineaste* a scathing takedown of the critical response to *2001*: "The innovational aspects of this film would seem to indicate the need for careful critical consideration and perhaps even a little encouragement but, with few exceptions, the major New York critics (sensitivity and influence usually in inverse proportion here) wrote insensitive and unfeeling reviews."

Crowdus blamed the generation gap for the difference of opinion: "Looking in vain for a traditional dramatic structure or elements of a plot, the older generation seems unable . . . to comprehend the purely visual narrative, or appreciate the visually abstract sequences of the film." Here Crowdus recalls media theorist Marshall McLuhan, who argued that the generation gap could be attributed in part to a shift from the "hot" medium of print, a more linear and logical form that emphasizes a single sense, to the "cool" medium of television, which is a multisensory, more participatory experience.[83] By the late 1960s McLuhan was a public intellectual with celebrity status, although his ideas about the generation gap were often reduced to a simple "verbal vs. visual" binary.[84] When trying to explain the disparate reactions to *2001*, *Variety* remarked, "As Marshall McLuhan has so laboriously pointed out, today's youth is visually oriented. Words do not have the importance they used to have, whether because the young aren't willing to exert themselves, or because they no longer trust a tool supposedly misused by politicians and advertisers."[85]

This perspective was further developed by critic William Kloman in the *New York Times* a month after *2001*'s premiere. For Kloman, *2001* was the ultimate countercultural artwork, a "deeply subversive film" that rejects easy categorization and old-fashioned attempts at literal interpretation. The film instead calls for "opening your senses to what is happening without anticipation or imposition of logical structures. . . . People restless to 'get on with the action' miss what the real action is."[86] Kubrick, for his part, encouraged this take on his film: "I wanted to make a nonverbal statement, one that would affect people on the visceral, emotional and psychological levels. People over 40 aren't used to breaking out of the straight-jacket of words and literal concepts, but the response so far from younger people has been terrific."[87]

The generation gap was also evident in the reaction to *2001* within the SF literature community. Rob Latham observes that debates over the merits of Kubrick's film mirrored to some extent internal discussions by authors and fans over the direction of literary SF.[88] In 1962, thirty-one-year-old SF author J. G. Ballard had written "Which Way to Inner Space?," an essay that dismissed most SF writing as juvenile, simplistic, and creatively stagnant. Ballard saw no reason why SF stories and novels should not meet the artistic standards set by the best literature; to this end he called for a rejection of the tired tropes of space travel, alien encounters, and time machines, in favor of a new emphasis on human psychology and cultural commentary: "It is *inner* space, not outer, that needs to be explored. . . . I'd like to see science fiction becoming abstract and 'cool,' inventing fresh situations and contents that illustrate its theme obliquely."[89] Ballard's manifesto anticipated the revitalization of SF literature in the 1960s and 1970s called "the New Wave," in reference to the

French cinematic *Nouvelle Vague*. New Wave authors like Ballard, Ursula K. Le Guin, and Samuel R. Delany rejected the jargony technophilia of '50s SF in favor of character subjectivity, formal experimentation, and controversial sociopolitical content.

Fans and writers devoted to the more conventional forms of the genre fiercely attacked the New Wave as, in Latham's words, "nothing less than a betrayal of what SF was all about."[90] To its detractors the New Wave was pretentious, nihilistic, and even obscene. This tension between old and new is evident in the *2001* reviews written by SF authors. Arthur C. Clarke was not considered a New Wave writer, and his novelization dulls the radical edge of the film by explaining and literalizing its more ambiguous aspects. But *2001*'s formal complexity made it a perfect cinematic counterpart to the New Wave. Writers like Delany (born 1942) praised *2001* as "exciting to look at, and . . . exciting to think about," while older establishment writers were much less enthusiastic, their reviews resembling the pans from newspaper critics.[91] Ray Bradbury (born 1920) criticized *2001* for lacking human interest, claiming that Clarke "has had the misfortune of crossing trajectories with the now inexplicably dull director, Stanley Kubrick. . . . Clarke should have done the screenplay totally on his own and not allowed Kubrick to lay hands on it."[92] Frederik Pohl (born 1919) described it as a "wasted opportunity. . . . It could have dealt honorably with the hard parts of what it had to say, instead of blurring them in a mess of imagery."[93] Lester del Rey (born 1915) took direct aim at the New Wave in his blisteringly negative review: "It's the first of the New Wave–Thing movies, with the usual empty symbolism. The New Wave advocates were exulting over it as a mind-blowing experience. It takes very little to blow some minds. But for the rest of us, it's a disaster. It will probably be a box-office disaster too, and thus set major science-fiction movie making back another ten years."[94]

Latham notes that New Wave SF was closely linked to the counterculture, with Ballard's "inner space" serving as a metaphor for mind expansion via psychotropic drugs.[95] Inspired by the psychedelic effects of the "star gate" climax, the counterculture audience turned *2001: A Space Odyssey* into the first "Grind Road Show" in history, to use *Variety*'s phrase.[96] Fancy downtown theaters normally populated by "older and affluent" road-show audiences were packed with hippies and "heads" who smoked

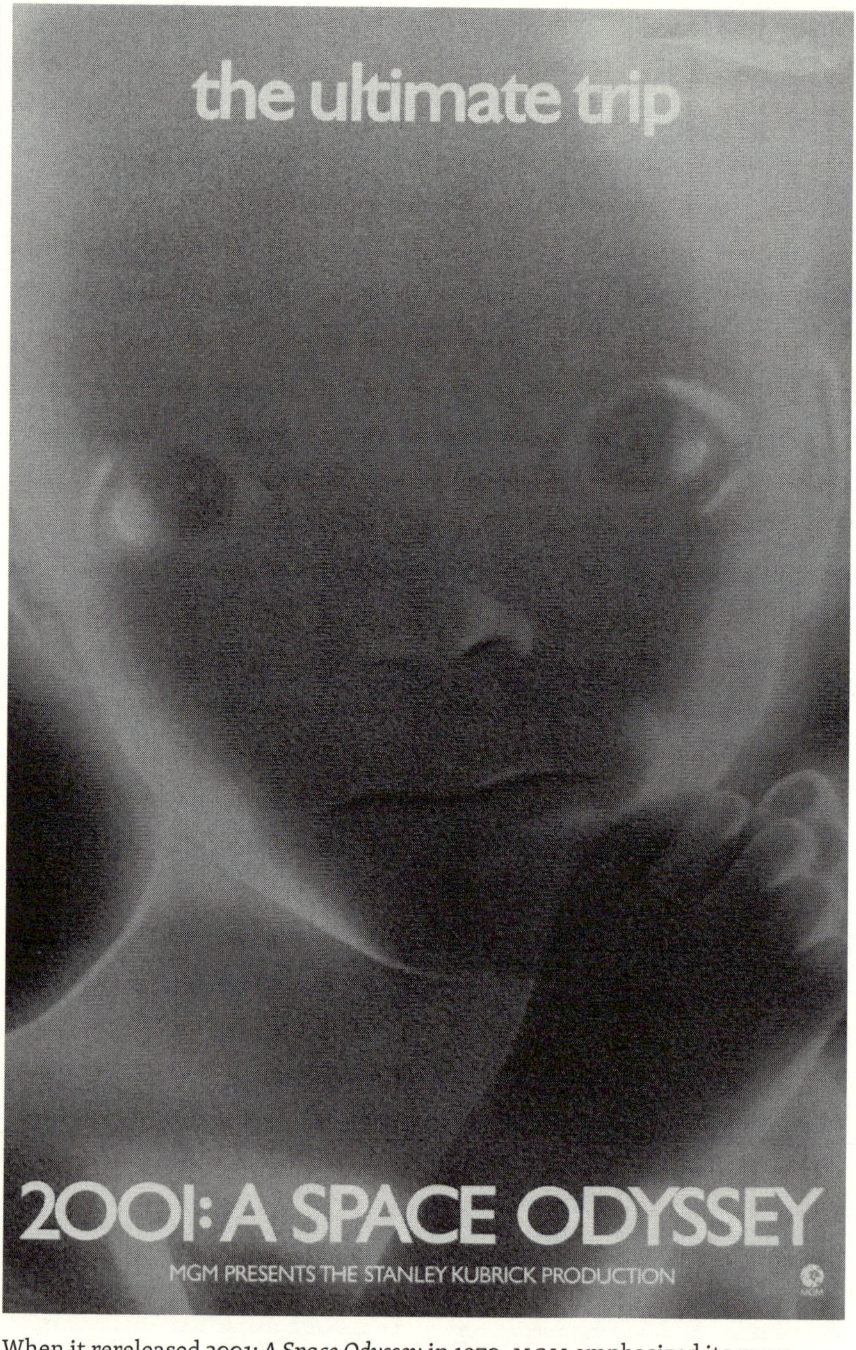

When it rereleased *2001: A Space Odyssey* in 1970, MGM emphasized its more surreal, psychedelic qualities.

marijuana in the balconies and scandalously flouted road-show tradition by neglecting to purchase their tickets in advance.[97] *Variety* describes audience members lying on their backs directly in front of the screen during the star gate sequence, and *Rolling Stone* reported that a young man actually leaped through the Cinerama screen during one showing, shouting "It's God! It's God!"[98] MGM was quick to "re-brand" the film to take into account this unexpected new audience. Less than two weeks after *2001*'s release, the studio was using a quote from *Time* in print ads that promised "the closest equivalent to a psychedelic experience this side of hallucinogens!"[99] Later ads in 1968 featured similar quotes, including "Kubrick's 2001 is the ultimate trip," pulled out of context from the *Christian Science Monitor*.[100] "The ultimate trip" was later used as a tagline for *2001*'s rerelease in 1970. Ironically, neither Clarke nor Kubrick was a drug user, and both attempted to disassociate the film from drug culture, with Kubrick complaining that LSD users "seem to completely lose their critical faculties" when under the influence.[101]

MGM expected a traditional road-show film and ended up with a countercultural phenomenon. But, as Peter Krämer observes, *2001*'s extraordinary commercial success indicates that the audience for the film consisted of far more than just college-age viewers.[102] Kubrick's film became a perennial favorite, reissued frequently throughout the 1970s. By the end of 1973, it had earned $20.3 million in domestic rentals, and $7.5 million from foreign markets, making it one of the highest-grossing films in MGM's history.[103] It was also nominated for four Academy Awards: Best Director, Best Original Screenplay, Best Art Direction, and Best Effects, winning the last. At the time the nominations were released in 1969, the critical consensus was apparently still too mixed for a Best Picture nomination. But some critics who had initially panned the film had revised their evaluations. *Newsday*'s Joseph Gelmis was the first, publishing a wildly positive second review only sixteen days after his first, mixed review.[104] Even Andrew Sarris in 1970 admitted *2001* was "a major work by a major artist."[105] By 1972, the film was a runner-up in a *Sight & Sound* poll of the greatest films ever made, tied with canonical works like *Sunrise* (1927) and *Grand Illusion* (1937).[106] A year later, a monograph on *2001* by scholar Carolyn Geduld was released, the first book of criticism to focus on a single SF film.[107]

More than any other film, *2001: A Space Odyssey* legitimated the SF film genre, both in the eyes of critics and mainstream audiences. First, its large-budget, high-profile distribution strategy and MGM's marketing campaign assured it would not go unnoticed in American popular culture. Then, the film's challenging form and the polarized reactions it elicited rendered it a cultural phenomenon that demanded to be seen. The film's thought-provoking themes about the evolution of mankind and our relationship to technology also made clear to viewers, critics, and filmmakers alike that SF cinema could be more than space opera and exploitation horror. The film's direct influence on SF filmmaking was attenuated, as I will discuss in chapter 4, but nonetheless its impact upon the genre as a whole was profound and unprecedented.

The Birth of SF Film Studies

The extraordinary amount of critical interest in *2001: A Space Odyssey* was crucial in the development of serious critical and scholarly analyses of SF cinema, particularly in specialized magazines or journals dealing exclusively with film or the arts, as opposed to the popular press, which targeted a wide audience. Kubrick's film redefined SF cinema not only for filmmakers and studios, but also for critics, who began to recognize the elasticity of the genre and its ability to depart from the pulp paradigm. Prior to the late 1960s, SF cinema was rarely discussed in film magazines —and when it was, it was usually in dismissive or highly critical terms. Richard Hodgens's essay "A Brief, Tragical History of the Science Fiction Film," published in *Film Quarterly* in 1959, is representative. For Hodgens, SF films had "come close to ruining the reputation of the category of fiction from which they have malignantly sprouted."[108] A champion of SF literature, Hodgens attacked SF film for its lack of respect for science and its emphasis on horror: "Unfortunately, science fiction films have associated science, the future, the different, and the unknown with nothing but irrational fear."[109] Hodgens's article was a systematic critique of nearly every American SF film of the 1950s, although he did spare *Destination Moon*, which he considered "a good semi-documentary, educational film."[110]

Hodgens's attitude toward SF cinema was common among SF literature aficionados in particular. SF author Frederik Pohl, writing for *Film Society*

Review, was considerably blunter than Hodgens: "Nearly every science-fiction movie made is pure crap, made by schlock merchants for an audience of cretins."[111] However, by the time Pohl wrote this invective in 1970, a number of film scholars and critics had begun to turn their enthusiastic attention to the genre. Not only had *2001* legitimated SF cinema, but according to Steve Neale, "it was not until the late 1960s and early 1970s that the study of genre and genres began to establish itself more fully in Britain and in the U.S., in tandem with the establishment of Film Studies as a formal, academic discipline."[112] As Neale notes, the rise of interest in genre films could be attributed to a new generation that had grown up watching critically disreputable films and was now eager to study them as adults. Many of the writers who first made a case for the critical legitimacy of SF film were in their twenties and thirties and had encountered 1950s SF films in their youth, either in the theater or later on television—as opposed to someone like Frederik Pohl, born in 1919, who was already in his mid-thirties when the genre began to proliferate.

SF would not receive the amount of scholarly attention in the 1960s and '70s that the more semantically consistent, easily definable genres such as the western or the melodrama would receive, yet a number of books and articles were published that challenged the prevailing, dismissive critical views of SF cinema by revealing the complexity of even the most lowly examples. These works called for a broad reassessment of the genre and expanded the critical lexicon for future writers. Three key foundational books for SF studies were Carlos Clarens's *Illustrated History of the Horror Film* (1968), John Baxter's *Science Fiction in the Cinema* (1970), and William Johnson's *Focus on the Science Fiction Film* (1972). Clarens, who had previously worked as a production assistant for Robert Bresson and Jacques Demy, devoted two chapters of his book to SF—one on the '50s cycle and the other on SF art films of the '60s like *La Jetée* (1962) and *Alphaville* (1965).[113] Both Baxter's and Johnson's books were released in the wake of *2001: A Space Odyssey* and use that film as an end point for their histories, as a realization of SF cinema's potential. Baxter, at the time a thirty-one-year-old SF writer who had published in *New Worlds*, segmented his fairly comprehensive history of SF film into a variety of topics—for instance, one chapter on SF serials, another on *Things to Come*. Johnson's book was an anthology that reprinted production histories and reviews of SF films from the days of the Kinetoscope in 1895 through the late 1960s.

Reflecting the limited availability of the films to readers and writers alike, Clarens's and Baxter's books emphasize plot synopsis and production details over close analysis. Yet critical evaluation was not absent, with Baxter championing *Invaders from Mars* (1953) and *The Incredible Shrinking Man* (1957), and Clarens calling attention to low-budget obscurities like *The Day Mars Invaded Earth* (1963). The very discussion of films like *Red Planet Mars* (1952) and *The Space Children* (1958) in sober works of film criticism (rather than fan magazines) was something of a radical act. As critic J. Hoberman notes, "Clarens talks knowledgably of movies . . . that hardly anyone else would admit to having seen."[114] Yet while Clarens and Baxter clearly enjoyed SF cinema, they were careful not to undermine their critical credibility by overstating the artistic value of the works in question, as fan discourse might. For both writers, SF film was still generally inferior to SF literature, which trafficked in ideas more than purely action and spectacle. Clarens argued that 1950s SF film "demanded of the filmmaker little beyond an awareness of the headlines and a technical dazzle," while Baxter claimed outright that "the two fields of sf and cinema do not mesh; sf films usually succeed as cinema in proportion to the degree in which they fail as sf."[115] In this respect they were not as far from Hodgens and Pohl as it might otherwise seem. Both books however, concluded with a sense of optimism, with Clarens praising *Alphaville* as "science-poetry"[116] and Baxter remarking that *2001* was as close a union between SF and SF film as may ever be achieved.[117]

Johnson's book was perhaps the most valuable, compiling twenty-two articles from widely disparate authors and sources, including translations of articles originally printed in French and Italian. For the first time, English-speaking audiences were widely introduced to European criticism of SF cinema, including a young François Truffaut's 1953 review of Paramount's *Dr. Cyclops* (1940) for *Cahiers du Cinéma*, and Michel Ciment's analysis of *2001: A Space Odyssey*, originally published in *Positif*. Johnson himself penned an introductory essay that offered a brief historical survey of the genre and, more importantly, defended SF cinema against its critics from the literary world, whom Johnson called "hypercritical." He argued that SF cinema had developed independently from SF literature and should be treated with distinct critical criteria: "Writing can be richer in ideas; the film, in experience . . . filmic qualities of vitality and intensity can transcend the limitations of the genre." Johnson also argued that SF cinema exhibited an ambivalence toward the unknown that lent it a thematic richness elevating it above other popular genres such as the western or thriller. These claims helped to establish a unique critical tradition for SF film that exists outside the usual comparisons to literature, where SF film was relentlessly criticized as simpleminded and inferior.[118]

In the wake of Clarens, Baxter, and Johnson, other critics, many with a scholarly background, fashioned complex analyses of '50s and '60s SF films. Occasionally they argued for the intrinsic artistic merits of a film, as Martin Rubin did in the pages of *Film Comment* where he claimed in 1974 that *The Incredible Shrinking Man* was at "the very forefront of its genre" owing to the relative subtlety of its atomic-age critique and its exploration of "the confines of middle-class life."[119] And although Rubin compared the film to the work of modern artists Magritte, Warhol, and Duchamp, his praise was ultimately backhanded: "The film's only limitation is the limitation of its genre, because for some reason it seems that science-fiction films are best served by bland or mediocre talents" such as Jack Arnold and Don Siegel. Rubin's comment was a broadside against auteur critics who believed filmmakers could enhance formulaic genre material through a distinctive personal style.

Rubin's appraisals of Arnold and Siegel were so polemical precisely because the two had both received the auteur treatment by other critics. Baxter devoted an entire chapter to Arnold in his book, calling him "the great genius of American fantasy film." For Baxter, Arnold's general lack of visual flair and lack of interest in symbolism were actually assets that made him unpretentious and "cool like the great jazzmen." Arnold "was in the movies for money, and because it was what he did best. Any art was incidental. But because of his insouciant attitude, his work had a calculated cynicism and a special poetry."[120] Siegel was even more celebrated; Andrew Sarris included him in his famous 1968 auteurist manifesto *The American Cinema* and described *Invasion of the Body Snatchers* as "one of the few authentic science fiction classics."[121] In 1972 Charles T. Gregory wrote that "a close examination of Don Siegel's work indicates how wrong Stanley Kauffmann was to dismiss him as a competent professional with nothing personal to say."[122] Gregory argued that the celebration of the individual over group conformity in the *Body Snatchers* was a central theme running through Siegel's body of work. For Gregory and other proponents of the auteur theory, these recurring themes served to elevate films like *Body Snatchers* that might otherwise have been considered routine.

Overall, however, critics in the 1960s and '70s did not often advocate for '50s SF films on their aesthetic merits. Making a case for Don Siegel as an auteur was one thing; championing journeymen like *Forbidden Planet*'s Fred M. Wilcox or *The Deadly Mantis*'s Nathan Juran was something else entirely. More common was to argue for the legitimacy of '50s SF cinema via its social relevance. Films whose pulp narratives might seem silly on first glance can be interpreted as full of potent subtextual sociopolitical meaning — Sontag's "The Imagination of Disaster" is perhaps the most influential essay in this vein. Another early example was Raymond Durgnat's "The Wedding of Poetry and Pulp — Can They Live Happily Ever After and Have Many Beautiful Children?," which contains an extended thematic interpretation of Universal's programmer *This Island Earth*. Durgnat writes: "*This Island Earth* has everything against it . . . it's science fiction, it's slanted at adolescents, it's a routine product from a studio with no intellectual pretensions, it has no auteurs . . . and for all that, it has a genuine charge of poetry and of significant social feeling."[123] While he identifies an undercurrent of thematic ambivalence in the film, ultimately Durgnat argues that *This Island Earth* exhibits a "resonance with certain psychopathological traits in American political thought," namely the right-wing paranoia and bellicosity of 1950s America.[124] The peaceful planet Metaluna, under attack by the warlike Zagons, is equated with a complacent, "too-liberal U.S.A." that has failed to adequately arm itself against its enemies. Regardless of one's evaluation of Durgnat's analysis, he makes the crucial point that "the emotional and moral 'catchment-area' of an apparently 'escapist' film may be far more extensive, and realistic than its overt content."[125]

Durgnat also identifies a number of Freudian symbols and Oedipal structures in *This Island Earth*, and implausibilities in the narrative are said to be using "dream-reasoning."[126] Applying a psychoanalytic frame was another strategy used by scholars and critics who wished to make a case for the intellectual legitimacy of SF cinema. Margaret Tarratt surveyed classic SF cinema from a Freudian perspective in her 1970 article "Monsters from the Id." She wrote that SF films "may deal with society as a whole, but they arrive at social comment through a dramatization of the individual's anxiety about his or her own repressed sexual desires, which are incompatible with the morals of civilized life. . . . The battles with sinister monsters or extraterrestrial forces are an externalization of the civilized person's conflict with his or her primitive subconscious or id."[127] *Forbidden Planet* was an obvious example, as it overtly addressed this theme. But Tarratt applied this interpretative schema to other films, such as *The Thing from Another World*. Other films, like *The Incredible Shrinking Man*, deal with castration anxiety: the title character is gradually emasculated as he shrinks, and redeems his masculinity only in the climax when he impales a (to him) giant spider with his phallic sewing needle. For Tarratt, the spider is the phallic mother that represents female domination and elicits horror and dread from the man.[128] Much like Durgnat, Tarratt believed that the seemingly trivial narratives of pulp SF/horror films belied their complex psychological and social underpinnings.

When it came to the wave of art cinema–influenced American SF films beginning with *2001*, critics naturally had a much easier time arguing the genre's merits. It was one thing to claim that exploitation films like *The Leech Woman* (1960) were worthy of serious analysis, another to argue the same for formally and thematically complex auteur films such as *THX 1138* or *A Clockwork Orange* (both 1971).[129] Films like these allowed SF film to achieve a new level of prominence and respectability in the popular press; yet popular reviewers remained limited by their assigned format. Intended for a general audience and relatively short, reviews could not approach the level of detail or intellectual depth possible in specialized film magazines and journals. Also, as we will see in chapter 4, popular critics were prone to dismiss SF art films as pretentious. In the case of these more challenging SF films, specialized film magazines and journals sometimes provided the only venue for sustained critical analysis. The critical reception of John Boorman's *Zardoz* (1974) provides an excellent case study that highlights the value of these sources in helping to establish a "serious" critical tradition for SF film.

Boorman's previous film *Deliverance* was among the twenty highest grossers of 1972 and was nominated for three Oscars, including Best

Picture and Best Director.[130] This emboldened the filmmaker to write *Zardoz*, a complex SF allegory with roots in both Boorman's recent visit to a commune in northern California and his aborted attempt to adapt J. R. R. Tolkien's *The Lord of the Rings* for the screen. *Zardoz* posits a 2293 in which the human race is bifurcated into separate societies. The ruling class, known as the Eternals, has discovered how to halt aging, cure disease, end war, and ultimately defeat death. They live in a seemingly harmonious paradise called the Vortex while using the false god Zardoz to pacify the Brutals, the primitive mortals who exist in the violent post-apocalyptic Outlands. Zardoz (a play on "Wizard of Oz," another story of a false god), takes the form of a massive flying stone head that spits out guns and bullets for the use of Exterminators, a warrior class ordered to keep the Brutal population in check. The protagonist is Zed, an Exterminator who sneaks aboard the stone head and travels to the Vortex when he learns the truth about Zardoz. Little does Zed know he has been genetically engineered by a rebellious Eternal who seeks to disrupt the dull conformity and perfection of the Vortex. Zed introduces to the Eternals sex, anger, jealousy, and eventually death, which the terminally bored Eternals welcome with open arms. The film ends with the collapse of the barrier between the Eternals and the Brutals, with a coterie of Eternal women inseminated by Zed leaving for a new life in the Outlands, and a group of Exterminators massacring the remaining Eternals.

Zardoz is replete, arguably overburdened, with meaning; Boorman intended the film to be, among other things, a critique of the Catholic Church, New Age communes, ageism, the class divide, and modernity.[131] Despite his considerable cachet in the industry at the time, Boorman struggled to find a studio willing to fund his project. Eventually Twentieth Century-Fox agreed to distribute the film, setting its budget at $1.5 million, an almost impossibly low sum for a film with the scope and ambition of *Zardoz*.[132] Even worse for Boorman, Fox would offer only a negative pickup deal, meaning Boorman (serving as writer, director, and producer) was responsible for the initial financing and would be repaid by Fox only when the film was completed. Boorman had to spend $200,000 on casting Sean Connery, a star whose career was floundering after he abandoned the James Bond role in 1971. Further underscoring the threadbare nature of the production, Connery would be Boorman's houseguest

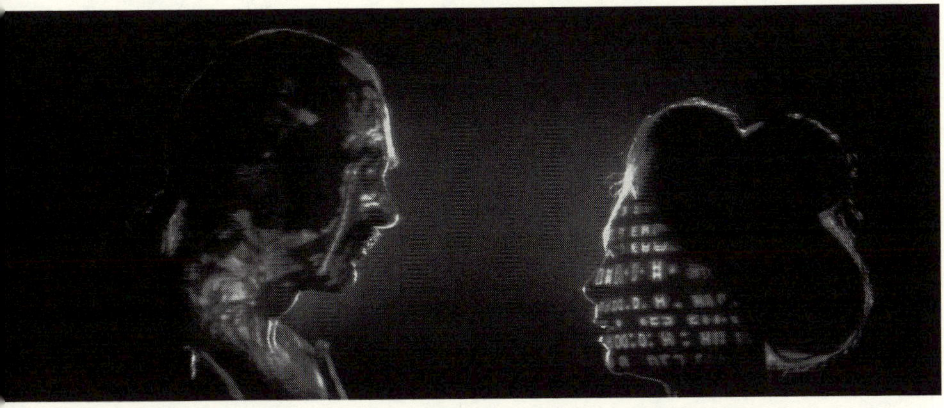

The special effects of *Zardoz* (John Boorman Productions/Twentieth Century-Fox, 1974) have a distinct avant-garde quality, which contributed to the mystified reaction of popular critics to the film. Here, Zed (Sean Connery) is "touch taught" by May (Sara Kestelman).

for the duration of the shoot, which took place in the nearby Wicklow Mountains in Ireland.[133]

Perhaps Boorman's most important hire was master cinematographer Geoffrey Unsworth, who had recently shot *2001* and *Cabaret* (1972). Unsworth favored the heavily diffuse, soft look that was fashionable in the late 1960s and early '70s. "Fog filters" placed over the lens and the use of smoke on the set created an evocative, otherworldly atmosphere. Working within the limits of the film's relatively low budget, Unsworth and Boorman used mirrors and 16mm projectors to produce *Zardoz*'s special effects "in-camera" rather than optically. This ingenious strategy led to most of the film's standout sequences, including the scene in which the women of the Vortex "touch teach" Zed, offering their limitless wisdom in exchange for their insemination (male Eternals are sterile). To externalize this psychological process, Boorman and Unsworth project a variety of culturally potent images such as classical paintings and mathematic formulas onto the hands of the actresses, then onto Zed's body as he reclines. The images are rendered abstract as they blend with one another and distort from their projection on the uneven surface of the human body. Soon the camera begins to spin, rendering the patterns indecipherable until the screen is awash in nothing but flashes of light and color.

Like the star gate sequence of *2001*, the images are motivated by the story line, yet in their abstraction they exceed the bounds of the narrative.

Zardoz, released in early February 1974, was a misfire at the box office, earning only $1.8 million in rentals.[134] The film was also poorly received by the popular press, with only three of sixteen reviews out of New York favorable.[135] Critics tended to praise Unsworth's visuals, particularly the scene described above, but overall *Zardoz* was condemned as thematically muddled and pretentious to the point of absurdity. Gary Arnold of the *Washington Post* described it as "a hopelessly ludicrous science fiction allegory,"[136] while *Variety* warned that "both sophisticated and general audiences may emerge confused, for opposite reasons."[137] Perhaps anticipating these objections, Fox ordered Boorman to insert an explanatory prologue in which a character directly addresses the audience, briefly explaining the film's "false god" conceit and describing *Zardoz* as "rich in irony, and most satirical," suggesting that Boorman is in on the joke. A glossary and guide to the world of the film was also distributed to critics.

Zardoz was certainly left vulnerable to criticism by Boorman's bizarre mix of solemn sociopolitical commentary, allegory, and camp imagery—such as the floating stone head intoning "the gun is good, the penis is evil," and the sight of Sean Connery in a skimpy loincloth and, in one scene, a wedding dress disguise. The film is also weighted down by a surplus of concepts—some delivered with sledgehammer subtlety, others utterly ephemeral. For instance, one of the Eternals notes that their technology, including the ability to resurrect the dead, was originally intended to aid in interstellar travel, but when Zed inquires further, the Eternal dismisses space travel as "another dead end," and the issue is never raised again. Boorman's novelization of the film helps to clarify some of these matters and provides the access to Zed's psychology denied by the film, yet even Boorman admitted years later that "there were maybe too many ideas in this picture. . . . I'm astonished at my hubris in making this extraordinary farrago."[138]

At least the negative reviews made an effort to engage with the film; perhaps more damning was the response *Zardoz* engendered in the popular press, which treated Boorman's film as little more than a vanity project, unworthy of serious discussion. Gene Siskel in the *Chicago Tribune* warned, "Never finance the next production of a director who's just had a big hit. Every director . . . has a secret script he's just dying to put on film . . . and, experience proves, it will be both an artistic and financial disaster."[139] Pauline Kael may have panned the film ("Everybody is entitled to a certain amount of craziness, but John Boorman may have exceeded the quota"), but at least it merited a thoughtful, lengthy lead review in her *New Yorker* column.[140] In contrast, Stanley Kauffmann (not a Boorman fan) did not review the film at all, and the *New York Times* buried a short review — written by "thirdstring staffer" A. H. Weiler rather than lead critic Vincent Canby — at the bottom of the page. According to *Variety*, Twentieth Century-Fox was "incensed over the treatment given" to *Zardoz* by the popular press, saying that the studio's "ire is not so much sparked by negative reviews but by the alleged 'dismissal' of the work of a major director."[141]

In contrast, specialized film magazines and journals, receptive to auteur-driven, thematically rich films, provided a more welcome critical environment for *Zardoz* and other ambitious SF films of the period, like *Slaughterhouse-Five* (1972) and *The Man Who Fell to Earth* (1976). This was crucial for a genre like SF film, which was just beginning to develop a tradition of serious criticism. Whereas Siskel chided *Zardoz* as "simple-minded" and insulting to the intelligence of its audience, a number of magazines and journals devoted lengthy essays to the film's themes.[142] In her eight-and-a-half-page analysis in *Film Quarterly*, film professor Marsha Kinder argued that *Zardoz* was "liberated and experimental in form, yet fascist and sexist in content." Kinder compared the crystalline artificial intelligence of *Zardoz* known as the Tabernacle to crystalline imagery in William S. Burroughs's *Naked Lunch* (1959) and Norman Mailer's *Why Are We in Vietnam?* (1967), thus linking Boorman to these formally innovative yet arguably misogynistic writers. Kinder interpreted Zed's overthrow of the Vortex as a response against the peace movement and feminism; a peaceful, classless, matriarchal commune is destroyed, allowing for the restoration of the violent patriarchal order, including the nuclear family.[143]

In a five-thousand-word review for *Jump Cut*, Fredric Jameson agreed that *Zardoz* could be understood as reactionary, particularly in its rejection of the Vortex's Marxist utopia. At the same time, Jameson held that the film could conversely be seen as a critique of capitalism: "We

Americans are ourselves the Vortex's immortals, freed by the service economy from the drudgery of real labor and sheltered cosmetically from any real experience of death. Yet our world's leisure and privileges are dependent on the effectiveness with which, through the violence of our mercenaries and the power of superstition and enforced ignorance, we are able to extract the necessary riches from servile and miserable populations abroad." While Jameson admired the aesthetics of *Zardoz*, he found its thematic ambiguity a "cop-out" and argued that "an outright commitment to science fiction would have forced Boorman into an honesty and a speculation about future history which his other aesthetic all too cheaply and easily allows him to elude."[144] Even if scholars like Kinder and Jameson found *Zardoz* to be just as flawed as did the popular critics, their thoughtful, sophisticated analyses were far removed from the superficial pans of most of the reviewers.

Aside from the specialized film magazines and academic journals, certain fan magazines provided another haven for the serious analysis of SF cinema. When it came to SF film, some fanzines were arguably even more progressive than the academic journals, in that they devoted their attention not only to art-cinema-influenced auteur films, but also to exploitation films and other culturally devalued product. Most of the fanzines of the late '50s to the '70s that dealt with SF were focused primarily on the horror film. The best known, most widely read horror film "prozine" (a fanzine with wide commercial distribution) of the period was *Famous Monsters of Filmland* (191 issues, 1958–1983), published by James Warren and edited by SF pulp writer and collector Forrest J. Ackerman and with a circulation of approximately 150,000.[145] Its success was closely linked to the television revival of classic horror and SF films that began in the late 1950s. Distribution packages such as Columbia's "Shock!" introduced the horror and SF films of the '30s to the '50s to a new generation; these "monster kids," as they are described in fan circles today, are baby boomers who grew up not only on Bela Lugosi and Boris Karloff, but on SF films like *The Thing from Another World* as well. According to Matt Yockey, Ackerman and *Famous Monsters* "legitimated fans' interest in the culturally marginalized pleasures of horror films, empowering them to assert an increased degree of social authority and control."[146] As we shall see in chapter 5, by the late 1970s, readers of *Famous Monsters* like Steven Spielberg had grown up and begun to introduce the "monster kid" sensibility into mainstream culture.

As popular as *Famous Monsters* was, it was not exactly a bastion of serious criticism. The magazine consisted mostly of large black-and-white stills, with plot synopses and quippy captions provided by Ackerman. As Bob Rehak notes, the images served as a kind of cinematic repository in the days before home video, allowing readers to revisit their favorite films while waiting for them to reappear on television.[147] While *Famous Monsters* continued to appeal to younger readers until its cancellation in 1983, other fanzines inspired by Ackerman targeted an older audience. Calvin Beck's *Castle of Frankenstein* (twenty-five issues, 1962–1975) was formatted similarly to *Famous Monsters*, with an emphasis on large stills from classic films, but offered much more sophisticated articles written by reputable contributors such as film historian and professor William K. Everson. But the most sophisticated of all genre fanzines of the period was undoubtedly *Photon* (twenty-seven issues, 1963–1977), published by Mark Frank. In the words of film historian Scott MacQueen, *Photon* "was the closest thing in the day to a 'peer review' academic journal, in the best sense of that stuffy phrase, signaling the seriousness of intent."[148] *Photon* jettisoned any *Famous Monsters* trappings, and targeted adults instead of children with a more sober look at horror and SF films. For instance, an issue from 1974 contains an exceptionally erudite twelve-page analysis of *2001* that would not have been out of place in academic film journals. In his lengthy exegesis, author David MacDowall relates the film's evolutionary themes to Shakespeare's "Seven Ages of Man," applies numerology to analyze the number three as a key motif, reviews the Clarke novel, discusses the film's special effects, and debates the film's critics. While he does not use citations, MacDowall quotes numerous sources from the trade and popular presses. But alongside the intelligence and professionalism of MacDowall's essay lurks the outrage of the fan: "Many people and critics see in science fiction a basically adolescent infatuation. . . . How fatuous we know this to be. . . . Yet this is precisely the stance many cinemaddicts and professional critics have taken upon viewing *2001*—a vicious and mocking condescension."[149]

Often resembling an academic journal more than a fanzine, *Photon* positioned critically disreputable genre films within the context of contemporary critical theories. For instance, Dale Winogura's "The Auteur in Science Fiction" places directors of SF films into a critical hierarchy, à la Andrew Sarris. Winogura begins with a textbook defense of the auteur theory as propagated by Sarris: "Screenplays are blueprints, and the director constructs the building. . . . The major concern of this article is with the personality of the director, both in person and technical terms." Like all good auteurists, Winogura cannot help but indulge in a few idiosyncratic opinions, such as elevating Robert Altman to the first tier for his early, minor film *Countdown* (1968), and referring to *Forbidden Planet* as "the worst acted, written, and especially directed of all the major science fiction films."[150]

Despite its remarkably high quality, the impact of *Photon* outside the tightest circles of SF and horror fandom was limited by its relatively low print run of only a few thousand copies per issue. Distribution was almost entirely mail order, reliant on word of mouth and advertising in other fanzines.[151] In contrast, the magazine most responsible for the cultural circulation of sophisticated criticism of SF cinema was Frederick S. Clarke's *Cinefantastique* (1970–2006). Clarke first began publishing *Cinefantastique* in mimeograph form in 1968 and upgraded it to a slick paper prozine in 1970, when he was twenty-two years old. Sold to both subscribers and newsstands, *Cinefantastique* had a professional look that set it apart from magazines like *Famous Monsters*. As prozine publisher Tim Lucas would later relate, "It's hard to explain to later generations raised on slick color periodicals how stunning it was to behold, for the first time, a genre film magazine printed on slick paper. . . . The interior layout was clean, streamlined, and impeccable — horror and fantasy films presented with taste!"[152] In 1975, with *Cinefantastique* at a circulation of about five thousand (including four thousand newsstand sales per issue), Clarke quit his job and began to edit and publish the magazine full-time. Circulation took off beginning with the SF boom of the late 1970s and leveled out at approximately thirty thousand copies per issue by the mid-1980s.[153]

Cinefantastique was notable not only in the professionalism of its presentation, but also in its fervent defense of the artistic legitimacy of horror, fantasy, and SF films. In the opening editorial essay of issue number 1, Clarke wrote, "There is absolutely no difference between 'cinema' and 'those crazy science fiction films.' . . . Those poor mainstream critics.

Their brains have turned to marble. They haven't entertained an original thought since high school. Their 'sense of wonder' has atrophied."[154] Clarke was dedicated to giving *Cinefantastique* an oppositional, independent voice, as opposed to the mainstream press or prozine competitors like *Starlog*, which sold about two hundred thousand copies per issue but was often little more than a promotional mouthpiece for the studios. Given this impulse, Clarke would frequently find himself in the position of harshly criticizing films to which he had devoted a great deal of prerelease coverage. The spring 1980 issue, for instance, contains a sixty-page article on *The Black Hole* (1979), based on twenty-three hours of interviews conducted by freelance writer Paul M. Sammon, whom Disney did not allow to see the film before the issue's deadline.[155] Frederick Clarke *had* seen the film before the issue was published, however, and wrote: "I wish I had something good to say about *The Black Hole*, [which exhibits] a total lack of understanding on the part of its makers as to what constitutes good science fiction, or even good filmmaking for that matter."[156]

Clarke seemed to take pleasure in arguing with readers whose letters expressed exhaustion with his combative, highly critical tone. One letter reads: "I should think that despair would have squashed your so-called 'sense of wonder.' After all, hardly any films nowadays meet your approval"—to which Clarke responded, "You may be one of those doomed to sit, zombie-like, through an endless stream of mediocrity that passes for horror, fantasy, and science fiction on the screen today, without even questioning what you see."[157] This exemplifies the "caustic rhetoric" of the "paracinema" subculture, as discussed by Jeffrey Sconce.[158] But whereas paracinema is a celebration of "trash" in defiance of traditional norms of quality, Clarke's tastes were less predictable: he panned some Hollywood blockbusters, like *Star Wars* and *Close Encounters of the Third Kind*, while praising others, like *E.T. the Extra-Terrestrial* (1982) and *Star Trek II: The Wrath of Khan*.[159] Likewise, some low-budget horror films were celebrated, while others were not. As idiosyncratic as Clarke's tastes might have been, they seemed uninfluenced by budget category or cultural status. Clarke's iconoclast credentials were solidified when both Spielberg and George Lucas refused to allow *Cinefantastique* access to their films, after Clarke had published unauthorized special-effects photos of *E.T.* and spoiled the ending of *Return of the Jedi* (1983) before its release.[160]

Clarke's contrary opinions may have grown tiresome for readers, and contributors often found him a difficult man to work for.[161] But he was crucial in bridging the gap in SF film criticism between uncritical fan discourse and the dismissive hostility of many mainstream critics and fans of SF literature. Reflecting Clarke's expansive tastes, there were few boundaries on the films that could be covered by *Cinefantastique*: in the premiere issue, reviews of *Catch-22* (1970) and *Fellini Satyricon* (1969) were published alongside those of *Beneath the Planet of the Apes* (1970), Ishiro Honda's *Latitude Zero* (1969), and Jess Franco's *Eugenie, the Story of Her Journey into Perversion* (1969). By conflating art cinema, exploitation, and Hollywood films into a single category of the "cinefantastique," Clarke made a case for the serious critical consideration of all films, regardless of genre or cultural status. In an early issue he wrote, "Our intention is to span the entire spectrum, and if this unduely disturbes [*sic*] some of the purists, so be it. No doubt some of the more narrow minded will have trouble accommodating such a variety of theme under a single concept."[162]

Cinefantastique's importance extended beyond the critical realm: it also pioneered the industrial historiography of '50s SF film. In the late 1970s Clarke began publishing several lengthy and groundbreaking retrospectives, rooted in archival research and cast and crew interviews, of films such as *The War of the Worlds* and *Forbidden Planet*.[163] Even as these articles were being published, however, *Cinefantastique*'s critical essays were being marginalized in favor of extensive special-effects coverage. David Sanjek has criticized the magazine for its "cult of the technician" and idolization of special-effects workers.[164] For instance, sixty of the seventy pages of *Close Encounters of the Third Kind* coverage were devoted exclusively to special effects, the only exception being a ten-page interview with Spielberg (which also deals, in part, with effects). Nevertheless, Michele Pierson notes that the magazine's production coverage offers valuable insights into the creative process, particularly in terms of establishing a film's visual style.[165]

Cinefantastique was only one prominent example of the tremendous development in SF film criticism over the course of the 1970s. Before the late '60s, even brief mentions of SF films in works of serious film criticism or scholarship were rare. By the late '70s, both cultural and aesthetic

AUTHOR'S COLLECTION

Cinefantastique was known for its well-researched retrospectives of classic SF films, such as an article on *The War of the Worlds* (Paramount, 1953) in the spring 1977 issue.

analyses were widespread in specialized film magazines and academic journals. In 1980, the first scholarly book on the American SF film, Vivian Sobchack's *The Limits of Infinity*, was published. Looking to give SF the same close theoretical attention that the western and gangster film had already received, Sobchack provides a structuralism-influenced analysis of "one of the least critically observed genres in American cinema."[166] She works to define the genre (particularly as it is differentiated from SF literature and horror film), details its iconography and narrative tropes, and uses a discussion of sound and dialogue in SF film to explore questions of satire and humor. For Sobchack, SF film is characterized by a tension between the visual, which looks to "the temporal and spatial freedom" of the future, and the verbal, which reiterates the banality of the status quo.[167] While today the book may be best known for its chapter on SF and postmodern theory, added in 1987, the original version of Sobchack's work remains a crucial milestone in the legitimation of SF film within academic film studies.

The wider acknowledgment by critics of SF cinema's aesthetic and philosophical potential, and SF's rapid ascent as a mainstream genre in the 1970s, can be traced to the epochal release of *2001: A Space Odyssey*, a sui generis masterpiece that pulled SF out of the cultural morass of parody and Z-level exploitation and influenced a generation of fans, filmmakers, and critics. *Cinefantastique* ceased publication in 2006, after thirty-six years and 194 issues. Six years earlier, Frederick Clarke had committed suicide after struggling with depression. "What keeps me going?" Clarke asked in 1979. "I can still feel the buzz from seeing *2001: A Space Odyssey* in 1968, and that could last me the rest of my life."[168]

4

RETURN TO RELEVANCE

///

Art, Exploitation, and Politics in SF Film, 1968–1976

According to Rick Altman's "Producer's Game" of genre cycles, it would seem only logical for the major studios to follow up *2001: A Space Odyssey* with a series of equally extravagant, formally challenging, and thematically complex SF films. And while there was never any guarantee the majors would have gambled on further big-budget SF art films, the collapse of the road-show market shortly after the release of *2001* ensured they would not. The success of mid-1960s blockbusters like *Dr. Zhivago* had led an overeager industry to invest in a surfeit of elaborate, costly films. There was insufficient audience interest (and dollars) to support them all, and by the end of the '60s Hollywood faced its biggest recession since the end of the '40s. The major studios collectively lost over $200 million in 1969 alone.[1] The big-budget flops continued through 1970; most of the remaining films that cost in excess of $10 million, like *The Battle of Britain* (UA, 1969), *The Only Game in Town* (Fox, 1970), and *Darling Lili* (Paramount, 1970), returned only a small fraction of their production costs.[2]

The downfall of the Zanuck regime at Twentieth Century-Fox served as one cautionary tale. Darryl F. Zanuck had run the studio, on and off, since its inception in the mid-1930s; his son, Richard, had been head of production since 1962. In 1970 Fox released three very pricy films: *Tora! Tora! Tora!* ($25.5 million cost), *Hello, Dolly!* ($25.3 million), and *Patton* ($12.6 million).[3] Only *Patton* would justify its big budget, and even it would be outgrossed by the same studio's *M*A*S*H* (1970), made for only $3 million.[4] Fox lost $77.4 million in 1970 alone, and both Zanucks were eventually ousted by the studio's board of directors.[5] Fox was not alone in its financial woes: in 1969 MGM lost $35.4 million and replaced its president twice within a year.[6] Even Columbia was $127.5 million in debt by 1973, despite inexpensive sleeper hits like *Easy Rider* and *The Last Picture Show* (1971).[7]

Unlike in the 1950s, this slump could not be blamed on audience attrition. Theatrical attendance, which had been in decline since the mid-'50s, had largely stabilized by the mid-'60s: average weekly attendance from 1966 to 1974 hovered consistently between sixteen million and nineteen million.[8] Although this was partly a result of rising ticket prices, box office revenue actually increased every year, save one, from 1962 to 1975.[9] The recession of 1969–1971 was due less to a lack of interest from moviegoers than to the disastrous misallocation of funds to a small number of extremely expensive blockbusters. Hollywood responded by backing away from the blockbuster strategy that had been in place since at least the 1950s. From 1971 to 1975, the major studios cut production budgets sharply: during that period, only ten films cost $10 million or more. And of those, some were over budget, like *The Exorcist* (1973) or *Jaws* (1975), or were coproductions between two studios (Fox and Warners split the $14 million cost of *The Towering Inferno* in 1974).[10]

With blockbuster budgets in decline, budget categories were reconfigured across the board in the early 1970s. Most high-profile studio releases were priced roughly in the $4 million to $8 million range, rather than $10 million or more. The traditional A/B distinction of the classical period was meaningless by this period, as double features were confined to dilapidated independent "grind house" theaters and were no longer an economically significant exhibition strategy in America.[11] However, we can retain the term "A film" to refer to this budget category, as the films correlate closely to the classical studio A film: sizable, while not blockbuster-level, budgets, featuring a popular star or two, and aimed at general adult audiences. Examples include *Dirty Harry* (1971), *The Godfather* (1972), *The Sting* (1973), and *Shampoo* (1974).[12] The majors also continued their distribution (and in some cases, production) of low-budget exploitation pictures, generally costing between $500,000 and $750,000 each. Especially popular were horror films like *The Brotherhood of Satan* and *Countess Dracula* (both 1971) and action films, including martial arts and blaxploitation movies like *That Man Bolt* (1973) and *Black Samson* (1974).

Many films released by the majors in the early 1970s lie between the A-film and exploitation categories, however, costing between $1 million and $3 million each. These modest budgets often precluded the casting of a major star, so the appeal of these films was largely genre-based. David A. Cook has connected the surge in genre film production in this period to the majors' retrenchment strategies; the genre boom "was underwritten by the studios as a form of risk reduction since genre films, like stars, were inherently 'pre-sold' and easy to package."[13] Crime and action dramas were especially prolific, as these genres contained strong marketing appeals but did not require expensive sets or special effects. With their intermediate budgets, these films, like *Vanishing Point* (1971) and *The French Connection* (1971), can be considered programmers—the 1970s equivalent of the films that existed between the A and B genres in the classical studio era.[14]

Unlike programmers from the '30s through the '50s, there was no question that '70s programmers were anything but major, high-quality product. They played in first-run theaters and were not limited to drive-ins or grind houses, as exploitation films often were. However, as programmers represented a smaller investment than the typical star-driven A film, they typically received less promotion and performed only modestly at the box office. Their purpose was to allow their studios to tread water financially—the relatively small profits from programmers were preferable to risking disaster with a blockbuster. Typical was *The Other* (1972), an "evil twin" horror film distributed by Twentieth Century Fox. Produced for $2.25 million, it generated $3.5 million in domestic rentals.[15] The small but relatively consistent profits from the '70s programmers recall the B films and programmers of the studio era. And like those films, there was always the possibility that an inexpensive film could become a sleeper hit. Fox's action film *Dirty Mary, Crazy Larry* (1974) cost $1.14 million but earned $12.1 million in domestic rentals.[16] The revenue from the unexpected successes more than compensated for the losses from programmers that failed to find an audience.

MGM's output in the early-to-mid-1970s is perhaps the epitome of the era's low-risk production strategy. In 1969 businessman Kirk Kerkorian purchased a controlling interest in MGM and appointed former CBS president James Aubrey to head the studio. Aubrey's mandate was to drag MGM into solvency, using whatever means necessary. This involved, notoriously, not only firing half the studio's employees, but also selling much of the studio's back lot and auctioning most of its vintage wardrobe and props from classic films.[17] Aubrey, who ran the studio until late 1973, set a $2 million limit on budgets and filled MGM's production slate with genre programmers and exploitation films.[18] Aubrey's attitude mirrored the wider industry logic at the time: "If a movie costs $2 million, you get your costs back. If it costs $17 million, you can lose a lot if it is not a worldwide hit."[19] There were a few surprise programmer hits, including *Shaft* (1971), but overall the films of Aubrey's tenure were unremarkable both artistically and financially. MGM's timid approach to budgeting was mirrored at Fox, which spent over $5 million on precisely two films from 1971 to 1975 (*The Towering Inferno* and *At Long Last, Love*, 1975), and Columbia, which instituted a $3 million budget cap in 1973, partly in response to its $12 million flop *Lost Horizon* (1973).[20]

In terms of SF, the dual successes in 1968 of *2001: A Space Odyssey* and *Planet of the Apes* facilitated its revival as a mainstream genre in the early '70s. Approximately thirty major-studio SF productions were released between 1969 and 1975, alongside many low-budget exploitation films from independents like AIP. While a few of these films, such as *The Andromeda Strain* (1971) and *Slaughterhouse-Five* (1972), were budgeted in the A category, most were programmers. The majors' SF films of the late '60s to mid-'70s can be divided into two categories, each representing the influence of one of the two breakout SF hits of 1968. First were the action-oriented films reminiscent of *Planet of the Apes*, which placed SF concepts into traditional Hollywood genres and used sociopolitical content to lure audiences with promises of "relevance." Less commercially successful overall were the films of the second category, SF art films influenced by *2001*, even as these films tried to incorporate their formal experimentation into more classical structures.

Both of these categories of SF film were concerned with differentiating themselves from exploitation SF, something that became more difficult as loosened content regulation led to a new emphasis on explicit sex and violence in major-studio films, and a concomitant blurring of the boundaries between art, mainstream, and exploitation cinema. The critical and commercial failure of Norman Jewison's SF film *Rollerball* (1975) is tied to the way it awkwardly straddles these three cinematic modes. *Rollerball* serves as a key example of how adult content threatened to conflict with the primary strategies of legitimation used by SF films in this period, namely the incorporation of political content and art cinema techniques. While there were no breakout SF hits in the late '60s to mid-'70s to rival *Planet of the Apes* or *2001*, the genre was firmly established for the first time as consistently successful in the mainstream marketplace, if only at the more modest programmer level. The films of this period also deepened the complexity of American SF cinema, demonstrating that it could be a genre of ideas, as it was in literature, and not just a genre of visual extravagance.

Planet of the Apes and the Political SF Programmer

While *2001: A Space Odyssey* may have been crucial in legitimating SF cinema in mainstream American culture, it was the other great SF hit of 1968, the more conventional *Planet of the Apes*, that provided a more economically successful model for SF through the mid-1970s. Ironically, although *Planet of the Apes* was a much more accessible film than *2001*, its producer, Arthur P. Jacobs, had a considerably more difficult time than Stanley Kubrick persuading a major studio to finance an SF project. In 1963 Jacobs, a former publicist who had yet to produce a film, purchased the rights to *Bridge on the River Kwai* author Pierre Boulle's new SF novel, *La planète des singes*, in which astronauts explore a planet where apes have replaced humans as the dominant species. An ambitious Jacobs endeavored to put together a package of top talent, such as Marlon Brando, Paul Newman, J. Lee Thompson, and Paddy Chayefsky, but they were either uninterested or unavailable. Studios were also hesitant to finance *Planet of the Apes*; first, the epic scale of Boulle's novel suggested that a large budget would be necessary. Second, SF cinema was arguably at its commercial nadir in 1963. A serious SF A film set in the far future and dealing with space travel had not been attempted since *Forbidden Planet*, seven years earlier, and even that film had underperformed. Third, studio executives feared that a novel featuring talking apes could not be successfully adapted to the screen without becoming an unintentional comedy.[21]

After Fox, Paramount, and United Artists passed on *Planet of the Apes*, Jacobs managed to sign Blake Edwards as director and Rod Serling as screenwriter. This prestigious talent drew the attention of Warner Bros., which in 1964 agreed to make the film. As development continued, however, the estimated cost of *Planet of the Apes* ballooned to $7.5 million, which would have made it one of the most expensive films of 1965.[22] A gun-shy Warners pulled the plug before production began. Blake Edwards left the project, and Jacobs turned to Twentieth Century-Fox, for which he had just produced the star-studded hit *What a Way to Go!* (1964). Head of production Richard Zanuck repeatedly refused to green-light *Planet of the Apes*, even after makeup tests demonstrated that talking apes could be believably achieved without inciting audience laughter, and Charlton Heston agreed to star in the film. Heston's career had peaked several years earlier with *Ben-Hur* (1959), but he was still a major star who would bring considerable legitimacy to the project. Heston, for his part, was looking to update his image, which was still based on the stoic biblical characters he portrayed in the 1950s.

Zanuck eventually changed his mind, based largely on the performance of Fox's *Fantastic Voyage*, released in August 1966. Costing $5 million, *Fantastic Voyage* was the most expensive American SF film to that point, along with *20,000 Leagues under the Sea*, also directed by Richard Fleisher.[23] Originally a period piece like *20,000 Leagues* and *Journey to the Center of the Earth*, *Fantastic Voyage*, following the generic trends of the mid-1960s, was eventually reconceived as a Cold War thriller in which doctors are miniaturized and injected into the body of an injured Soviet defector in order to perform delicate brain surgery on him. Ultimately the film earned an impressive $5.5 million in domestic rentals.[24] According to associate producer Mort Abrahams, he and Jacobs pitched *Planet of the Apes* again to Zanuck, arguing that "*Fantastic Voyage* was doing this fantastic business, and who the hell was in it, and nobody ever heard of it, and it wasn't based on a bestselling book. . . . If you look at grosses, it shows you a gimmick picture can work, and [*Planet of the Apes*] is the greatest gimmick picture of them all."[25] Zanuck was convinced, and agreed to finance

Apes at a budget similar to that of *Fantastic Voyage*. Franklin J. Schaffner, who had just directed Heston in *The War Lord* (1965), replaced Blake Edwards, and Michael Wilson rewrote Serling's script.

Planet of the Apes was released in April 1968 (two months earlier in New York City) to generally warm reviews, with Charles Champlin in the *Los Angeles Times* calling it "a triumph of artistry and imagination"[26] and Pauline Kael praising it as "one of the best science fiction-fantasies ever to come out of Hollywood" (although she was careful to add, "That doesn't mean it is art").[27] In *Boxoffice*, a manager of a Kansas City theater chain urged his fellow exhibitors to treat *Planet of the Apes* as a "class" film, "not just another science-fiction potboiler, designed for a quick exploitation playoff."[28] The film's substantial budget (ultimately $5.8 million) and brilliant makeup by John Chambers helped counteract any negative preconceptions spectators might have had about its genre or concept.[29] The *Motion Picture Herald*'s review emphasized the film's excellent production values and ambition when compared to previous SF pictures and noted that Heston's involvement would ensure "a much larger audience than that of the average S-F film."[30] Indeed, *Planet of the Apes* did tremendous business — its $15 million in domestic rentals made it the sixth-highest-grossing film of 1968 and Fox's second-biggest film of the year.[31] *Apes* also won an honorary Academy Award for its makeup and received two other nominations (for costume design and Jerry Goldsmith's score).

Planet of the Apes was arguably just as crucial as *2001* in establishing SF as a viable first-run genre. Although Kubrick's film was more polarizing and controversial, and therefore more widely discussed in the national media, *Planet of the Apes* significantly outperformed *2001* in its initial run in theaters, at half the budget.[32] And in the end, it was the films made in the *Apes* model that proved more financially successful, giving SF cinema its first consistent mainstream success in America. The *Planet of the Apes* production model was characterized by the incorporation of political content within the action-oriented framework of conventional genre cinema and by the avoidance of space travel and futuristic environments — not only to distance itself from the pulp exploitation tradition, but as a cost-cutting strategy.

The key legitimating tactic in *Planet of the Apes* was its use of political commentary and social satire. The film famously ends with the protagonist cursing the human race at the base of the ruined Statue of Liberty, as he realizes he has been on Earth all along, and a nuclear holocaust has allowed the apes to become the dominant species. Postapocalyptic stories were nothing new for SF cinema, of course. But mainstream postapocalyptic films, such as *On the Beach* or *The World, the Flesh and the Devil* (both 1959), were more strictly realistic, avoiding pulp SF tropes to the point where they were not described as SF at all by critics. Such was the genre's low reputation at the time, and so prevalent was the association with pulp exploitation, that even Franklin Schaffner claimed, "I had never thought of [*Planet of the Apes*] in terms of being science fiction. More or less, it was a political film, with a certain amount of Swiftian satire, and perhaps science fiction last."[33] In fact, the general plot of *Planet of the Apes* would not have been out of place in *Astounding Science Fiction*; yet it also manages to be the most overtly political SF A film since *The Day the Earth Stood Still*.

Critics praised the social critique of *Planet of the Apes*, with the *Cleveland Plain Dealer* remarking, "The script is a compliment rather than an insult to the intelligence. There is biting social satire like Jonathan Swift in 'Gulliver's Travels.' . . . Its attack on the futility of war at the end may find some people in tears. It is a sermon in itself."[34] This critic mirrors Schaffner's citation of Swift, suggesting that the film's talking apes are acceptable to sophisticated tastes, like the civilized horses the Houyhnhnms in *Gulliver's Travels*, because they are allegorical. *Variety*, in a bit of uncharacteristically abstract commentary, elaborates upon this line of thought: "Rather precise parallels exist in the allegoric writing to real world events over, say, the past 20 years. Suppression of dissent by fair means and foul; peremptory rejection of scientific data by maintainers of the status quo; double standard evaluation of people and events. It's all here. Screenplay probably could not have been filmed 10 years ago, and the disturbing thought lingers that it might not be possible in another 10 years, when engineered public and political opinion again swings into another distorted extreme."[35] According to a profile in *Boxoffice*, Fox's advertising campaign emphasized the film's "startling theme," seeking to position *Planet of the Apes* as "a totally new approach to 'science fiction'—a fantastic, frightening idea molded into a meaningful, thrillingly believable action story by a distinguished author."[36] Words such as "totally new," "meaningful," "believable," and "distinguished" give a sense of Fox's ardent efforts to estab-

The violent climax of *Conquest of the Planet of the Apes* (Twentieth Century-Fox, 1974) was intended to call to mind the 1965 Watts Riots in Los Angeles.

lish *Planet of the Apes* as culturally legitimate, and distinct from the usual SF fare.

Eric Greene has written compellingly on the *Apes* films as political discourse, arguing that they "depicted, commented upon, and engaged in, the painful convulsions of the changing times."[37] Greene identifies a number of political themes besides the obvious antinuclear commentary, including the conflict between science and religion, and the government suppression of information deemed dangerous to its own interests. But Greene's emphasis is on the film's critique of racism, seen in the tensions among the ape species, and of course the apes' brutal treatment of humans.[38] The racial allegory becomes even more pronounced in the four *Planet of the Apes* sequels, released from 1970 to 1974. In the third film, *Escape from the Planet of the Apes* (1971), two apes travel from the future to contemporary Earth, where they are treated as racial "others" by the populace. Likewise, the fourth film, *Conquest of the Planet of the Apes* (1972), is a clear allegory for the civil rights conflict in the United States. In the film, set in the near future, apes have become the slaves of mankind: mistreated, degraded, and forced to perform manual labor. Caesar, a superintelligent ape introduced in the previous installment, leads his brethren in a violent revolution against their human oppressors. Screenwriter Paul Dehn recalls, "We wanted that film to be very angry; to be the counterpart of the riot in Chicago and Watts."[39]

By the time of *Conquest*, the series' political commentary, praised in 1968, was wearing thin for some critics. The *Village Voice* criticized *Conquest*'s "simple-minded metaphor,"[40] and the *Oregonian*'s Ted Mahar wondered why "pure entertainment is evidently seen as some kind of pornography which must somewhere be justified with socially redeeming value."[41] The lack of subtlety in *Conquest* might have been an artistic deficit (and the films' correlation of African Americans and apes certainly gives one pause), but from a marketing perspective it was an effective hook to draw crowds to otherwise routine genre films. Producer Frank Capra Jr. reported that *Conquest* played particularly well with African American audiences: "The marketing guys at Fox began to get the message and so began to play it in more and more black theaters. . . . I was at a theater in Long Beach, which was predominantly African-American, and it was a very enthusiastic audience complete with people yelling at the screen, encouraging Caesar and all the rest."[42]

The original *Planet of the Apes* was the pioneer in a general shift from the late '60s through the '70s toward political SF cinema. Instead of being buried in the subtext, as with many 1950s films, sociopolitical commentary became the dominant organizing principle and thematic center of the film, as it was with much SF literature of the time. This political turn was instigated by the major studios' pursuit of the counterculture, discussed in more detail below. But once again the mainstream was simply following the lead of the exploitation studios, which had been attracting young audiences with "torn from the headlines" topics for over a decade. American International Pictures pioneered counterculture SF in 1968 with *Wild in the Streets*, which used an SF conceit to address the frustration of young Americans about their exclusion from the political process. The film postulated a near future in which the voting age is lowered to fifteen — a rock star is elected president, and all citizens over thirty-five are placed in concentration camps where LSD keeps them docile. Costing $700,000, *Wild in the Streets* attracted audiences with its mix of social satire and youth appeal, and grossed an outstanding $4 million.[43] The film was praised by Pauline Kael and even secured an Oscar nomination for editing.[44]

Because the majors targeted a wider audience than did a relatively small independent studio like AIP, their SF films tended toward broader sociopolitical issues, such as the state of the environment. In 1970, the first nationwide Earth Day led to environmentally conscious legislation and the foundation of the Environmental Protection Agency.[45] By the early '70s, ecological topics replaced nuclear warfare as the most salient political issue in SF cinema. Films like *No Blade of Grass* and *Soylent Green* addressed fears that overpopulation would lead to worldwide famine.[46] In Douglas Trumbull's *Silent Running* (1972), space hippie Bruce Dern tends to the last remaining vegetation from Earth, which has been shot into space by a short-sighted government. And Paramount's *Z.P.G.* (1972) (Zero Population Growth) is packed with a litany of hot-button issues including overpopulation, pollution, nuclear war, and abortion. Even exploitation films reflected this new interest in ecology—in AIP's *Frogs* (1972), animals attack humans in retaliation for the spraying of pesticides on a private island in South Florida.

Another important political plotline, originating with *Planet of the Apes* but becoming more potent in the Watergate era, was the protagonist's defeat or unmasking of some malevolent government conspiracy. In the climax of *Apes*, Heston's character Taylor learns that the ape ruling class has been hiding from the general population the fact that their world is built on the ruins of a human civilization. Heston uncovers a similar mystery in *Soylent Green*, when his character discovers that the government has solved a global famine (associated with overpopulation) through cannibalism. Post-Watergate, an entire subgenre of conspiracy thrillers would emerge, including SF films like *Futureworld* (1976), *Logan's Run* (1976), and *Capricorn One* (1977), in which a Mars landing is faked by NASA in order to prevent federal budget cuts, and shady government agents try to kill the astronauts involved. The post-Watergate pessimism and suspicion of authority reflected in these films reveal what John G. Cawelti in 1979 called the "tragic inadequacy" of traditional American genres.[47] For Cawelti, by placing conventional genre stories within a more realistic, morally ambiguous environment, filmmakers tacitly acknowledge that culture has progressed beyond "the underlying mythology" represented by traditional generic forms.[48] The utopian optimism of the SF cinema of the 1950s and early '60s seemed naive a decade later.

In a 1978 article in the *Journal of Popular Film and Television*, Joan F. Dean proposes that SF's interest in sociopolitical issues and political conspiracies in this period, rather than the usual emphasis on outer space and aliens, reflects a shift in national priorities as a result of Vietnam and Watergate.[49] Dean's argument is cogent, in that SF film producers sought to tap into the rise in political activism in the United States and exploit the timeliness of current events. But there are a number of other factors behind the shift from space-travel narratives to earthbound SF. For one, SF films set on Earth were simply cheaper to produce. Any SF film set in space would naturally be compared to *2001: A Space Odyssey*, a very high standard to meet, particularly with a low budget. In 1969 Hammer Films released a programmer titled *Moon Zero Two*, a "space western" that takes place on a lunar colony in 2021. Co-financed with Warner Bros., the film was nearly twice as expensive as the average Hammer horror and as such was a considerable risk for the independent British studio.[50] *Moon Zero Two*'s ultimate failure at the box office was blamed in part on the low effects budget. Director Roy Ward Baker remarked, "What nobody realized at the time is that you simply cannot make a space fiction picture at those prices at a double or even treble normal Hammer budget. As we've seen happen since, people go to forty, fifty, and sixty million dollars to make such a picture and that's what it costs."[51]

Rather than trying to produce a film set in outer space that would not be laughable given the small budgets of the early 1970s, filmmakers focused on a different type of SF entirely—one that would resonate with politically conscious young audiences and could be convincingly achieved with a programmer budget. Again, *Planet of the Apes* was an important influence, as it made use of a number of cost-cutting strategies that were easily reproduced by subsequent, cheaper films. Whereas for *2001* MGM had spent millions on the construction of intricate models and immense sets, *Apes* achieved its science-fictional mise-en-scène largely through location shooting. According to cinematographer Leon Shamroy, the crew found in the deserts of Utah and Arizona and the shoreline of California "a landscape weird and 'unearthly' enough to suggest the possible terrain of another planet."[52] *Apes* also cleverly projected a future that had devolved technologically as a result of nuclear war. The primitive adobe architecture of the simian civilization enabled the film's major sets to be built with only polyurethane foam and paper.[53] Most of the major SF films of the 1970s followed the lead of *Planet of the Apes* and avoided both space travel and civilizations with futuristic technologies. Instead films took place in contemporary times (*No Blade of Grass*; *Colossus: The Forbin Project*) or in a "not-too-distant" future that resembles modern times aside from minor technological flourishes (*Soylent Green*, *Westworld*, *Rollerball*).

Another important reason for the emphasis on earthbound SF stories was the differentiation of major SF films from the exploitation tradition of the past. This was a concern for "serious" SF filmmakers in the 1970s, just as it was two decades earlier. SF was just beginning to emerge as a major genre after years of parodies and Z-level releases, and the specter of Buck Rogers lingered despite the relative dearth of low-budget SF at the time.[54] In the wake of films like *Santa Claus Conquers the Martians* (1964) and *The Reluctant Astronaut* (1967) with Don Knotts, a safer strategy was the incorporation of SF concepts into traditional earthbound genres like the detective film (*Soylent Green*), the western (*Westworld*), or the war film (*Battle for the Planet of the Apes*).

If a major studio SF film dealt with space travel at all, it usually did so in a "realistic" fashion—as an account of the American space program, which reached its apex with the 1969 moon landing. Films like Warner Bros.' *Countdown* (1968) and Columbia's *Marooned* (1969), released to cash in on the Apollo program, are the direct descendants of *Destination Moon* in their adherence to known scientific knowledge, their eschewal of pulp SF tropes, and their use of technological obstacles like rocket failure and the unexpected depletion of oxygen levels. Although these films did not directly engage with sociopolitical issues like racism or the environment, they were similarly branded as "relevant" in the marketplace via their close association to current events. *Marooned* was still in theaters during the 1970 Apollo 13 incident, when a manned lunar spacecraft was almost lost owing to an oxygen tank rupture. Columbia limited its advertising campaign for the film while the astronauts were still in danger, but after they had returned safely, the studio took advantage of the crisis with ads proclaiming "Now *Marooned* Is More Than Just a Thrilling Motion Picture!"[55] So close was their relationship to actual events, space program films like *Marooned* were not considered SF films by the trade and popular presses, which labeled them "space dramas" or "space melodramas."[56] Likewise, writer-director Michael Crichton's 1970s techno-thrillers such as *The Andromeda Strain* and *Coma* (1978), similar to Ivan Tors's '50s films in their basis in plausible technological innovations, were sometimes called "science fact," a term of differentiation from the fantasies of pulp SF. For instance, *Variety* on *Westworld*: "The story is too plausible today to call it futuristic, nor is science fiction an appropriate label. It is all horrifyingly credible."[57] SF, then, is only the domain of the incredible.

The trend toward relevance in SF cinema was no guarantee of success—*Silent Running* and *Z.P.G.* were two conspicuous flops (although the former has since developed a cult following). And sometimes the political appeals backfired spectacularly: Columbia invited one hundred prominent feminists to a promotional screening of *The Stepford Wives* (1975) and a post-screening "awareness session" where they were asked to discuss their opinions of the film. Based on Ira Levin's novel, *The Stepford Wives* deals with a group of husbands who replace their feminist wives with submissive androids. The screening itself was peppered with "hisses, groans, and guffaws," and afterward *The Feminine Mystique* author Betty Friedan stood and announced, "I think we should all leave here. I don't think we should help publicize this movie. It's a rip-off of the women's movement."[58] *The Stepford Wives* went on to earn $4 million in domestic rentals.[59] This is a typical number for the political SF programmer of the 1970s, which were modest but solid successes, particularly in relation to their cost. Even when Fox, anticipating audience attrition, slashed the budget of each successive *Planet of the Apes* sequel, the series continued to attract audiences. The final installment, the poorly received *Battle for the Planet of the Apes*, still made $4 million in domestic rentals against a budget of only $1.7 million.[60] The individual grosses may have been small, but the cumulative profits of genre programmers kept the studios afloat during the learn years of the early 1970s.

The key to the success of the political SF programmers was their accessibility. Political themes were used to lend them a sense of immediacy and social relevance, but divisive or pessimistic political statements were generally avoided. A few of the SF conspiracy films like *Soylent Green* and Philip Kaufman's 1978 remake of *Invasion of the Body Snatchers* have bleak conclusions in which the protagonist is overwhelmed by the vast, sinister institution he faces. But generally the revolutionary political messages in '70s SF films are softened by happy endings that ultimately serve to reconfirm the dominant order. For instance, in *Z.P.G.* the protagonists and their baby escape their polluted, totalitarian society into open waters (an ending that was later appropriated by Alfonso Cuarón's similarly themed *Children of Men*, 2003). By revealing that a clean, safe environment exists outside its dystopian civilization, the film assures audiences that it is not too late — mankind can "start over" with a more ecological attitude.

Likewise, the original ending of *Conquest of the Planet of the Apes*, in which ape leader Caesar executes the human governor and urges immediate armed rebellion, was drastically softened by studio fiat. After a preview screening, Fox feared that the ending would alienate family audiences and potentially incite race riots.[61] The studio ordered that the (white) governor be spared, and that Caesar take a more benevolent, conciliatory approach. Director J. Lee Thompson: "It was correct in terms of film entertainment to cop out, because I have no right to take an *Apes* film and really make it such a strong political platform. . . . If it gets too strong and you're really beginning to upset people, then cool it."[62] Political statements were limited by the desire to adhere to conventional happy endings and avoid offending audiences. In this sense, despite their radical sheen, Hollywood genre films of the 1970s are no different from their antecedents of the classical studio era. The incorporation of political themes into genre films in the 1970s represents less the political awakening of the major studios than the canny use of exploitation tactics to appeal to the perceived changing demands of the American film audience. The combination of politics and SF action established by *Planet of the Apes* allowed SF to proliferate and establish itself as a legitimate A genre.

The American SF Art Film, 1971–1974

The second key production strategy for SF films in this period certainly did not avoid politics, but rather than the conventional style and accessible action narratives of the political SF programmers, these films were influenced by the art cinema experimentation of *2001: A Space Odyssey*. The success of Kubrick's film with the counterculture was further evidence to the studios that audience demographics were shifting in the late 1960s. A 1968 Motion Picture Association of American (MPAA) survey indicated that nearly half of moviegoers were between the ages of sixteen and twenty-four.[63] Two youth-oriented breakout hits released in 1967, *Bonnie and Clyde* and *The Graduate*, seen alongside the failure of the family musical *Doctor Dolittle* (1967), suggested that instead of the traditional "invisible style" and a focus on appealing to general audiences, studios should target the "Lost Audience" of young, educated moviegoers by emphasizing ostentatious formal techniques, increased levels of sex and violence, and a countercultural ethos. When Columbia's drugs-and-bikers film *Easy Rider* (1969) produced $7.2 million in domestic rentals against a cost of approximately a half million dollars, it seemed as though Hollywood had found a new model for profitability: cheap, art cinema–influenced films with huge profit potential.[64] In 1970 the *New York Times* pronounced the old Hollywood dead, and studio executives like MGM's James Aubrey expressed their desire to tailor their films to the new youth market: "The audience, I think, is ahead of the business and we've got to get ahead of them. . . . Irreverence and honesty are two subjects which appeal in today's market."[65]

Young, untried filmmakers were the beneficiaries of this new industrial strategy. As Warner Bros. executive John Calley said in 1970, "When formulas break down in times of uncertainty, it's a breeding ground for young talent. Everyone is ready to listen to wilder forms and concepts."[66] True to Calley's word, Warner Bros. financed and distributed George Lucas's first feature, the SF film *THX 1138* (1971). A remake of an award-winning short film written and directed by Lucas while at the University of Southern California film school, *THX 1138* was the first release of American Zoetrope, an independent studio operating out of San Francisco that was founded in 1969 by Lucas and his friend and mentor Francis Ford Coppola. Through Zoetrope Lucas looked to revive the independent spirit of his film school days, while Coppola's aims were more ambitious. In Lucas's words, Coppola hoped to "get a lot of young talent for nothing, make these movies, hope that one of them would be a hit, and eventually build a studio that way."

Hoping for the next *Easy Rider*, Warner Bros. agreed to finance *THX 1138* and lent Zoetrope an additional $600,000 to develop more scripts and build its production infrastructure.[67] Warner Bros.' level of risk was practically nonexistent; the budget of *THX 1138* was only $777,000 (seven was Coppola's lucky number), Lucas did not have the right to final cut, and Zoetrope was on the hook for the development money if Warners decided not to green-light any future projects. Lucas immediately put *THX 1138* on

In this scene from *THX 1138* (American Zoetrope/Warner Bros., 1971), depth cues are removed and combine with a decentered composition to create a nearly abstract image.

the fast track: "I realized that I might never get the chance again to make this totally off-the-wall movie without any real supervision."[68] The film's plot is fairly conventional, mixing a variety of well-worn tropes of dystopian SF: the title character rebels from an underground police state in which the population is drugged into complacency, forbidden from having sex, and pacified by a religion of meaningless consumerism.

While its story may not be particularly original, *THX 1138* is one of the most formally unusual major studio releases of the period. The influence of *2001: A Space Odyssey* is apparent, particularly in the subdued, affectless acting style, antiseptic mise-en-scène, and open-ended conclusion (the protagonist THX escapes the underground civilization and stands alone in the open air as the sun sets). Lucas's interest in avant-garde cinema led him to construct an SF film that surpasses even Kubrick's in its bold use of abstract imagery. Visually, the futuristic society of *THX 1138* is based almost entirely around the contrast of black and white. In certain scenes, such as when THX is imprisoned, the white backgrounds remove all depth cues from the composition, so the characters' positions in space are uncertain. This minimalist visual style was balanced by a highly aggressive and innovative soundtrack, designed by Walter Murch, that included as many as twenty layers of sound, including experiments with tape speed, sound distortion, and microphone placement. William Whittington argues that Murch's complex sound montage challenged conventional

Hollywood norms of realism and effacement, and influenced the development of sound design as a mainstream cinematic practice.[69]

Reviews for *THX 1138* were mixed. Some critics approached Lucas's film as an heir to *2001* and adjusted their critical schemata accordingly. Charles Champlin of the *Los Angeles Times* suggested, "The real excitement of *THX 1138* is not the message but the medium — the use of film not to tell a story so much as to convey an experience."[70] The *New York Times*'s Vincent Canby described the film as "a stunning montage of light, color, and sound effects that create their own emotional impact,"[71] while the *Dallas Morning News* claimed that *THX 1138* "should be seen primarily as a visual symphony."[72] But, as with *2001*, some critics found the slow narrative pace and visual/aural emphasis dull. Stanley Kauffmann, who strongly disliked *2001*, was unconvinced by this similar approach to SF: "Lucas has clearly made his bet on cinematic display, and to his credit, he sustains interest on that score for about fifteen minutes. . . . 'Shut your eyes and open your mind,' films of this type suggest. 'Nuts,' is what I suggest in return."[73] *Variety* offered the ultimate backhanded compliment: "Likely not to be an artistic or commercial success in its own time, [*THX 1138*] just might in time become a classic of stylistic, abstract cinema."[74]

Unfortunately for Lucas and American Zoetrope, *Variety*'s review was prescient. When Warner Bros. executives screened the finished *THX 1138*, they were not pleased, finding its challenging formal system incomprehensible and its commercial prospects nonexistent.[75] The studio canceled its development deal with American Zoetrope (which included *Apocalypse Now* and *The Conversation*, two films that would later win the Palme d'Or at Cannes) and demanded that Zoetrope return the $600,000 of development money, essentially shuttering the fledgling studio.[76] Then, to Lucas's lasting horror, Warner took *THX 1138* out of his hands and recut it slightly in an attempt to make it more accessible. Their efforts failed, and the film returned only $956,000 in domestic rentals.[77]

The performance of *THX 1138* at the box office was typical of the post–*Easy Rider* youth cycle: other conspicuous flops included *The Last Movie* (1971), Dennis Hopper's follow-up to *Easy Rider*; Michelangelo Antonioni's *Zabriskie Point* (1970), which lost $6 million for MGM;[78] and *Two-Lane Blacktop* (1971), which *Esquire* had prematurely proclaimed "the movie of the year" before its release.[79] When the studios realized that *The Graduate*,

Bonnie and Clyde, and *Easy Rider* were anomalies, they simply pulled the relatively meager funds they had allotted for counterculture art pictures. As early as February 1971 a *Variety* headline warned: "'Teen Power' Fading at B.O.," and by 1972 studios had stopped making films aimed primarily at the counterculture.[80] Steve Neale points out that, media rhetoric aside, these films were only a relatively minor component of each studio's annual production slate; the box office was still dominated by classical product, such as musicals like *Oliver!* (1968) and children's films like *The Love Bug* (1969). Neale indicates that the large amount of retrospective critical attention paid to the films is a reflection of their aesthetic and political interest rather than their economic value to the studios.[81]

The influence of art cinema did not evaporate from Hollywood, however. Paul Ramaeker argues that after the failure of the initial youth cycle, the art cinema influence in Hollywood was transferred to genre films, on the basis of hits like *The French Connection* and *The Godfather*.[82] These films used generic conventions to provide a familiarity that reduced the disruptive effects of their art cinema techniques, while retaining their novelty. This hybridity between classical and art cinema is characteristic of the "Hollywood Renaissance" period of the late 1960s to mid-1970s. Robert B. Ray notes that even seemingly transgressive films like *Bonnie and Clyde* and *The Graduate* were ultimately "formally conservative, surrounding the borrowed New Wave devices with long stretches that completely conformed to traditional continuity rules."[83] David Bordwell characterizes the classical Hollywood cinema as one that readily assimilates avant-garde influences and reworks them until they fit comfortably within the preexisting norms of mainstream filmmaking.[84] By incorporating art cinema techniques into the classical model, filmmakers could avoid the commercial failure of more challenging films like *THX 1138* and *Zardoz*.

The turn toward "art-genre" films, to use Ramaeker's term, was particularly fortuitous for SF as, the failure of *THX 1138* notwithstanding, intelligent SF film and literature seemed on the cusp of a commercial breakthrough in the early 1970s. In the wake of *2001* and the literary New Wave, SF was poised to shake off the pulp clichés that had hindered its development and find a new, potentially larger audience among college students and other intellectuals. The market for paperback SF novels had exploded in the mid-to-late '60s, reportedly due to interest by "a wider, more sophisticated audience for science fiction in the college campuses."[85] The centralization of SF courses within university English departments contributed to a shift within the genre toward literary-type fiction that emphasized characterization and the social sciences more than technology and the "hard sciences."[86] This further broadened the potential audience for SF. In 1970, Science Fiction Writers of America president Gordon R. Dickson noted: "The tendency has been to look at science fiction as something separate from other forms of literature, but now this is changing. . . . The work is aimed not necessarily at the scientifically sophisticated, but at the intelligent everywhere."[87]

SF writer and editor Judith Merril was particularly committed to integrating SF into the literary mainstream; her "Year's Best S-F" series in the 1960s included stories not only from New Wave writers like Thomas M. Disch and Brian W. Aldiss, but prestigious authors from the literary world like John Updike, Jorge Luis Borges, and Günter Grass.[88] In 1972 the *New Yorker* published a lengthy survey of contemporary SF literature, emphasizing the mainstream legitimation of the genre and focusing on New Wave writers like J. G. Ballard, who employs "a narrative style that is virtually indistinguishable from experimental fiction in general."[89] In the article, English professor and SF scholar Thomas D. Clareson argues that the decline of literary realism and naturalism had created an opportunity for SF to become a prominent literary category: "The continued segregation of science fiction into a small, self-sufficient genre, with its own inbred audience and its own narrow standards of taste, is getting harder and harder to justify."[90]

One film that sought to exploit this new audience for SF was Universal's *Slaughterhouse-Five* (1972), directed by George Roy Hill and adapted from Kurt Vonnegut Jr.'s 1969 novel. The book was a commercial breakthrough for Vonnegut, who had been writing SF since 1950. Vonnegut was well regarded within the SF community, with two Hugo nominations for best novel, but his unique brand of SF, satirical and humanistic, was also accessible to mainstream readers. *Slaughterhouse-Five*, his sixth novel, appeared on the *New York Times* bestseller list for sixteen weeks and was listed as one of the twelve best books of the year by the *Times Book Review*. The book tells the story of Billy Pilgrim, a World War II veteran who has come "unstuck in time" and leaps from one stage of his life to another. The core event of *Slaughterhouse-Five* is the 1945 bombing of Dresden by Allied forces, which Vonnegut experienced. The seriousness of this topic, and the clearly satirical use of SF tropes like flying saucers and aliens from the planet Tralfamadore, pulled the book out of the SF ghetto and into the hands of mainstream readers and critics.

For the film adaptation of *Slaughterhouse-Five*, Universal allotted $5 million, a substantial sum in the era of Hollywood austerity. Director George Roy Hill's previous two films, *Thoroughly Modern Millie* (1967) and *Butch Cassidy and the Sundance Kid* (1969), had been huge hits. *Slaughterhouse-Five*'s large budget and prestigious director indicates that Universal saw the film not as an SF project with the concomitant niche audience, but as an adaptation of a mainstream bestseller, intended for general adult audiences. College students were targeted in particular. Vonnegut's acerbic wit and antiwar message had made him hugely popular on college campuses, both as a writer and a guest speaker. Universal's press book for *Slaughterhouse-Five* notes: "Aim at the College Audience. While his novels are read by people of all ages, Kurt Vonnegut Jr.'s popularity as an international author is greatest among college men and women. 'Vonnegut Cults' exist on many University campuses."[91] At the same time, *Slaughterhouse-Five* was not another low-budget counterculture film; to recoup its sizable production costs, it would need to attract more than just college students.

Slaughterhouse-Five exemplifies the "art genre" film in the way it incorporates art cinema techniques into a largely classical structure. Whereas art films like *2001* and *THX 1138* employ an overt style that deviates from classical norms by tacitly acknowledging the hand of the director and calling attention to the constructed nature of the film text, less radical films like *Slaughterhouse-Five* contain their unorthodox stylistic techniques through some narrative justification. As a genre, SF is particularly adept at providing narrative motivations for overt stylistic techniques. Because SF is not bound to traditional conventions of realism, its imaginative, speculative plots allow a filmmaker to invent any number of scenarios with which art cinema techniques can be rationalized. For instance, *Slaughterhouse-Five*'s fragmented plot disorients the viewer by continually leaping from one time and place to another: from the battlefields of the European theater, to postwar domesticity in America, to

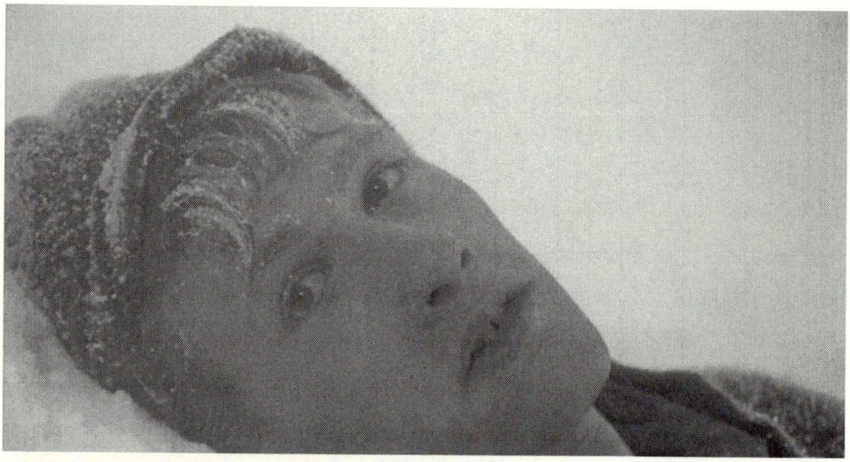

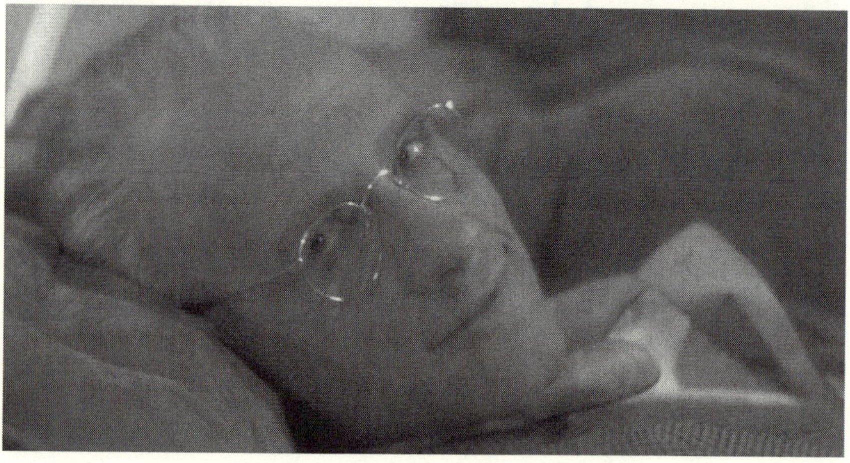

Tralfamadore where Pilgrim is observed by the aliens that abducted him. Conventional scene structure is dismantled by the film's fluid representation of temporality, as it weaves interconnecting plotlines into a coherent whole. But the disruptive effect of this fractured storytelling is reduced through narrativization. The flashbacks and flash-forwards are not explained by character subjectivity (that is, by Pilgrim merely remembering a past event or anticipating future events) or through the objectivity of conventional filmic narration (for instance, the film showing us past or future events in order to relay important information to the audience). Instead, the temporal and spatial shifts are motivated by an SF concept; Pilgrim is literally being transported from one time and space to another. This is established in the film's first scene, in which Pilgrim types a letter to the editor of the *Ilium Daily News*: "I come unstuck in time. I jump back and forth in my life and I have no control over where — " The sound of the typewriter suddenly merges with the noise of a tank. This acts as a sound bridge to the next scene, which takes place on a snowy battleground in the Second World War.

Slaughterhouse-Five takes care to make its disjointed narrative structure as easy to comprehend as possible. Not only does it give a concrete narrative explanation for the jumps; it uses stylistic devices to soften their disorienting effect. Early in the film, Pilgrim is lying in the snow, hiding from German troops. We hear the disembodied voice of the character Montana Wildhack call "Billy?"; Pilgrim turns his head in response. "You time tripping again?" asks Wildhack, who lives with a future version of Pilgrim on Trafalmadore. The young Pilgrim, still in World War II, smiles. His reaction links the two scenes together, as Pilgrim seems to be living in both places (and times) at once. Further connecting the two scenes, the film next creates a false eye-line by cutting from World War II Billy to a medium close-up of Montana on Tralfamadore. The shot/reverse-shot sequence suggests a spatial relationship that does not quite

opposite:
Slaughterhouse-Five (Universal, 1972) employs a graphic match to make the transition less jarring as Billy Pilgrim (Michael Sacks) "time trips" from World War II to a zoo on an alien planet, where he lives with Montana Wildhack (Valerie Perrine).

exist. Montana explains that she can always tell when Pilgrim has been time tripping, and there is a conventional shot/reverse-shot cut to Pilgrim, much older, on Tralfamadore. The composition and placement of the actor, with his head resting at an angle, is identical to the previous close-up of Pilgrim back in the war. *Slaughterhouse-Five* uses techniques like graphic matches, false eye-line matches, and sound bridges to make the transitions between scenes less jarring than in an art film like Alain Resnais's *Last Year at Marienbad* (1961), for instance, which cuts between past and present with no warning, and where the relationship between scenes is rarely obvious.

Slaughterhouse-Five was well received critically, winning the Jury Prize at Cannes and eliciting mostly positive reviews from major American critics. Charles Champlin at the *Los Angeles Times* described it as "a startling, complex, engrossing, affecting, and provocative film,"[92] and *New York*'s Judith Crist praised its "ability to . . . blend the past, the fleeting present and the endless future without a moment's confusion."[93] But despite the film's efforts to make its complex narrative as accessible as possible, it earned only $2.4 million in domestic rentals, a major disappointment for Universal.[94]

Other SF films of the period employed art cinema techniques in an even more limited, conservative fashion. Robert B. Ray writes, "The increasingly rapid dissemination of every cinematic innovation quickly co-opted the power of all but the most radical departures, converting the New Wave's revelatory defamiliarizations (e.g., freeze-framing, slow motion) into mere cosmetic flourishes assimilable by Hollywood's conventional forms."[95] For instance, Robert Wise's adaptation of Michael Crichton's 1969 novel *The Andromeda Strain* contains a number of split-screen sequences. But unlike the use of split screen in experimental cinema of the era, *The Andromeda Strain* tends to use the technique as a simple substitute for conventional editing patterns. For instance, in the film's first act, scientists investigate a town stricken by a deadly virus. As they look through windows, the periphery of the screen fills with images of the corpses the scientists observe. Rather than using the eye-line match technique and cutting to a shot of the corpses, we get the bearer of the look and its object on the screen simultaneously. More interesting is when Wise uses the split screen to represent character subjectivity.

Around the fifty-three-minute mark, the screen becomes segmented into a number of boxes; the largest box is the image of one of the scientists in thought, while the smaller boxes contain images that represent the memories or concepts he is pondering. Here the split screen allows the film to communicate that the character is considering a number of things simultaneously, something that consecutive flashback sequences, for instance, could not achieve. While creative, even this technique is only a slight reworking of stylistic convention. It does nothing to undermine the diegetic effect or encourage a more demanding form of spectatorship.

Although the major studios were more willing than usual in the early 1970s to experiment and take chances with film content, in the end very few SF films attempted to reproduce the uncompromising art cinema style and narration of *2001: A Space Odyssey* — and the films that did invariably disappointed at the box office. Even films that exhibited the influence of *2001* in a more limited way found it difficult to attract an audience. In 1974 graphic designer Saul Bass harked back to *2001* in the finale of his directorial debut, the killer-ant film *Phase IV*. Although it is a subtler and more understated film than one would expect from its subject matter, *Phase IV* is fairly conventional until its conclusion, a stunningly bizarre five-minute sequence in which the lead romantic couple appear to be experimented upon by the hive mind of the ants that have captured them. The scene as originally produced features double exposure, projections (reminiscent of *Zardoz*), rapid editing, time-lapse photography, and surreal imagery like a gasping fish with human legs, and human fingers pushing out through a human skull. In retrospect, even Bass admitted he could not articulate exactly what it all meant.[96] Objecting to the scene, one of the strangest in all of 1970s Hollywood cinema, Paramount cut it down to a single minute and added an explanatory voiceover ("We knew then we were being changed, and made a part of their world"). Even with the more comprehensible ending, *Phase IV* endured the same fate as the rest of the more unconventional SF films of the period — commercial failure.

In retrospect, the studios' hope that formally experimental films, usually limited to a niche audience, would proliferate in the mainstream seems misguided and more than a little desperate. The success of *The Godfather* and *The Exorcist* would dictate a more comfortable, classical model of genre film production for the industry. Rather than leading to a successful cycle of SF art films, *2001*'s influence was limited primarily to its special effects, beginning in the late 1970s, and the elaboration of the "killer computer" trope in films like *Colossus: the Forbin Project* (1970) and *Demon Seed* (1977). The Hollywood Renaissance has been nostalgically recalled as "the last good time we ever had," a time when Hollywood placed art over commerce.[97] However, the introduction of art cinema practices into mainstream filmmaking was simply another strategy to perpetuate the major studios' hegemony. The period saw numerous groundbreaking films like *2001*, but the classical system quickly absorbed and conventionalized their achievements.

Sex, Violence, and *Rollerball*: Art and Exploitation in 1970s SF

I have defined art cinema in terms of experimental style and narration; however, historically the term has held other connotations. Eric Schaefer has shown that beginning in the early 1960s the categories "art films" and "European films" were often associated not with formal innovation, but rather with nudity.[98] The success of risqué art films like *Blow-Up* (1966) contributed to the Motion Picture Association of America's October 1968 decision to replace the Production Code with a ratings system. This would, in theory, allow filmmakers complete creative freedom while also placating conservative critics worried about the increased sex and violence in Hollywood films. Most importantly, as David A. Cook notes, the ratings acted as promotional tools meant to lure viewers to theaters with the promise of titillating or shocking content they could not get from television.[99] The box office performance of *The Graduate*, among other films, indicated that audiences were receptive to controversial material; the ratings system was a strategy by the majors to legitimate this content in the eyes of mainstream American culture. As with the incorporation of art cinema techniques and progressive political themes, more "adult" content also marked a film as cutting edge and distinguished it from the classical cinema of the past.

At the same time, the ratings system brought mainstream cinema ever closer to the realm of exploitation, as films like *The Last Picture Show* (1971) and *Deliverance* (1972) drew audiences with teen sex and intense violence, respectively. Yet these were respectable major studio films, with eleven Oscar nominations between them. The boundaries between art cinema and exploitation cinema also began to blur. There was a substantial crossover audience for exploitation and art cinema; Joan Hawkins describes them as "the two extreme tastes of the postwar youthful filmgoing public."[100] At the level of distribution, Roger Corman's New World Pictures released Bergman's *Cries and Whispers* (1972) and Fellini's *Amarcord* (1973) alongside films like *The Clones* (1973) and *Caged Heat* (1974). By the '70s, art house theaters were sustained by "midnight movies" like *El Topo* (1970) and *Pink Flamingos* (1972), which were informed by both art cinema and exploitation traditions.[101] In the world of genre cinema, we saw in the previous chapter how art films were reviewed alongside exploitation SF, fantasy, and horror in *Cinefantastique*.

The early-to-mid-1970s remain the era in which the boundaries between mainstream, art, and exploitation cinema were the most fluid and imprecise. As they often reflect the simultaneous influence of these disparate production traditions, films from this period are among the most complex and contradictory texts in American film history. An SF film that cogently exemplifies these characteristics is *Rollerball* (1975), produced and directed by Norman Jewison. *Rollerball*'s mixture of art cinema techniques, social critique, and violent action makes it the perfect summation of SF cinema of its era; but this uneasy combination also renders the film thematically incoherent and categorically uncertain, factors that contributed to its poor critical reception and box office. *Rollerball* demonstrates how by taking advantage of the new ratings system and dabbling in more explicit content, mainstream SF filmmakers ran the risk of reversing the cultural ground gained by the genre since 1968.

The most expensive SF film since *2001: A Space Odyssey*, *Rollerball* is a transitional film, bridging the modestly budgeted political SF of the early 1970s and the SF blockbusters of the latter part of the decade. Its distributor, United Artists, was in something of a transitional period itself at the time. By 1974 the studio had finally recovered from its massive losses of 1968–1970, when it had gambled on a number of pricey counterculture films and lost.[102] Like the other studios, UA returned to solvency by focusing on smaller films, with an average budget of only $1.4 million.[103]

Additionally, in 1973 UA became the domestic distributor for MGM, a deal that proved profitable for UA on the basis of successes like the MGM musical compilation film *That's Entertainment!* (1974).[104] UA's new financial stability allowed it to venture into slightly more expensive projects, such as the Oscar-winning *One Flew over the Cuckoo's Nest* (1975) and *Rollerball*. Despite SF's modest track record at the time, UA gave *Rollerball* a $4.7 million budget, making it the studio's most expensive film in years.[105] This reflected UA's confidence in Norman Jewison, whom it had just signed to a multi-film deal.[106] Jewison was a highly respected filmmaker who had already been nominated for the Best Director Academy Award three times. UA had recently distributed Jewison's enormously successful *Fiddler on the Roof* (1971), and Jewison's last film, *Jesus Christ Superstar* (1973), had made $10.8 million for Universal.[107]

Jewison was known for incorporating political themes into traditional genres; his racially charged police procedural *In the Heat of the Night* (1967) was a Best Picture winner, and *Jesus Christ Superstar* replayed the biblical passion play through the lens of the '60s counterculture. SF was a logical choice for Jewison's next project, considering the political direction the genre had taken since *Planet of the Apes*. Like *Apes*, *Rollerball* is an allegorical social critique, specifically an indictment of big business. In the year 2018, nations have been replaced by corporations representing resources such as "energy," "food," and "transport."[108] Rollerball is a violent state-subsidized sport used to pacify the public, redirecting its aggression away from revolution. When one rollerballer, Jonathan E., grows too popular, his individuality threatens to stir up the somnambulant populace. The corporations respond by gradually increasing the danger of the rollerball game, hoping that Jonathan will be killed. Jonathan rebels against the system, refusing to retire and ultimately defeating all his opponents, rallying the bloodthirsty spectators to his cause, in defiance of all authority. The film's portentous print advertisements underscored its antiestablishment theme: "It made him a hero / In a future without heroes / It made him a man of action / In a world of spectators / It made him an individual / In an age of conformists."[109] As an action-oriented alpha male who takes a stand against a far-reaching institutional conspiracy, Jonathan E. is a typical SF protagonist of the period.

Rollerball exhibits the influence of European art cinema throughout;

however, Jewison is no avant-gardist. *Rollerball* is closer to *The Andromeda Strain* than *THX 1138* in its limited use of experimental technique to add a sense of novelty to an otherwise classical structure. Many of the film's narrational and stylistic flourishes seem dated or derivative in the context of 1975, like its freeze-framed, open-ended conclusion, recalling *400 Blows* (1959), and its use of classical music (here, Bach's *Toccata and Fugue in D Minor*) that can only be seen as an imitation of Kubrick. Also, in his representation of aristocratic life beyond the rollerball track as languorous and hedonistic, Jewison seems to reference Fellini and Antonioni. He peppers each party scene with long, slow tracking shots, including a thirty-eight-second shot in a fireside scene between Jonathan and friends, and a twenty-eight-second shot at a larger corporate party. Jewison retrospectively described the film's style as "more European than American . . . I think I move the camera slower. I took my time."[110] The slow pace of these scenes contrast sharply with the rapidly cut rollerball sequences. The average shot length of the first rollerball game is only 2.39 seconds, very quick for the time.[111] Jewison generally follows continuity norms during these sequences, respecting screen direction and using well-timed match cuts, but his incorporation of handheld shots and sweeping, fluid camera movements gives the scenes a visual energy that would come to define the intensified continuity style of contemporary Hollywood.

While its frenetic action scenes distinguished *Rollerball* in the marketplace, those same scenes aroused a good deal of unwanted controversy. Many critics identified a disconnect between *Rollerball*'s ostensible message and its representation of violence. In the words of Kevin Kelly at the *Boston Globe*, "*Rollerball* is an entirely hypocritical movie. It gloats over what it pretends to despise."[112] *The Milwaukee Journal* continued: "The savage action scenes that we are invited to condemn are the most engaging part."[113] Jewison went on the defensive in the *Los Angeles Times*, arguing that the film's violence was meant to be critically reflexive: "If the film itself is accused of exploiting violence, I would ask how you make a statement about violence without showing any violence. . . . I know certain people will be excited by the violence in *Rollerball*. I just hope they understand why they're being excited, and by the end of the picture perhaps realize that the violence is appealing to their more base instincts."[114] Anecdotes from screenings suggest that the film was not being received in

Critics felt that the graphic violence of *Rollerball* (United Artists, 1975) undercut the critique of violent sports intended by director Norman Jewison.

this fashion. Critic Hollis Alpert wrote, "I saw the film with a paying audience of about 1,000. And when James Caan . . . strews his opponents about the arena on his way to scoring winning goals, a good many in the audience appeared to forget that their minds were supposed to be involved, and cheered as though they were watching the Philadelphia Flyers in action."[115] Likewise, in a review from the United Kingdom: "The most chilling element of last Sunday's performance proved to be the audience. . . . As the movie progressed and they grew more vociferous, it became apparent that they were identifying with neither teams nor players but rather with the film's mindless masses cheering and clapping every kill."[116]

Appropriately enough, given Jewison's artistic debt to Stanley Kubrick, the debate over the alleged hypocrisy of *Rollerball* mirrored the one surrounding *A Clockwork Orange* three and a half years earlier. The violence of Kubrick's film, in which a sociopathic youth commits random acts of murder and rape until he is arrested and "reformed" at the hands of the government, inspired much critical vitriol. Whereas *2001* was merely accused of being pretentious or boring, Roger Ebert labeled *A Clockwork Orange* "a paranoid right-wing fantasy," and Pauline Kael called it "an abhorrent viewing experience."[117] The film was accused of encouraging copycat crimes via its detached, artful depiction of violence and its sympathetic treatment of the protagonist, Alex.[118] *A Clockwork Orange* received an X rating from the MPAA, which restricted the film's audience to those above seventeen. Although the X rating was initially a legitimate "adults-only" rating, by 1972 it was associated primarily with pornography, and nearly half of all theaters in America refused to show X-rated films.[119]

In April 1972 the controversy over *A Clockwork Orange* came to a head when the conservative *Detroit News* instituted a policy in which it refused to review or publish advertising for any X-rated film, arguing that "a sick motion picture industry is using pornography and an appeal to prurience to bolster theater attendance."[120] Kubrick responded, comparing the newspaper editors to Hitler and arguing, "To start to ban films . . . on the grounds of offensiveness is to take the first step on a course that history has shown to end in the suppression of many other liberties."[121] However, in order to broaden the potential audience for the film, Kubrick eventually acquiesced, replacing thirty seconds of footage with alternate takes and reissuing the film in late 1972. Ironically, although most of the outcry surrounding the film was due to its violence, the only footage replaced for the R-rated cut was sexual in nature.[122] By the end of 1972, *A Clockwork Orange* had earned $12 million in domestic rentals, making it the sixth-highest-grossing film of the year.[123]

Rollerball ran into its own ratings difficulty when the MPAA's Code and Ratings Administration (CARA) slapped it with an R rating, which meant that children could not attend the film without an adult. This was a serious problem for United Artists, which reportedly expected the film to gross as much as $150 million.[124] Only *The Godfather* and *The Exorcist* had earned that much with an R rating; *Rollerball*'s path to blockbuster grosses would be much easier with the less restrictive PG rating. UA and Jewison immediately protested the rating board's decision.[125] Jewison again complained to the media: "The R rating will prevent young people from seeing the film and achieving an understanding of what life could be like, if many present-day trends evolve to their logical conclusion."[126] He compared the film to *Jaws*, released the same week as *Rollerball* and well on its way to becoming the highest-grossing film of all time. For Jewison, Spielberg's film lacked the necessary social-educational content that would justify its violence: "It's got severed legs, mutilated bodies, and people being eaten alive by a shark and it's PG . . . [whereas] I think *Rollerball* has something valid to say about the future of our lives."[127]

The reproducibility of the violence was a factor in the ratings discrepancy; for the ratings board, it was a crucial distinction that the violence in *Jaws* could not be replicated by impressionable youths, as they presumably lacked access to a twenty-five-foot great white shark.[128] *Rollerball's* violent scenes, however, could be mimicked by any kid at the local roller derby. In private correspondence, UA head Arthur Krim appealed to CARA chairman Richard Heffner: "The question is not whether there is violence, but whether it has crossed the line of what may be considered the common experience of all of us. . . . No youngster who has witnessed contact sports . . . let alone having witnessed day-to-day war on television, is likely to be traumatized by *Rollerball*. . . . *Rollerball* does not depict criminal violence, let alone brutality or sadism."[129]

Heffner was not convinced. While in a letter to Jewison he proclaimed *Rollerball* "a masterpiece" and "one of the most magnificent productions I have ever seen," he also admitted that he thought the film actually should have received an X rating, as it was "much too strong a film for not-yet-mature minds."[130] Unfortunately for UA, CARA was cracking down on violence at the time, having recently awarded the first X rating for violence to the 1974 martial arts film *The Street Fighter*.[131] UA twice appealed the R rating, which was nearly unprecedented, but the appeal was rejected on both occasions.[132] The *Los Angeles Times* film critic Charles Champlin speculated that CARA did not want to appear to fold in the face of industry pressure, as *Rollerball's* R rating was damaging its box office performance.[133] The film finished with a paltry $6.2 million in domestic rentals, compared to $102.7 for *Jaws*.[134] Even Roger Corman's low-budget *Rollerball* knockoff, the exciting and campy *Death Race 2000* (1975), made nearly as much, with $4.8 million.[135]

Rollerball's R rating certainly contributed to its disappointing box office performance, but it was not the only factor. As the *Washington Post's* Gary Arnold observes, the film's "expository scenes are so solemn, monotonous, and attenuated that Jewison is in danger of losing his audience in the lengthy intervals between game days."[136] Only the few-and-far-between action scenes seemed to work, in a summer when audiences were thrilling to *Jaws*. But even the rollerball sequences are undercut by the film's mixed messages, as it attempts to be an action film and politically conscious art film simultaneously. Outside the rollerball rink, Jewison looks to criticize the tranquilized, ennui-ridden aristocracy and the masses' gleeful acceptance of the "bread and circuses." But the rollerball scenes themselves are structured like a conventional sports film in which the audience is guided to root for the protagonist, an unvarnished hero whose tenacity against the totalitarian government engenders nothing but our esteem. Again a comparison with *A Clockwork Orange* is instructive, as both protagonists are depicted as lone representatives of individuality in a mechanized, conformist society. But Kubrick asks viewers to engage in a "perverse allegiance" with Alex, a character who has admirable traits that complicate the audience's distaste for his criminal behavior.[137] This allegiance draws the audience into a state of complicity with Alex's actions and gives the film a troubling, ambivalent quality. *Rollerball's* portrayal of Jonathan E. has no such complexity. The film condones his violence as an integral part of the rollerball sport, which has grown more violent owing to powers beyond his control. And even the most progressive viewers are free to cheer his bloody victories, as each brutal act thwarts the efforts of the authorities to stifle his righteous rebellion.

The thematic contradictions within *Rollerball* are partly a function of the film's industrial status. At a cost of only $2 million, *A Clockwork Orange* could afford to unsettle its audiences, which because of its X rating would be limited to adults. The more expensive *Rollerball* needed to cast a wider net, hence the mix of appeals. Audiences looking for a politically conscious art film and those looking for an exciting action film could both, in theory, enjoy Jewison's film. United Artists' elaborate marketing campaign for *Rollerball,* which cost nearly as much as the film, only underscored its fundamental incoherence. At times, the film was presented as serious sociopolitical commentary. Arthur Krim held a preview screening for a group of U.S. congressmen (mostly Democrats, as Krim had been an adviser to Lyndon B. Johnson), in which he emphasized *Rollerball's* critique of privatization and called it "a prophecy based on certain trends."[138] Norman Jewison also gave interviews and wrote a defensive letter to the *New York Times* in which he decried "a society that increasingly tends to both glorify violence and applaud human brutality" and described American football as "a brutal and punishing game, teaching techniques of controlled violence." At the same time, UA marketed the film to sports fans, with segments running on ABC's *Wide World of Sports*,[139] and a preview article in *Sports Illustrated*, in which the writer describes "the dead and maimed" of the rollerball games, then bafflingly suggests that the sport could "catch on" in the real world, and "spark a new sport."[140] Likewise, the print ads depict *Rollerball* as an action film rather than a social critique: "It is war. It is ROLLERBALL," reads the copy, against an image of star James Caan in his militaristic rollerball armor.[141]

The thematic tensions within *Rollerball* and the negative reception of the film highlight the uncertain boundaries between exploitation, art, and mainstream cinema in the mid-1970s, as filmmakers experimented with more-explicit content. Even films made by reputable directors like Jewison were susceptible to charges of exploitation — that they included graphic violence solely to titillate and thus improve the film's box office performance. Ultimately *Rollerball* was undone by its muddled collection of disparate appeals. Jewison had attempted to make a socially critical film in the vein of *A Clockwork Orange*, but this aspect of the film was overwhelmed by the visceral intensity of the rollerball sequences. And even *A Clockwork Orange*, nominated for Best Director and Best Picture Oscars, was labeled "the purest exploitation" by Pauline Kael for what she saw as its gratuitous female nudity.[142]

By the late 1970s, the exploitation influence was absorbed into the mainstream, and its more controversial aspects were largely neutralized. Classical norms were reestablished as studios sought once again to attract general audiences and generate massive box office income from individual films. SF filmmakers had spent the last twenty years desperately avoiding pulp tropes — even Jewison was careful to note that *Rollerball* would have "no ray guns or silver suits or Flash Gordon fighting the monster"[143] — but the changing demands of the market and two wildly successful films would, in many ways, take the genre back to the 1950s. The success of the SF blockbusters of the late 1970s would not have been possible, however, without the legitimation provided by the SF art films and political programmers that immediately preceded them.

5

REVENGE OF THE NERDS

///

The Pulp SF Blockbuster, 1977–1982

Nearly twenty years after they had been dismissed as outmoded, pulp SF tropes like flying saucers, monstrous aliens, and interstellar battles were suddenly flung back into the mainstream with the success of blockbusters like *Star Wars*, *Close Encounters of the Third Kind*, and *Alien*. High-profile young directors like George Lucas and Steven Spielberg who had grown up with '50s SF were in a position to explore the less reputable side of the genre with the vast resources of major studios at their disposal. But these filmmakers were not interested in simply reproducing the films of their youth — they wanted to produce big-budget SF films with near-universal appeal. To achieve this goal they needed to combat the camp response that had become a popular reception strategy for SF cinema, due to years of bad exploitation films and deliberate camp like *Barbarella* (1969). Directors of the new SF blockbusters used a number of legitimating strategies, including photorealistic special effects, visual world-building, and, in some cases, graphic violence in order to help ensure that audiences could suspend their disbelief and receive these SF blockbusters with the appropriate level of seriousness and credulity, rather than mocking laughter.

The extraordinary success of the big-budget SF films of the late 1970s led to the widespread industrial and cultural acceptance of pulp SF as a major American subgenre. Rather than keeping their distance from pulp elements as they had done earlier in the decade, the major studios instead eagerly sought out old space action franchises like *Star Trek* and *Flash Gordon* in an effort to reproduce the *Star Wars* formula. Mainstream critics and audiences alike found films like *Star Wars* and *Close Encounters* to be refreshing, exciting escapism. However, not everyone was enamored of the new direction that SF, and American filmmaking in general, was taking. The revival of the blockbuster was accompanied by the widespread abandonment of the art cinema–inspired, more political filmmaking that had proliferated earlier in the decade. In SF, the social critique of films like *A Clockwork Orange* was replaced by PG-rated, family-friendly action and sentimentality. The widespread merchandising that accompanied *Star Wars* and *E.T.* threatened to make a film's aesthetics secondary to the number of tie-in products it could generate. A new blockbuster era had begun.

SF and the Birth of the Contemporary Blockbuster

The film that crushed *Rollerball* at the box office in the summer of 1975, Steven Spielberg's *Jaws*, is usually identified by historians as the film that kicked off the contemporary blockbuster era.[1] The unprecedented success of films like *The Godfather* (1972) and *The Exorcist* (1973) indicated that the recession of 1969–1971 was over, but it was not until *Jaws* earned a record $102.7 million domestically in its first year of release that the major studios returned to the consistent production of big-budget films.[2] *Jaws* was reminiscent of previous blockbusters in many respects: it was expensive (although this was primarily due to a troubled shoot that went over budget), and presold, based on a best-selling novel. But unlike roadshow blockbusters of the 1960s or *The Godfather* and *The Exorcist*, which opened in a few theaters and gradually expanded, *Jaws* received a national television advertising campaign and nationwide saturation release that were key to its unprecedented success.

Sheldon Hall and Steve Neale note that *Jaws* was not the first big-budget film of the 1970s to receive this treatment, but its record-breaking performance at the box office established the nationwide saturation release as the standard for all future blockbusters.[3] Regional saturation releases date back at least as far as the blockbuster western *Duel in the Sun* (1946), but in the 1950s they were largely associated with exploitation films, as discussed in chapter 2. The strategy continued into the 1970s for a number of studio programmers with exploitation appeal; for instance, MGM's *Westworld* (1973) played at 275 theaters in Chicago, Detroit, and Cleveland in its first month before moving to Boston, Philadelphia, Minneapolis, and Toronto.[4] Rather than a regional saturation release, however, *Jaws* premiered on 464 screens across North America on a single day—June 20, the height of the summer season.[5] Releasing the film in all major markets on the same day added efficacy to Universal's nationwide television advertising campaign—the studio ran prime-time ads on all three networks in the week leading up to the film's release.[6]

Regional saturation releases typically employed short runs of one or two weeks; the idea was to build a brief bubble of excitement before the local audience for cheap exploitation fare had been exhausted. The nationwide saturation release of a blockbuster featured much longer runs of at least ten to twelve weeks, marking the film as a major cultural event. As David A. Cook puts it, "What had been a means of throwing a movie away . . . became a way of signaling its importance."[7] The hype generated by a saturation release also helped to mitigate the risk of financial disaster. For instance, in 1970 Paramount's road-show musical *Darling Lili* earned only $3.3 million in rentals, against a cost of $22 million.[8] Six years later, post-*Jaws*, Paramount opened its $24 million remake of *King Kong* on over a thousand screens in North America on December 17, 1976.[9] Producer Dino De Laurentiis promoted the remake as "the greatest love story of all time," compared it to David Lean's *Brief Encounter* (1945), and predicted it would best *Jaws* with a $200 million domestic gross.[10] Such were the expectations surrounding the film that it was considered a major disappointment at the box office despite grossing $52.6 million domestically.[11] Crucially, $35 million of that final gross was earned in the first seventeen days of release, after which ticket sales plummeted.[12] Gulf and Western chairman Charles Bluhdorn blamed bad weather, but the lukewarm reviews for *King Kong* suggest that poor word of mouth played a role. Importantly, however, the saturation release led to front-loaded grosses that ensured the film would perform relatively well, regardless of word of mouth. Had *Kong* been released as a road show, it is unlikely that it would have achieved the success it did.

The contemporary blockbuster's great profit potential led the majors to loosen their purse strings in the late 1970s. As discussed in the previous chapter, before 1976 studios rarely spent more than $5 million to $7 million on a film — even *Jaws* was originally budgeted at a mere $3.5 million.[13] From 1971 to 1975, only two films cost $15 million or more; in 1980 alone seventeen films were that expensive, with another twenty-one in 1981.[14] The average cost of a Hollywood film nearly doubled from 1976 to 1979.[15] Inflation, rising star salaries, and a new emphasis on special effects were all factors, but in general the explosion in production budgets reflected the studios' increased confidence in the blockbuster. By the late 1970s the market was crowded with spectacular, big-budget films — not all of which could be successful. Saturation releases helped to minimize risk, but flops still occurred. American International Pictures' disaster film *Meteor* (1979) cost $16 million, plus an additional $3 million in marketing costs, and opened in six hundred theaters,[16] but by the end of 1979 it had earned only $4.2 million domestically.[17] "The picture never really opened," griped AIP head Samuel Z. Arkoff. "It used to be if you had a big promotion, at least you did business the first week."[18] Undeterred, studios were willing to gamble that the extraordinary grosses of the blockbusters that were hits would more than compensate for the films that were not. Even struggling AIP, which merged with the independent production company Filmways in 1979, had two breakout successes that same year: *The Amityville Horror* and *Love at First Bite*.

The increase in Hollywood budgets allowed SF to move out of the programmer category and return, on an even larger scale, to the kind of spectacular, effects-driven films innovated by George Pal in the 1950s. But this transition was not instantaneous; a year after the release of *Jaws*, SF was still considered unworthy of blockbuster budgets, particularly after the relative failure of *Rollerball*. An expensive exception was MGM's *Logan's Run*, an adaptation of the 1967 cult SF novel that proposes a futuristic society in which citizens are euthanized at age thirty (twenty-one in the novel). The film was originally budgeted at $5 million, but elaborate special-effects work led to costs ballooning to $9 million in postproduction.[19] *Logan's Run* was reconceptualized as a major blockbuster, with distributor United Artists supplying a saturation release and even striking 70mm prints for select theaters.[20]

Aside from its cost, *Logan's Run* is a fairly typical mid-1970s SF studio film: featuring an action-oriented white male protagonist who rebels against a far-reaching conspiracy, it mixes action and social commentary in the mode of *Planet of the Apes*. The film received largely negative reviews, with Gene Siskel calling it "the worst major motion picture I've seen this year."[21] Especially vocal in their criticisms were SF fans who initially were intrigued by the largest SF budget since *2001: A Space Odyssey*; a cover story in *Cinefantastique* was subtitled "The science fiction film boom begins with a bomb."[22] In 1977, two members of the Academy of Motion Picture Arts and Sciences visual effects award committee resigned in protest after *Logan's Run* and *King Kong* were awarded "special achievement" Oscars. One of them remarked, "I can't think of any two films in the last few years that got such scathing criticism in the press, and yet we give them our award. It's a pretty sad business."[23] Despite the pans, *Logan's Run* earned $8.7 million in box office rentals — a respectable amount, but quite modest in relation to its cost. Like *Rollerball*, *Logan's Run* was yet another SF film that had failed to become an "event picture" like *The Exorcist* or *Jaws*. It would take another year for SF to truly establish itself as the quintessential contemporary blockbuster genre, which it did with the release of Fox's *Star Wars* and Columbia's *Close Encounters of the Third Kind*.

At the time of their production both films were considered extremely risky investments. When it first expressed interest in Lucas's *Star Wars* project in 1973, Fox envisioned it as a $3 million film, the first entry in a series of programmers along the lines of the studio's successful *Planet of the Apes* franchise.[24] In his account of the making of *Star Wars*, J. W. Rinzler portrays Fox as highly skeptical of Lucas's project and reluctant to invest, to the extent that it refused to fund nearly $500,000 worth of preproduction work, which Lucas was forced to pay out of pocket.[25] When the film's budget increased to $8.2 million in mid-1975, Fox actually froze preproduction pending the outcome of a board of directors meeting at year's end. Fortunately, Lucas had an ally in production head Alan Ladd Jr., who persuaded the board to green-light the film.[26]

While his struggles with Fox would permanently sour Lucas on Hollywood, the studio's lack of enthusiasm for *Star Wars* is perhaps understandable, given SF's track record at the box office. Indicating that the audience for the genre was still quite limited, SF films in the early 1970s earned between $2 million and $5 million in domestic rentals, almost without exception. Therefore, budgets needed to be kept low if an SF film had any chance at profitability—the success of the *Planet of the Apes* sequels, for instance, was due more to their modest budgets than the number of tickets sold. Lucas himself estimated that his film, meant to appeal primarily to children and SF fans, would gross between $16 million and $25 million (or approximately $8 million to $12.5 million in film rentals), and even those numbers meant it would need to be the most successful SF film since *A Clockwork Orange*.[27] Ultimately, *Star Wars* would cost $11.3 million, which according to Lucas biographer Dale Pollock meant it needed to gross at least $32 million simply to break even.[28]

The odds of *Star Wars* attaining profitability seemed slim, if prerelease exhibitor interest was any indication. Exhibitor advances and guarantees were another important factor behind the increase in budgets in the late 1970s; they allowed a studio to proceed with a blockbuster budget, confident that it would recover a substantial portion of its investment regardless of the film's ultimate reception at the box office.[29] In a summer that included such promising box office attractions as *The Spy Who Loved Me*, *The Deep*, and *Exorcist II: The Heretic*, theater owners were not interested in booking an SF film with no major stars (save the geriatric Alec Guinness), even if it was made by the director of the surprise hit *American Graffiti*. Pollock writes that *Star Wars* received only $1.5 million in guarantees, "rather than the $10 million expected of big movies."[30] Acknowledging this exhibitor indifference, Fox opened *Star Wars* on only forty-three screens on Memorial Day weekend, which was considered too early in the year to be a desirable slot.[31] Of course, *Star Wars* defied predictions and went on to earn $127 million in domestic rentals in its initial release, plus an additional $38.4 million in a 1978 rerelease.[32] Unlikely as it might have seemed at the time, an SF film had become the highest-grossing movie in the history of American cinema.

Although he was pleased for his friend George Lucas, Steven Spielberg was privately perturbed by the success of *Star Wars*, as he felt it took attention from his own SF blockbuster, the UFO abduction drama *Close Encounters of the Third Kind*, released seven months later.[33] As the director of

Jaws, Spielberg did not receive the obstructive treatment Lucas suffered at the hands of Fox. Yet in other respects the productions of *Star Wars* and *Close Encounters* were much alike — both were originally intended as moderately priced A films, only to have their budgets increase dramatically, due largely to their complex special effects.[34] The original budget for *Close Encounters* was $4.1 million; as it turned out, that amount barely covered the film's effects budget.[35] The final cost of *Close Encounters* was $19.4 million, plus another $5 million to $6 million for marketing.[36] The risk for Columbia was enormous; however, it reduced this risk considerably by asking for stiff terms in its guarantees with exhibitors. Theater owners were much more eager to play Spielberg's new film than they were with *Star Wars*. *Close Encounters* secured an extraordinary $24 million in guaranteed bookings, which meant the film was close to breaking even before it even opened.[37] It finished its initial theatrical run with $77 million in domestic rentals, plus an additional $5.7 million from a 1980 "special edition" reissue that featured new footage.[38]

The grosses from *Star Wars* and *Close Encounters* had a major impact on the fortunes of their respective studios. Fox took one-third of the rentals for *Star Wars* as a distribution fee and then split the remaining rentals 60/40 with Lucas.[39] For a film that grossed $524 million worldwide by the end of the decade, this was an extraordinary windfall for the studio.[40] Aubrey Solomon reports: "Fox's stock rose from a low of $6 per share in June 1976 to nearly $27 after *Star Wars*' release. [The studio's] revenues rose from $195 million in 1976 to $301 million in 1977."[41] Investors were keenly aware of this boost to Fox's stock when *Close Encounters* was readied for release in late 1977: shares in Columbia Pictures dropped sharply when *New York* magazine published an early review that suggested the film would be "a colossal flop."[42] But the studio got the last laugh — Columbia's quarterly profits in April 1978 shot up 169 percent from the previous year, due almost entirely to the performance of *Close Encounters*.[43]

The success of Lucas's and Spielberg's films led to an explosion of SF production by the major studios. In 1976, only one SF film (*Logan's Run*) was not a low-budget exploitation film or foreign import. By 1979, most of the majors had jumped on board the SF bandwagon, including Paramount with *Star Trek: The Motion Picture* (which had been developed as a new television series until *Star Wars* debuted) and UA's *Moonraker*, featuring

James Bond in outer space. Just as *2001* and *Planet of the Apes* had done a decade earlier, *Star Wars* and *Close Encounters* proved that SF had legitimate crossover potential. This time, however, the films were unabashedly embracing the tropes of pulp SF, rather than employing them obliquely, as *2001* and *Apes* had. Spielberg and Lucas were "monster kids" who had grown up with exploitation SF, both in theaters and on television. As a child Lucas had been obsessed with comics, including EC's SF books and DC's *Tommy Tomorrow*, as well as pulp SF magazines like *Amazing Stories*.[44] He also watched classic B movies and serials on *Adventure Theater*, a nightly television show broadcast out of San Francisco.[45] Spielberg was a regular reader of Forrest Ackerman's *Famous Monsters of Filmland*; in 1987 he claimed that the fanzine gave him "much needed inspiration" to make his own amateur films as a youngster.[46] The roots of *Close Encounters* can be found in *Firelight*, a feature film about UFO investigation and alien abduction made by Spielberg in 1964 when he was only seventeen years old.[47] It was only natural for filmmakers like Lucas and Spielberg to gravitate toward the SF genre as they looked to develop projects that would entertain the whole family. The challenge they faced, however, was translating the SF conventions they loved to an audience who found them childish and absurd.

Pulp Verisimilitude vs. Camp

The classic pulp SF that inspired Lucas and Spielberg was by the 1970s appreciated almost solely as camp. Broadly defined, camp is an alternative reading strategy that playfully celebrates a work of art for the ways in which it challenges conventional notions of quality and good taste. Chuck Kleinhans writes, "Camp is an ironic and parodic appreciation of an extravagant form that is out of proportion to its content, especially when that content is banal or trivial."[48] In her influential 1964 article "Notes on 'Camp,'" Susan Sontag wrote that camp "is art that proposes itself seriously, but cannot be taken altogether seriously because it is 'too much.'"[49] SF examples cited by Sontag include Flash Gordon comics and Japanese films like *Rodan* (1956) and *The Mysterians* (1957).[50] Low-budget exploitation SF cinema of the 1950s and 1960s lends itself especially well to a camp reception, as its poor production values, shoddy special effects, narrative improbabilities, and amateurish acting diverge from normative conceptions of "quality" cinema. Rather than condemning a film for these characteristics, a camp reading celebrates them as stylized, exaggerated, and artificial, a break from the contrived realism of conventional filmmaking.

While Sontag has been subsequently criticized for effacing the role of queer identity and the aesthetics of 1960s gay subculture in the construction of camp, her article was important in popularizing the concept. Soon after "Notes on 'Camp'" was published, camp was being used intentionally by the culture industry to appeal to mainstream (that is, heteronormative) audiences. Shows like *Batman* (ABC, 1966–1968) were intentionally faux-serious parodies that encouraged a camp reception with their hyperbolic melodrama.[51] These deliberate "mass camp" or "pop camp" texts self-consciously attempted to reproduce the naive charm of "pure" camp texts, and explicitly cued a camp response from the audience. Whereas at first camp was an oppositional reading method that challenged the dominant order by refusing to accept Hollywood's codes of realism, its assimilation into popular culture created a relationship of complicity in which the culture industry guides its audience toward a preferred reading. Thus, mass camp lacks the radicalism of a "pure" camp response.

It might seem as though the proliferation of deliberate camp SF like Irwin Allen's television show *Lost in Space* would only further damage SF's already low cultural reputation by playing up its more absurd qualities. Instead, camp represents a strategy through which studios and filmmakers made pulp SF palatable to adult audiences, by directly acknowledging the genre's tendencies toward cartoonish, juvenile excess. Sasha Torres writes that *Batman*'s use of camp represents "a way to circumvent Batman's associations with low culture and children's entertainment."[52] By treating the comic book character with a sense of camp exaggeration, the show gave adults "permission" to enjoy the program. A detached, ironic reading strategy confirms the adult audience's conception of itself as sophisticated and superior to juvenile media texts like comic books and pulp SF.

Roger Vadim's comic book adaptation *Barbarella* (1968) was the first big-budget SF film to employ camp intentionally. Called the apotheosis of pop camp by sociologist Andrew Ross, *Barbarella* carefully maintains a façade of seriousness, thereby reproducing the tone of "naive" camp.[53] Jane Fonda portrays the title character, a wide-eyed adventurer who travels from one sexually charged situation to another in her quest to rescue scientist Durand Durand. *Barbarella*'s outlandish sets and costume design combine the pulp SF iconography of Jean-Claude Forest's 1962 comic with late-1960s contemporary fashion, contributing to the "anything goes" sense of camp hyperbole. Some critics were offended by *Barbarella*'s playfully uninhibited sexuality, although it only made overt the erotic (including sadomasochistic) subtexts that coursed through earlier space operas like *Flash Gordon*. Calling it "pure sub-adolescent junk, bereft of redeeming social *or* artistic importance," *Film Quarterly* sniffed, "In the year that Stanley Kubrick and Franklin Schaffner finally elevated the science-fiction movie beyond the abyss of the kiddie show, Roger Vadim . . . has knocked it right back again."[54] Likewise, *Variety* condemned *Barbarella* as an "artless, tasteless, misdirected vulgarity."[55] Charles Champlin of the *Los Angeles Times* was more insightful, identifying the film as "the highest high camp has ever been" and a "tribute (fraught with the wry) to the whole ray-gun, space-ship, bug-eyed-monster field of fiction."[56] Mixed reviews were typical for camp films, whose excesses inspired polarized reactions.

Although *Barbarella* was a costly flop for Paramount and producer Dino De Laurentiis, it developed a cult following and was a direct influence on several films produced during the space opera revival of the late 1970s. Intentionally campy independent films like *Starcrash* (1979) and *Galaxina* (1980), though battered by critics who were not in on the joke, were still able to find modest success at the box office because of their low budgets. This would not be the case for *Flash Gordon* (1980), another De Laurentiis production, which cost $20 million. When considering an approach for the SF blockbuster, director Mike Hodges saw no alternative but camp: "What else are you meant to do but laugh at a comic strip? When Alex Raymond had first created the strip in the 1930s, man was a long way from landing on the moon. But by 1980 we'd been there, done that! It *had* to be tongue-in-cheek."[57] Long before the release of Hodges's *Flash Gordon*, the 1930s pulp iconography of the original *Flash* had been reduced to camp by low-budget exploitation films and co-opted by intentional camp like *Barbarella*. In 1966 the Flash Gordon and Buck Rogers serials were repurposed as camp comedies, as ABC films licensed them to television stations looking to take advantage of the popularity of *Batman*.[58]

Max von Sydow (as Ming the Merciless) and Ornella Muti (as Princess Aura) give campy, exaggerated performances as the villains of *Flash Gordon* (Dino De Laurentiis/Universal, 1980).

The plot of the 1980 *Flash Gordon* follows its comic strip source material fairly closely, but from its garish use of color to its pseudoscientific gadgets (Ming the Merciless employs a weather machine with buttons marked "Earthquake" and "Typhoon"), the film employs a stylized camp approach meant to reassure adult audiences that it does not take its fantastic scenario too seriously. The performances are broad, with Sam J. Jones performing a variation on Jane Fonda's innocent routine from *Barbarella*, and the dialogue (by former *Batman* television writer Lorenzo Semple) is wildly melodramatic, with Ming intoning portentously, "Pathetic Earthlings," and Dale Arden breathlessly exclaiming, "Flash, I love you, but we only have fourteen hours to save the earth!" Clinching the campy tone is a flamboyant soundtrack from the glam rock band Queen.

Flash Gordon employed a tone of faux-seriousness and avoids self-aware humor that "winks" at the audience, as this would make the film an overt parody. Like Barbarella, the characters in *Flash Gordon* react as though the stakes are high and the drama is legitimate. In this way, the film attempts a "dual-address" strategy, characteristic of mainstream camp, in which the text can be taken seriously by "naive" viewers such as children and accepted as parody by "sophisticated" viewers. However, this strategy is complicated by *Flash Gordon*'s attempt to oscillate between faux-seriousness, outright comedy (as when New York Jets quarterback Flash assaults Ming's guards with a makeshift football), and a legitimately dramatic tone, as in the suspenseful duel between Flash and Barin on the forest moon Arboria. *Flash Gordon* exemplifies a trend identified by scholar Ken Feil, in which contemporary blockbusters are "ambivalent parodies" that mix camp irony with sincerity so that "audience members can both experience a genre as well as a mockery of it."[59] Rather than dividing the audience into naive vs. sophisticated viewers, the film allows for the possibility that audience members will "travel between those poles" of irony and sincerity.[60] In *Flash Gordon*, this leads to incoherence, as the film cannot seem to decide whether it wants the audience to become emotionally invested in the plot or to maintain an ironic distance.

Flash Gordon earned $14.9 million in domestic rentals, a pittance compared to the same year's *Star Wars* sequel *The Empire Strikes Back*, which made $141.6 million.[61] *Flash Gordon*'s failure was typical of camp blockbusters of the 1980s, which were almost invariably box office disappointments, if not utter disasters. The litany includes *Superman III* (1983), *The Adventures of Buckaroo Banzai across the 8th Dimension* (1984), *Supergirl* (1984), *Ice Pirates* (1984), and *Howard the Duck* (1986). The consistent failure of camp SF films in the '80s suggests that general audiences found their mixture of comic and dramatic cues confusing or unsatisfying. Because of their faux-dramatic tone, deliberate camp films lacked the overt comedic appeal of broad farces like *Porky's* (1982) or *Police Academy* (1984). At the same time, their campy humor ensured that, for sophisticated audiences, the films could not provide the emotional catharsis of a straightforward drama either. The two tiers of camp reception are contradictory and therefore exclusive to some extent. Feil argues that mass camp films must emphasize sincerity at certain points, especially in their conclusions, to avoid alienating general audiences that expect dramatic catharsis.[62] He writes, "The more extreme a film's camp address, the more it risks appealing to only 'insider' audiences."[63] It is likely that *Flash Gordon*'s cartoonish, hyperbolic melodrama inhibited character identification and the audience's emotional investment in the story line.

Flash Gordon was produced on the back of the success of *Star Wars*, but its campiness differs sharply from Lucas's approach to similar material. With its broad melodrama, unabashed use of genre clichés, and somewhat amateurish performances from the young leads, *Star Wars* could certainly be received as unintentional camp by some spectators. For instance, Robert B. Ray claims that "*Star Wars*, with its elephantine score . . . and cartoon characters was inescapably camp for anyone over twelve."[64] However, the historical evidence overwhelmingly indicates that *Star Wars* was successful precisely because it was *not* "inescapably camp," even for adults. The film's reviews, Oscar nominations, and box office performance suggest that adult spectators and critics were able to suspend their disbelief and take *Star Wars* on its own terms as a lightweight but sincere adventure drama. Reports of early screenings suggest a "midnight movies" cult atmosphere, but, crucially, without the camp irony — a Beverly Hills theater owner remarked that "the audiences become deeply involved with the characters and the action. . . . They go in there and have a ball, cheering and applauding."[65]

Instead of using camp to acknowledge the hackneyed nature of the SF conventions it employs, *Star Wars* treats these conventions with the utmost earnestness. Dale Pollock writes, "Lucas insisted that his cast never play a scene for its camp humor, even if the script seemed to call for it. *Star Wars* was not a camp movie and there would be no double-takes or sly grins."[66] The film is funny, but the humor takes the form of lighthearted banter among the lead characters, with the effete droid C-3PO providing additional comic relief. Importantly, the humor never exceeds the boundaries of the diegesis, never damages the verisimilitude of the fantasy world, and never suggests that the narrative is not worth the audience's emotional investment. As critic Vincent Canby noted, "Everyone treats his material with the proper combination of solemnity and good humor that avoids condescension."[67] Roguish smuggler Han Solo (Harrison Ford) is characterized by a sarcasm and cynicism that has the potential to disrupt the integrity of the narrative, but ultimately reinforces it. Solo is initially skeptical of "the Force" — the mystical energy field that gives the Jedi their extraordinary powers. Here Solo acts as an audience surrogate, in that his skepticism anticipates the audience's own. Yet by the end of the film, Solo, with a measure of earnestness, tells protagonist Luke Skywalker "May the Force be with you" when the two part ways. Solo's character arc adds credence to the film's fantastic concepts.

Before *Star Wars*, humor in SF films was largely based in camp or parody. It is comparatively easy for somber films like *Blade Runner* (1982) or

The Thing, which contain graphic violence and complex themes, to appeal to older audiences. Even *The Empire Strikes Back* (1980) clearly skews older than its predecessor, as it is much darker, more violent, and more slowly paced. *Star Wars* demonstrated how a film rooted in pulp SF concepts could be funny while still remaining dramatically potent. By avoiding camp, Lucas was gambling that he could persuade adult audiences to suspend their disbelief and become immersed in the narrative. Some critics found this pastiche approach to be embarrassingly unsophisticated. Stanley Kauffmann wrote, "I kept looking for an 'edge,' to peer around the corny, solemn comic-book strophes."[68] But the film's unprecedented success and the fervor of its fan following indicate that Lucas achieved his goal.

Another strategy used by SF blockbusters to avoid a camp response was elaborate visual world-building via innovative special effects technology and production design. Julie A. Turnock argues that the special effects of SF films of the late 1970s, particularly *Star Wars* and *Close Encounters*, exhibit a tension between two competing aesthetics. First, the filmmakers seek to achieve a sense of "graphic dynamics." Influenced by the abstract imagery of avant-garde filmmakers like Jordan Belson, these effects (such as the jump to hyperspace in *Star Wars*) thrill the audience's senses and immerse them in the narrative action.[69] From a business standpoint, the combination of these spectacular effects with exhibition technologies like Dolby surround sound offered viewers a powerful, visceral theatrical experience. At the same time, achieving photorealism was also of utmost importance; Turnock defines George Lucas's philosophy as "the more seamlessly photoreal the effects, the more the audience accepts the diegetic world as visually convincing and therefore narratively and intellectually convincing."[70]

To achieve a photorealistic look, the *Star Wars* and *Close Encounters* teams worked to minimize distracting matte lines in composite shots of spacecraft, and sought a "first-generation" look rather than the washed-out, degraded, "dupey" effects shots that plagued low-budget films.[71] For *Star Wars*, Lucas demanded a great deal of camera movement during the space battles, to avoid the static quality that he felt bracketed or "locked off" effects sequences from the rest of the film, thereby calling attention to themselves. Special effects supervisor John Dykstra developed a motion control camera that could store and precisely duplicate intricate camera movements; this enabled *Star Wars* to feature effects shots containing a number of models (each of which needed to be photographed separately) along with dynamic, sweeping camera movements. Again realism was the key motivator. Dykstra explains: "If you start moving the camera, that is the subliminal cue to the person watching it, even if he knows nothing about film, that he's watching real live action photography. . . . Instead of viewing a postcard, he's seeing a three-dimensional reality."[72] Seamless special effects were not just a selling point; they were crucial in maintaining an audience's suspension of disbelief and warding off a camp response. For a film rooted in pulp SF like *Star Wars* to be effective, there had to be no room for the audience to snicker.

The groundbreaking special effects in *Star Wars* were part of a larger strategy of narrative world-building, something that would become a crucial marker of quality and legitimacy for subsequent SF A films.[73] World-building has been "an intrinsic part of the construction of a science fiction novel" for hundreds of years; however, in literature, successful world-building is generally associated with strict scientific accuracy.[74] "Hard SF" writers such as Poul Anderson were renowned for their attention to scientific detail when building their fictional worlds, and were kept honest by readers who would chide them for any inaccuracies or leaps of logic.[75] Lucas, however, was not interested in that type of realism, noting in 1977 that science "bogs you down. . . . I want to tell a fantasy story."[76] Lucas's world-building was closer to that of earlier fantasists like Edgar Rice Burroughs, Robert E. Howard, and J. R. R. Tolkien, who developed elaborate fictional worlds with their own complex histories. Tolkien famously created not only a back history and maps for his Middle-earth, but languages, genealogies, songs, flora and fauna, and calendar systems. Films like *Star Wars* might be able to achieve the breadth of an SF novel's world-building, particular with the addition of sequels, but they cannot achieve the same depth. A time-bound medium like cinema cannot relay the elaborate back history of a fantasy world without impeding the progress of the narrative. Instead, close attention to visual detail in production design creates a believable environment that *suggests* the existence of the things Tolkien describes in his appendices.[77] Rather than attempting to match the comprehensiveness of literary world-building, films like

Star Wars use an accumulation of visual detail to provide the illusion of comprehensiveness.

As discussed earlier, SF films in the years immediately preceding *Star Wars* were typically set in the near future, which meant a believable SF environment could be created by simply tweaking existing locations and settings. As a space opera set "a long time ago, in a galaxy far, far away," *Star Wars* needed to create its narrative world from scratch. Therefore, production design became just as essential as special effects in establishing a realistic SF environment. One aspect of the film's production design that proved highly influential was the crafting of what Lucas in 1976 called a "used future." Inspired by the poor condition of the Apollo capsules after reentry, Lucas wanted sets and props to be deliberately weathered. This was a reaction against the often-antiseptic look of earlier SF films and television shows, which Lucas found distractingly unrealistic.[78] *Star Wars* production designer John Barry remarked in 1976, "My personal taste leans more toward *Barbarella*, which George didn't want to do. He wants to make *The Star Wars* [*sic*] look like it's shot on location on your average, everyday Death Star or Mos Eisley spaceport."[79] To that end, the environments needed to look functional and "lived-in." By filling *Star Wars* with ramshackle spaceships, dented robots, and gritty desert towns, Lucas enhances the verisimilitude of his fictional world. Rather than looking like the work of a single production designer, the props and sets seem organic to their particular environment. (Lucas: "I want it to look like one thing came from one part of the galaxy and another thing came from another part of the galaxy."[80]) When the "antiseptic" style is used in *Star Wars*, it serves a very different narrative function. In films like *2001*, the look communicates scientific efficiency and progress. In *Star Wars* (as in *THX 1138*), it is associated with a fascist government—the sterile halls of the Death Star seem menacing compared to the warm stylistic hodgepodge of the rebel base.

The "used future" look became almost de rigueur for SF films after the release of *Star Wars*. Despite its expensive, ornate sets, Disney's *The Black Hole* (1979) looks anachronistic with its sterile hallways and uniforms. Even *Star Trek* incorporated a more dilapidated aesthetic into its typically clean, utopian environments with the grungy costumes of Ricardo Montalbán and company in *Star Trek II: The Wrath of Khan* (1982). The "used

The clutter of the spaceship *Nostromo* in *Alien* (Twentieth Century-Fox, 1979) exemplifies the "used universe" look that became popular in SF after *Star Wars*.

universe" strategy would reach new levels of obsessive detail in Ridley Scott's *Alien* (1979) and *Blade Runner* (1982). In *Alien*, an R-rated horror film green-lighted by Fox after the success of *Star Wars*, a rapidly mutating, monstrous creature hunts and kills members of a mining spacecraft on its way home to Earth. The spaceship *Nostromo* is a dimly lit, cluttered industrial-domestic space, full of the crew's personal items and detritus like beer cans. This contrasts with the sleek organic design of H. R. Giger's alien, creating disturbing incongruities and emphasizing the alien's status as the threatening Other. *Blade Runner*, an SF noir set in the visually overwhelming postindustrial wasteland of 2019 Los Angeles, was even more elaborate and has since become one of the most heralded examples of production design in Hollywood history. The film's plot, adapted from a Philip K. Dick novel, deals with a private detective hired to hunt down and execute a group of rebellious androids.

Ridley Scott's SF films place viewers within fully realized science fictional environments, immersing them in the narrative rather than encouraging an ironic distance. For some critics, however, this careful attention to production detail became excessive and distracted from the story rather than enhancing it. *Cineaste* lauded the way the spacecraft *Nostromo* looked "worked in, lived in, with grimy pipes, strewn papers, and claustrophobic decks and corridors," but ultimately decided that *Alien* was nothing more than "a lightweight script imbalanced by lavish production values."[81] *Blade Runner* would receive much harsher criticism along the same lines. The film's reviews, which were mostly negative, charged Ridley Scott with losing sight of the narrative amid all the detailed mise-en-scène. Typical was the review from the *New Orleans Times-Picayune*, which remarked, "The sets all too often overwhelm the narrative content — in fact, the sets all but *become* the content."[82] Pauline Kael wrote, "A suspenseless thriller; [*Blade Runner*] appears to be a victim of its own imaginative use of hardware and miniatures and mattes. . . . The people we're watching are so remote from us they might be shadows of people who aren't there."[83]

By emphasizing production design so strongly, and employing an emotionally distant protagonist, *Blade Runner* violates the mainstream critics' standards of quality, rooted in character arcs and audience identification, and aligns the film more closely with the exploitation tradition, in which character is subordinated to spectacle. For these critics, visual components such as production design are meant to tastefully accent the drama without calling attention to themselves. However, by drawing a dichotomy between production design and story, these critics ignore the important narrative function of such visual elements, namely the way in which they create a believable, immersive science fictional or fantasy world, crucial in establishing a film's dramatic plausibility. Without this close attention to detail, films run the risk of looking bare, their settings too artificial and contrived. With films like *Alien* and *Blade Runner*, the production design also works to generate a grim, unsettling tone, crucial for the films' overall emotional impact.

Ridley Scott's SF films were also at the center of controversies surrounding the final strategy employed by SF blockbusters to avoid a camp reception — the use of intense, graphic violence. Again, visceral responses could bind audiences to the narrative — *Star Wars* elicited feelings of exhilaration and awe, but fear and disgust could be just as effective. *Alien* in particular was understood at the time to have expanded the boundaries of what could be shown in major motion pictures in terms of gore. The alien's jaws plunge into human skulls, and a robot is decapitated with a fire extinguisher, but most horrific was the infamous scene in which the alien is born by bursting out of crewman's chest cavity, where it had been incubating. Despite its violent, pulpy content, *Alien* was still to some extent marked as a "sophisticated" film upon its release in June 1979: the art cinema proclivities of Ridley Scott (whose previous film, *The Duellists* [1977], had won Best Debut Film at Cannes) combined with the inimitable and unsettling designs of H. R. Giger to give the film a distinct auteur sensibility. And indeed, *Alien*'s visual style was lauded by critics. Tom Figenshu in *Film Comment* wrote, "[Scott] forgot that *Alien* was just a horror film, and he tried to give us a terrific movie by any standards. Some of the images . . . possess a beauty quite unlike anything we've seen in horror films before."[84]

This praise was often tempered, however, by a vigorous critique of *Alien*'s violence and unrelenting tension. Janet Maslin in the *New York Times* complained, "Fun is nowhere to be found in 'Alien,' a movie whose sole and very mystifying purpose seems to be making its audience miserable. People are lined up around the block to see it. I don't understand why. . . . [It has] a mirthless, one-track dedication to turning the audience's collective stomach."[85] David Denby was even stronger, writing that *Alien* "is so 'effective' it has practically turned me off movies altogether. . . . [It] works on your nerves and emotions with the practiced hand of a torturer extracting a confession. The movie is terrifying, but not in a way that is remotely enjoyable. I came out of it feeling drained and exhausted."[86] Two months after *Alien*'s release, the *Los Angeles Times* published a letter to the editor arguing that it was "an evil movie" and wondering, "Why are we paying [the filmmakers] to do these awful things to our poor sensibilities?"[87]

Even more controversial was Universal's $15 million remake of *The Thing* (1982), green-lighted based on the success of *Alien*. Directed by Howard Hawks fanatic John Carpenter, the remake exploited advances in special effects and makeup to reproduce the shape-shifting alien from John W. Campbell's original story. The horrific creations of makeup effects artist Rob Bottin and the film's bleak tone proved too much for both critics and audiences at the time. *The Thing* received almost universally negative reviews upon release, with critics lambasting it in particular for its gore. "*The Thing* is bereft, despairing, and nihilistic," argued Linda Gross in the *Los Angeles Times*. "It is also overpowered by Rob Botin's [*sic*] visceral and vicious special effects." Vincent Canby wrote: "Sometimes it looks as if it aspires to be the quintessential moron movie of the '80s — a

Critics blasted the extreme gore of John Carpenter's remake of *The Thing* (Universal, 1982), considering it inartistic and in poor taste.

virtual storyless feature composed of lots of laboratory-concocted special effects, with the actors used merely as props to be hacked, slashed, disemboweled, and decapitated." In his review of *The Thing* in *New York* magazine, David Denby continued his campaign against graphic violence in horror films: "The tendency among recent horror filmmakers to split open the human body in the quest for weirder and weirder thrills comes close to outright obscenity."[88]

These critiques were part of a wider outcry against violence in cinema that included *Alien* producer Walter Hill's action film *The Warriors* (1979) and peaked with the slasher horror films of the early 1980s, which were accused by critics of appealing to "pruriently sadistic impulses."[89] The effects of violent content on young people were a concern, just as they were during the 1950s horror cycle. "Have Horror Films Gone Too Far?" read the headline of one 1982 *New York Times* article, which wondered, "What do horror films do to people who see them — not merely to 8-year-olds but to others, especially adolescents?" It continues, "As the audience's tolerance threshold for thrills and chills went up and the technical capacities to create monstrous and grotesque effects increased, horror films have come to rely more on sheer, explicit representations of the ugly and the terrible — and less on psychological fable, artful suggestion, and the filmgoer's imagination."[90]

Putting aside the issue of whether children should be watching violent, R-rated horror films, the question again becomes largely one of taste: subtlety and inference are considered tastefully effective, while explicit gore is crass and potentially harmful psychologically. The physiological effects of horror were also troublesome for critics. *Alien* was criticized for the way it elicits an instinctual fear response, as though it were poor filmmaking to not give the audience a choice in the matter. Pauline Kael observed, "Many people were angry at how mechanically they'd been worked over."[91] Implicit, psychological terror could be skillful, but exploiting the human disgust reflex was going too far. Scholar William Paul observes that "gross-out" films like *Alien* represent a "perverse reversal" of conventional standards of good taste: "Not only does it embrace bad taste, it transforms revulsion into a sought-after goal."[92] For Paul, the critical disdain for gross-out films represents a privileging of the spiritual over the material; also, "less subtle" genres like horror leave less room for the critical exegesis that defines critical and scholarly analysis.[93]

Whether or not films like *Alien* were socially irresponsible, bad art, or just plain "evil," in the marketplace their graphic violence was soon seen as a liability more than an attraction. On the back of a massive $15 million marketing campaign (including the eerie "In space . . . no one can hear you scream" teaser trailer), *Alien* opened to a record-breaking $4.7 million in only ninety-one North American theaters.[94] There were concerns, however, that the film's R rating would limit its audience, and indeed by the end of 1979 *Alien* had earned only $40 million in domestic rentals.[95] It was a fine number, given the film's $10 million budget, but a far cry from *Star Wars* or *Jaws*—not even as much as the PG-rated *Jaws 2* (1978), for that matter. According to a (much-contested) financial analysis by Fox, *Alien* was not even profitable until July 1980, owing to its substantial marketing, distribution, and production costs.[96] *The Thing*, in comparison, was an outright flop, with only $10.5 million in domestic rentals.[97] The grim, gory film was a tough sell in a summer where Universal's other SF blockbuster, the family-oriented *E.T. the Extra-Terrestrial*, was breaking box office records. *Thing* producer Stuart Cohen argued, "*The Thing* is the flip side of *E.T.*, and the reaction to Steven's film mitigated against us. I don't think anyone in America was interested in seeing the flip side this summer. The timing couldn't have been worse."[98] Facing terrible reviews and poor box office results two weeks after *The Thing*'s release, John

Carpenter mused that graphic horror films "probably have reached their saturation level."[99]

While in 1981 *Variety* praised "the ongoing strength of the horror-violence market," the films it cited, such as *Friday the 13th Part 2* (1981) and *Graduation Day* (1981), were low-budget slasher films. Big-budget, R-rated horror and SF films of the early '80s, in comparison—such as *Altered States* (1980), *Saturn 3* (1980), *Wolfen* (1981), *Ghost Story* (1981), *Cat People* (1982), and *Blade Runner*—failed to justify their sizable production and marketing costs.[100] Even Kubrick's *The Shining* (1980) just barely broke even, owing to its large budget.[101] Just like the SF A films of the 1950s, these films interested only a comparatively small audience and lacked the universal appeal of family entertainment like *E.T.* Graphic SF/horror violence was much more successful at the level of low-budget exploitation cinema, where it began. Again the films were largely knock-offs of major studio blockbusters; *Alien* was the most influential, as exploitation filmmakers could easily reproduce its dark corridors and slimy creatures without breaking the bank. *Galaxy of Terror* (1981), distributed by Roger Corman's New World and featuring production design by a young James Cameron, was an amalgam of *Alien* and *Solaris* (1972) that featured a notorious scene in which a female astronaut is raped by a twelve-foot alien maggot. Reflecting a double standard, critics were largely unmoved by the film's gore, with the *Los Angeles Times* calling it "routine exploitation fare."[102] By keeping its budget relatively low ($1.8 million),[103] *Galaxy of Terror* could become profitable by appealing to the niche exploitation market—it finished its run with $4 million in domestic rentals.[104] Further inexpensive *Alien* knockoffs like *Insemenoid* (1981), *Parasite* (1982), and *Creature* (1985) would follow from independent distributors like Embassy and Trans World.

As I will discuss further in the conclusion, after a gap of approximately three years the big-budget R-rated SF film reemerged in the mid-to-late 1980s with critically and commercially successful films like *Aliens* (1986) and *Robocop* (1987), which were intensely violent and gory, yet in some cases also critically acclaimed. Overall, however, the most commercially successful SF films of the 1980s (and since) were those that followed the family-friendly model established by *Star Wars* and *E.T.* These films would also bring a critical respectability that heightened the status of the genre, to the point where the pulp SF paradigm was fully integrated into the cultural and critical mainstream.

Escapism or Regression: Mass Audiences and the SF Blockbuster

Decades later, when the *Star Wars* franchise has come to represent the epitome of the "critic-proof" blockbuster to which audiences flock despite antipathy from reviewers, it can be easy to forget that the first film received overwhelmingly positive notices upon release. *Star Wars* was hailed as "a breath of fresh air," a tonic to the cynical, adult-oriented dramas of the decade.[105] *Newsweek*'s review, titled "Fun in Space," is representative. "I loved *Star Wars* and so will you, unless you're . . . oh well, I hope you're not," writes Jack Kroll. "The rarest kind of movie—it's pure sweet fun all the way. I don't know how Lucas could make so buoyant and exuberant a film, without a smudge of corrupt consciousness, in these smudged times."[106] For Pete Hamill in the *New York Post*, the film marked the end of that "smudged," tumultuous period in American history: "It's not 'about' anything. It doesn't make you think. It doesn't preach. . . . *Star Wars* is a Big Dumb Flick, and a good one. It is a perfect film for a time when no Americans are dying anywhere in a war, when no American bombs are landing on anyone, when no President is facing indictment or impeachment."[107]

In press interviews, Lucas reinforced this sense of *Star Wars* as a throwback to simpler times: "My main reason for making it was to give young people an honest, wholesome fantasy life, the kind my generation had. . . . Where are the romance, the adventure, and the fun that used to be in practically every movie ever made?"[108] In another interview, the director who had been wounded by the failure of *THX 1138* remarked, "Rather than do some angry, socially relevant film, I realized there was another relevance that was even more important . . . getting children to believe there is more to life than garbage and killing and all that real stuff."[109] Lucas also made sure *Star Wars* was differentiated from the other space travel films of the period. While those films sought legitimacy through technological accuracy, Lucas found this boring: "Science fiction is OK, but it got so involved with science that it forgot the sense of adventure."[110] A number of critics agreed, proposing the unusual argument that realism in SF could, in fact, be a creative hindrance. Stephen Zito in *American Film* writes that the characters in *2001: A Space Odyssey* and *Silent Running* "are boxed in by probability, logic, and common sense. Not so *Star Wars*."[111] And Gary Arnold of the *Washington Post* noted of *Star Wars*, "The tone and tempo are utterly, happily different from *2001* or *A Clockwork Orange*. Lucas's film is jaunty rather than portentous."[112] By dusting off the dormant tropes of space opera, it was as though Lucas had created the genre anew. As the *Los Angeles Times* wrote when covering the film's production in 1976, "Lucas is unabashedly making a high-energy, Boy's Own adventure, complete with space pirates, an Imperial Death Star Satellite, good kids and their benevolent protector ranged against the forces of evil, chases, trickeries and hair's breadth 'scapes."[113]

There were voices of dissent amid the acclaim. Most reviews cited the all-ages appeal of *Star Wars* as one of its key assets; for instance, the *Dallas Morning News* predicted that it will be "enjoyed even more by nostalgic adults than by wide-eyed youngsters."[114] But a few prominent critics were unenthusiastic about what they saw as the juvenilization of the American moviegoing audience. For John Simon, the film's genre alone was enough to raise doubts about its relevance for adults: "I don't read science fiction, of which this may, for all I know, be a prime example. . . . *Star Wars* will do very nicely for those lucky enough to be children, or unlucky enough never to have grown up."[115] Critics who had championed the sophisticated, adult-oriented auteur cinema of the 1970s were deeply disappointed at the artistic conservatism and avoidance of sociopolitical realities implied by the success of *Star Wars*. In a brief review months after the film's release, Pauline Kael complained, "It's a film that's totally uninterested in anything that doesn't connect with a mass audience. . . . The excitement of those who call it the film of the year goes way past nostalgia to the feeling that now is the time to return to childhood."[116] Likewise, Stanley Kauffmann writes, "This picture was made for those (particularly males) who carry a portable shrine within them of their adolescence . . . before the world's affairs and — in any complex way — sex intruded."[117] Jonathan Rosenbaum, writing for the British film journal *Sight & Sound*, explored the film's political implications more directly. Comparing *Star Wars* to Jean-Luc Godard's experimental *Numéro Deux* (1975), which actively elicits audience displeasure, Rosenbaum sarcastically argues: "Better to take a calculated step backward in knowledge, sever communal and historical ties, hoot at heroes and villains alike, blow up invisible, imaginary enemies from a safe video distance, and enjoy it all as good, clean, healthy fun — marking time until the next real opportunities for automatic, xenophobic destruction arrive."[118] This type of ideological criticism would only intensify throughout the 1980s, particularly among academics and other specialized critics, as the *Star Wars* films were taken to exemplify the evacuation of progressive political thought in Reagan-era America.[119]

These critiques were in the minority, however, as most critics seemed to be charmed by the unpretentiousness of *Star Wars*. Even the leftist journal *Cineaste* argued that "people who see fascist overtones in its all-white population, nostalgia for feudalism and visual grandiosity, are probably taking it much too seriously."[120] Scholars began to defend the film in academic journals as well, often attempting to legitimate *Star Wars* via an association with mythology. For English professor Andrew Gordon, the film's characters are "intentionally flat" and "archetypal." He continues: "The movie's fundamental appeal to both young and old lies precisely in its deliberately old-fashioned plot, which has its roots deep in American popular fantasy, and deeper yet, in the epic structure of what Joseph Campbell in *The Hero with a Thousand Faces* calls 'the monomyth.'"[121] In other words, *Star Wars* only *seems* superficial; it actually courses with deep-seated meanings that are fundamental to human civilization. While Lucas did not publicly cite Campbell as an influence until 1983, by as early as 1977 the filmmaker was describing *Star Wars* as "a modern fairy tale, a myth."[122] In 1980 Lucas pushed this interpretive frame further, referring to himself as "a student of anthropology" and arguing that *Star Wars* is "a psychological tool that children can use to understand the world better and their place in it and how to adjust to that. . . . Fairy tales, religion, all were designed to teach man the right way to live and give him a moral anchor."[123] Both scholars like Gordon and George Lucas himself sought to legitimate what appeared to be a trivial children's film by positioning it as a crucial cultural artifact, part of an ancient mythological tradition that, in Gordon's words, "gives voice to our deepest longings, and speaks to our hopes about the future of our society and of ourselves."[124] For Lucas, the film was also an educational tool, instructing children in traditional morality.

Whether due to its mythological resonances or not, the near-universal appeal of *Star Wars* was the fulcrum that shifted Hollywood's definition of its mass audience. Whereas mainstream films in the classical studio system were aimed at adults but made acceptable for children, post-*Star Wars* blockbusters were aimed at children but made acceptable for adults. Importantly, *Star Wars* was not considered a "children's film" at the time, as that genre was considered to have very limited appeal to older audiences. *Star Wars* producer Gary Kurtz actually fought for a PG rather than a G rating, which would have ghettoized the film. According to *Variety*, Twentieth Century-Fox "feared a backlash effect from teenagers if the film was to receive a G, which is sometimes considered an 'uncool' rating in teenage circles, since G is usually associated with wholesome family-type pix."[125] Historian Peter Krämer notes that *Star Wars* helped to "overcome the commercial limitations of children's films by returning to an older conception of family entertainment, one which embraced all age groups and in particular the cinema's core audience of teenagers and young adults."[126]

While Krämer cites Disney's influential combination of family-oriented films and merchandising as a key antecedent for *Star Wars*, Lucas was clearly targeting a wider, slightly older audience than that of the typical live-action Disney fare of the time, such as *The Apple Dumpling Gang* (1975).[127] This is evident in Disney's reassessment of its production strategies in the wake of the success of *Star Wars*. Rather than continuing with its stagnating children's production slate (such as *Gus*, 1976, in which football coach Don Knotts recruits a Yugoslavian mule to kick field goals), Disney spent $20 million on *The Black Hole*, its first-ever PG production and "a calculated attempt to win back the 15-to-35-year-old age group that made up the preponderance of moviegoers."[128] Like *Star Wars*, the film contains appeals to children such as comic relief robots, but it skews older as well with its violence and profanity. In one respect, Disney's plan to attract an older audience succeeded — only one out of seven tickets sold to *The Black Hole* was to a young child.[129] Yet *The Black Hole* was a financial disappointment, with $25 million in domestic rentals (compared to $120 million for *The Empire Strikes Back*, released the following year).[130] Disney was undeterred; in 1982 it released *Tron*, a $21 million SF action film that was the first major motion picture to rely heavily on computer-generated imagery.[131] Like *The Black Hole*, *Tron* also received a tepid response at the box office, and Disney lost a reported $10.5 million on the project.[132]

Ironically, the biggest hit of 1982, and the film that would ultimately top *Star Wars* as the highest-grossing film in history, was an SF film aimed at the younger demographic usually served by Disney. Steven Spielberg's *E.T. the Extra-Terrestrial*, the story of a lovable alien befriended by a group of children after being accidentally stranded on Earth, was considered a high-risk proposition, despite Spielberg's incomparable track record. Columbia passed on the film in 1981, allegedly because market research indicated that *E.T.* was a "wimpy Disney movie" that would appeal exclusively to young children. The same studio research placed the film near the bottom of all summer 1982 movies in terms of box office potential. Furthermore, exhibitor interest was initially so low that *E.T.* was set to open in only five hundred theaters, at a time when blockbusters typically opened in at least twice that number.[133] Just days before the film's release, David Sterritt wrote in the *Christian Science Monitor*: "What's commercially risky about *E.T.* is that — as Spielberg readily admits — the hero is a lot younger than the 'core audience' of teens and young adults that Hollywood pursues so eagerly these days. And the action is gentle, with hardly a shred of violence or vehemence. What if teenagers find E.T. too tame, and adults consider it too coy? It could be the first Spielberg flop since 1941."[134] Instead, *E.T.* was an instant hit, becoming the first film to gross $100 million in its first month of release.[135] In January 1983 it broke the box office record of *Star Wars*, and parent company MCA's stock nearly doubled in value.[136]

If the critical acclaim for *Star Wars* was overwhelmingly positive, for *E.T.* it was even more so. "*E.T.* is a miracle movie, and one that confirms Spielberg as a master storyteller of his medium," wrote Richard Corliss in *Time*.[137] As with *Star Wars*, mainstream critics celebrated *E.T.*'s ability to appeal to both children and adults by stripping away adult viewers' cynicism and embracing an old-fashioned emotional sincerity. David Denby observed, "It makes you see things you had forgotten or blotted out and feel things you were embarrassed to feel. . . . I have never seen so many grown men weep at a screening. . . . I welcome this return to the honorable emotional fullness that was taken for granted in movies of the thirties and forties."[138] Even Pauline Kael, notoriously stingy with praise, wrote that *E.T.* "seems to clear all of the bad thoughts out of your head. It reminds you of the goofiest dreams you had as a kid, and rehabilitates them. . . . Spielberg has earned the tears that some in the audience—and not just children—shed. The tears are tokens of gratitude for the spell the picture has put on the audience."[139]

Again like *Star Wars*, *E.T.* was interpreted as a modern fairy tale whose profound emotional effect was due in part to deep cultural underpinnings. Influenced by child psychologist Bruno Bettelheim, who argued that fairy tales allow children to face real-world emotional struggles in a safe way, a researcher at the State University of New York interviewed fifty-four children who had just seen *E.T.*, and concluded that the film helps children deal with emotional traumas such as separation anxiety due to divorce.[140] (Spielberg has said that the film was based on his emotional response to his parents' divorce.[141]) As with *Star Wars*, appeals to mythology help to justify the fantastic elements of the film, rendering them acceptable for adult viewers. No longer would an SF film need to be scientifically accurate or politically sophisticated for it to be considered "safe" for adults—primal, emotional truth and the chance to relive the simplicity of youth were sufficient.

In 1982 *E.T.* was known not only for its tear-jerking climax and "E.T. phone home" catch phrase, but for paratextual elements as well—namely, the bevy of merchandise it elicited. As usual, *Star Wars* paved the way, revealing the untapped profit potential of merchandising. David A. Cook notes, "Before *Star Wars*, it was not uncommon for studios to give merchandising rights away for free publicity. . . . Even when licensed for profit, as in the case of *Jaws* and *King Kong*, product tie-ins like T-shirts, jewelry, and candy had little life or value apart from the film once its run was completed."[142] So low were the commercial expectations for *Star Wars* that the rights to produce action figures were not licensed to toy maker Kenner until April 1977, which meant that toys were not available for Christmas 1977, much less by the film's release in May.[143] Yet the film's popularity had only intensified by 1978 when the toys were finally released, and by 1979 toy sales alone exceeded $200 million.[144] By 1982, approximately $1.5 billion in *Star Wars* merchandise had been sold.[145] For *E.T.*, Universal initially licensed products like children's books, Halloween costumes, and bicycles, announcing in a *Variety* advertisement that it had

AUTHOR'S COLLECTION

Star Wars (Twentieth Century-Fox, 1977) action figures were not ready in time for Christmas 1977, so children had to settle for an empty box with a mail-in certificate for four characters, to be redeemed in spring 1978.

"planned one of Hollywood's most extensive merchandising efforts" for *E.T.*[146] After the film became a hit, a second wave of licensing occurred, for products including children's shoes and "women's undergarments."[147]

Although Spielberg reportedly insisted on working only with "quality manufacturers," for some the aggressive merchandising surrounding *E.T.* began to taint the movie's artistic accomplishments.[148] "Spielberg —who had personal control over merchandising—turned his film into a toy factory, trivializing the movie almost beyond recognition," griped Michael Ventura in *L.A. Weekly*.[149] In January 1983, the *Los Angeles Times*'s Sheila Benson wrote, "It's hard to remember now, with E.T.s goggling at us from every franchised surface possible, the feeling of love and wonder that came with our very first look at 'E.T.' back in June. . . . This is probably the best example I can remember of overmerchandising turning a whole population surly, but I am hearing and seeing it everywhere."[150] *E.T.* was nominated for nine Academy Awards, including Best Picture and Best Director, but shortly before the awards ceremony, industry reporters were suggesting that "MCA's avarice may cost E.T. the best-picture Oscar."[151] Whether Oscar voters were truly turned off by *E.T.*'s inescapable merchandising, or whether they simply preferred a more culturally legitimate film, *E.T.* lost all of its major nominations (including Best Picture, Director, Screenplay, and Cinematography) to Richard Attenborough's

Gandhi (1982). "There's always a backlash against anything that makes more than $50 million in film rentals," sniffed Spielberg afterward.[152]

Despite the defeat on Oscar night, the fact that *E.T.* was even a Best Picture nominee underscored just how far the SF genre had come in only a few years. Like *Star Wars* before it, *E.T.* had managed to break box office records and achieve critical acclaim while exploring a side of the SF genre that had been carefully avoided by mainstream filmmakers since the late 1950s. Twenty-five years earlier, the story of interstellar warfare or a boy and his alien friend would have been confined to low-budget exploitation or children's television. SF had arrived as the most popular film genre in the world.

Conclusion

SF FILM TODAY

The critical and commercial triumph of *E.T. the Extra-Terrestrial* was the culmination of SF's ascent to the top of the American film industry. The genre's high profile continued through the 1980s, a period in which three broad production trends in SF can be identified, corresponding to three MPAA ratings. Dominant economically were the PG movies, which targeted a wide general audience. These were usually action-adventure films that broadly followed the *Star Wars* SF variation of the monomyth, in which a young white male protagonist is pulled from his mundane existence and thrust into an exciting science fictional drama. The most popular of these films, aside from the third Star Wars installment, *Return of the Jedi* (1983), was director Robert Zemeckis's adventure comedy *Back to the Future*, produced by his mentor Steven Spielberg. The highest-grossing film of 1985, *Back to the Future* involved teenager Marty McFly (Michael J. Fox) traveling back in time to meet his parents. Teens could relate to Marty, while the nostalgic references to the 1950s delighted baby boomers. Likewise, the PG-rated Star Trek film series continued very successfully through the 1980s by appealing to the same bifurcated audience: adults who were fans of the original series, and children and teens who enjoyed the special effects and space action.

More specifically aimed at adults were the R-rated SF films, which typically combined the graphic violence of contemporary action cinema with the gore of modern horror movies. After the costly failure of films like *The Thing* and *Blade Runner*, the major studios backed away from this form of SF until James Cameron's *The Terminator*, an independent action programmer released by Orion Pictures, was a sleeper hit in 1984. The story of a futuristic android assassin sent back in time to kill the mother of a resistance leader, *The Terminator* featured relentless gun violence and a gory scene where the Terminator (Arnold Schwarzenegger) performs surgery on his own damaged robotic arm and eye. Based on that success, Cameron was hired by Twentieth Century-Fox to write and direct *Aliens* (1986), the $18 million sequel to *Alien*. Rather than reproducing the art-horror menace of the original, Cameron instead made a war film in which space marines battle hordes of gruesome creatures. Not only was *Aliens* the fifth-highest-grossing film of 1986; it was nominated for seven Academy Awards, including Best Actress for Sigourney Weaver—a rare acting nomination for a genre film.[1] Other R-rated SF action blockbusters followed intermittently through the early 1990s, with Schwarzenegger becoming something of a one-man cottage industry in the subgenre, starring in *Predator* (1987), *The Running Man* (1987), *Total Recall* (1990), and *Terminator 2: Judgment Day* (1991).

The audience for R-rated films in the theatrical market is by definition limited, as, according to MPAA policy, audience members under seventeen need an adult guardian to accompany them to the screening. Addressing this problem was the intermediary PG-13 rating, created in 1984 after public outcry over the violence in two high-profile hits, *Indiana Jones and the Temple of Doom* (1984), directed by Steven Spielberg and produced by George Lucas, and *Gremlins* (1984), directed by Joe Dante and produced by Spielberg. Spielberg worked personally with CARA's Richard Heffner and MPAA president Jack Valenti to develop the new rating. As James Kendrick explains, "The creation of the PG-13 rating was largely about resolving the disparity between the simultaneous popularity of screen violence and reservations about its supposed nefarious effect on small children."[2] Kendrick notes that PG-13 serves as a brand that carves out a specific marketplace, one targeting teen audiences rather than young children. Importantly, unlike the R rating, PG-13 merely "strongly cautioned" parents, without forbidding children under thirteen from buying tickets. This was ideal for the studios, in that they could now have it both ways: they could appease parents' groups and cultural critics with the new, stronger rating, while also intensifying the violence in PG films without crossing over into the restricted rating.[3]

In terms of big-budget SF films, the PG-13 rating gradually began to prevail in big-budget SF films over the course of the 1990s. Occasional R-rated SF action blockbusters are still released, such as Lana and Andy Wachowski's *Matrix* trilogy (1999–2003) or Ridley Scott's *Alien* prequel *Prometheus* (2012). And the first two installments in George Lucas's Star Wars prequel trilogy (*Star Wars: Episode I—The Phantom Menace* [1999] and *Star Wars: Episode II—Attack of the Clones* [2002]) were PG. In general, however, the R rating is today most often reserved for comedies or horror films that rely on adult content as their main attraction, while PG has become associated primarily with children's films. Most contemporary blockbusters aim for the PG-13 rating, as it is considered the sweet spot that will attract the widest possible audience.

Making a strong case for the value of the PG-13 rating was Spielberg's *Jurassic Park*, the film that, more than any other of the era, revitalized both the blockbuster film and the SF genre. In the six years before *Jurassic Park*'s release, SF had lost some of its luster as a preeminent blockbuster genre, with only five top-ten domestic box office hits from 1987 to 1992, compared to twelve top-ten hits from 1981 to 1986. However, the popularization of computer-generated effects by *Jurassic Park* (and *Terminator 2: Judgment Day* two years earlier) opened up new vistas for SF filmmakers. And both *Terminator 2* and *Jurassic Park* were the top box office attractions of their respective release years, with *Jurassic Park* exceeding the $1 billion mark globally, the first film ever to do so.[4] By the late '90s, SF blockbusters were flourishing at the box office once again, with over a dozen big-budget productions released each year beginning in 1997. A number of the biggest hits, like *Independence Day* (1996) and *Armageddon* (1998), are clear throwbacks to George Pal's SF A disaster films of the 1950s.

In the early twenty-first century, SF production continues across all budget categories. SF programmers like *Source Code* (2011) and *Looper* (2012) provide the same low-risk and high-profit potential for mini-majors like Summit as they did for Universal-International in the 1950s.

Contemporary programmers, budgeted in the $25 million to $50 million range, typically make between $75 million and $150 million at the worldwide box office. They also often act as "calling cards" for young directors that can lead to blockbuster assignments — *Source Code* director Duncan Jones's next project was the big-budget computer game adaptation *Warcraft* (2016), and *Looper*'s Rian Johnson was selected to direct *Star Wars: Episode VIII* (2017).

Low-budget SF films are produced in two primary categories: "indie" (if not always strictly independent) films, and exploitation. Since the revival of the blockbuster in the late 1970s, the majors have de-emphasized the wide release of the "art genre" films that prevailed earlier in that decade. But formally and thematically challenging genre films continue to flourish in the niche art-house market, produced both by independent distributors and the "independent" branches of major studios, like Fox Searchlight. Independent filmmaker Shane Carruth has specialized in complex, narratively oblique SF films like *Primer* (2004), a time travel film that won Grand Prize at the Sundance Film Festival, and *Upstream Color* (2012), an avant-garde SF romance. While critically acclaimed, such is their formal complexity that SF indie films like Carruth's are commercially marginal and usually fail to cross over into the mainstream market, as other independent films like *Brokeback Mountain* (2005) have. Part of this is due to a conception of SF that differs from the pulpy, action-oriented model used in major studio product. Carruth comments, "There's the aesthetic of science fiction, with the aliens and chrome and neon and explosions in space, and then there's science fiction that's used as a literary device. That's the kind I'm interested in."[5] He cites Vonnegut's *Slaughterhouse-Five* as a key influence: "It's really brilliant for using sci-fi genre elements to get you into something else."[6]

Lacking the marketing muscle of major studio films, independent films are marginalized in American theaters, to the point where even highly commercial product like *The Signal* (2014), a Hollywood calling-card film if there ever was one, receive only limited theatrical releases and earn a pittance. These films rely instead on alternative distribution channels like home video, cable, video on demand, and Internet streaming to find an audience. Low-budget exploitation SF in particular is especially rare in the theatrical market. The popular association of the genre with state-of-the-art special effects serves as a barrier to entry for independent filmmakers, who cannot compete with the majors' resources. Instead, a camp approach is popular; with a tongue-in-cheek film, poor special effects are an asset rather than a distraction. Today's most prominent low-budget exploitation SF films are independent productions made for broadcast on the Syfy Channel, and later, distribution on home video. Syfy pays approximately half the budget (which in 2004 ranged from $1.4 to $1.8 million), with the producers earning a profit through the sale of foreign distribution rights.[7] The titles, such as *Mansquito* (2005) and *Chupacabra vs. the Alamo* (2013), suggest a gleefully over-the-top tone. While films such as these usually attract around two million viewers, in 2014 *Sharknado 2: The Second One*, produced by exploitation studio the Asylum, became a social media phenomenon, with 67.2 million mentions on Twitter. This social media buzz translated to mainstream media attention and, in turn, to 9.5 million viewers over six airings on Syfy.[8] Where the major studios traditionally avoid camp in their SF films, independent exploitation producers embrace it as a successful strategy for attracting viewers curious to see just how enjoyably bad a movie can be.

As relatively successful as SF has been in the programmer and low-budget categories, its industrial and cultural significance is, of course, primarily based on big-budget productions. Harrison Ford has said that George Lucas's direction to his *Star Wars* actors consisted mainly of repeating the words, "Faster, more intense."[9] That phrase neatly encapsulates the trajectory of blockbuster filmmaking since 1977. With each new blockbuster setting a standard for the next to surmount, average shot lengths have shrunk, action scenes have become more elaborate, and special effects have become more photorealistic and dynamic. Michael Bay's *Transformers* series, chronicling the exploits of giant alien robots that can change shape into cars and other mechanical items, has come to epitomize the "critic-proof" blockbuster of the twenty-first century—almost universally panned by professional reviewers, but extraordinarily successful around the world. The qualities that critics in 1977 found pleasurably novel in *Star Wars* have, for today's critics, become formulaic and exasperating in films like *Transformers*. Where the action scenes in *Star Wars* were exhilarating, *Transformers: Age of Extinction* (2014) is "the cinematic equivalent of being tied in a bag and beaten with pipes."[10] Where

Star Wars was a refreshing escape from harsh political realities, *Age of Extinction* is a military recruitment tool and apologia for American imperialism.[11] Where *Star Wars* was a pleasant return to the simplicity of childhood, *Transformers: Revenge of the Fallen* (2009) is "like the play date from hell, the kind where a crew of children reduce your home to rubble and conduct endless bouts of loud war on the living-room floor."[12]

And where in 1977 *Star Wars* was praised for departing from the grim and explicit adult-oriented films of the early '70s and appealing to a family audience, decades later some critics blame the film (along with *Jaws*) for ruining American cinema. In 2005 critic Charles Taylor charged, "The success of *Star Wars* devastated American movies, taking them from their high-water mark of the 1970s to their current progressive vegetative state. . . . Hollywood moviemaking is no longer about stories or emotions but about spectacle, concept and merchandising."[13] Other critics complain that *Star Wars* has seemingly permanently defined SF cinema in the popular consciousness as space opera and pulp, with no room for the more intellectually demanding forms of the genre. Critic Lewis Beale writes, "*Star Wars* has corrupted people's notion of a literary genre full of ideas, turning it into a Saturday afternoon serial. And that's more than a shame — it's an obscenity."[14]

Regardless of whether one agrees with these harsh assessments, it is inarguable that the ancillary market surrounding blockbusters has exploded in a way that makes *E.T.*'s marketing tie-ins look subtle and restrained. Merchandising is an essential component of the franchise logic that drives studio production in the twenty-first century. As Thomas Schatz writes, "The business of the major studios is making and selling franchise-sustaining blockbuster hits — i.e., calculated megafilms designed to sustain a product line of similar films and an ever-expanding array of related entertainment products, all of which benefit the parent conglomerates' various media-and-entertainment divisions."[15] The roots of contemporary franchise filmmaking lie, once again, in *Star Wars*. The elaborate narrative world-building that made the original *Star Wars* unique and compelling also made it an ideal vehicle for transmedia production — books, comics, toys, video games, and other products that continue the story begun in the films, and provide lucrative additional revenue streams. It has reached the point where the films are ancillary to the products surrounding them. By 2012, the *Star Wars* franchise had generated $33 billion in total revenue, with toys and video games accounting for twice as much as box office and home video sales.[16]

The merchandising power of *Star Wars* is partly what drove the Walt Disney Company to purchase Lucasfilm in 2012. Beyond the toy and game sales, and a new Star Wars film ever year, Disney also plans to incorporate Star Wars into its theme parks, and broadcast Star Wars television shows on its DisneyXD cable channel.[17] In a time of uncertainty and media convergence, Disney's deal for Lucasfilm illustrates the high value of popular, presold content that can be distributed across any number of platforms. According to media analyst Matthew Harrigan, "There's no one else who could extract as much value from *Star Wars* as Disney. On the merchandising side, Disney feels they can do a much better job than Lucasfilm has done as a standalone."[18] For some *Star Wars* fans, the association with Disney elicits fears that the films will be compromised as the studio focuses more on merchandising than storytelling—although, of course, Lucas had merchandising in mind when he wrote the first film in the mid-70s.[19]

Fortunately, the recent history of SF film is not so simple as a straightforward narrative of decline, with the genre losing critical acclaim and cultural prestige as it becomes associated with *Sharknado* and corporate blockbusters focused on toy sales. The *Transformers* films are something of an extreme case in their critical disreputability (and even Michael Bay has his advocates). There have in fact been many critically praised SF blockbusters released over the last few decades. Recently, the SF comic book adaptations of Disney's Marvel Studios such as Joss Whedon's *The Avengers* (2012) and James Gunn's *Guardians of the Galaxy* (2014) have been hailed for their wit and attention to character. *Rolling Stone*'s Peter Travers said of *Avengers*: "It's *Transformers* with a brain, a heart, and a working sense of humor. . . . Whedon knows that even the roaringest action sequences won't resonate without audience investment in the characters."[20]

This emphasis on character also serves an important economic function, as it fosters audience interest in the multitude of other related films in the "Marvel Cinematic Universe."[21] A bold experiment in synergy, the MCU reproduces the "shared universe" of Marvel Comics, in which superheroes do not exist in their own distinct and hermetic worlds but instead interact with one another. The economic advantage is obvious: Marvel can stir up interest in less popular or more obscure characters by connecting them to familiar characters like Captain America and Iron Man. Narrative interweaving allows Marvel to foster individual sub-franchises within the larger umbrella of the MCU, while making each of its films a must-see, if one is to stay current on the macro-plot. Plot threads are introduced in one film and picked up in another, even if the second film is not a direct sequel. For instance, *Iron Man 3* (2013), rather than the second Avengers film, deals with Iron Man's psychological fallout from the events of the first Avengers installment. The MCU approach has proven wildly successful, to say the least — not only have films like *The Avengers* (2012), which gathered the superheroes together for the first time, earned over $1 billion at the worldwide box office, but riskier films like *Guardians of the Galaxy* have also been massive hits, based, at least initially, on the Marvel brand alone. The "shared universe" model enables Disney to keep generating additional Marvel blockbuster sub-franchises that are relatively low risk. From an aesthetic perspective, it gives filmmakers the opportunity to engage in world-building that can far exceed what is possible with a single series of films. The rate at which this synergistic production model is being applied to other properties (including Warner Bros.' DC Comics characters and Disney's new series of Star Wars films), suggests that this new form of franchising will become the dominant mode of blockbuster filmmaking.

The proliferation of pulp SF tropes in blockbuster films and across American popular culture since the late 1970s has essentially solved the pulp paradox: no longer do studios have to fret about the low cultural status of a film like *Guardians of the Galaxy* that deals with interstellar fleets, alien bounty hunters, and space pirates. That does not mean that the strategies of legitimation employed in the 1950s through the 1980s are not still in wide use. For instance, the use of humor in *Guardians* — whimsical, but never campy or at the expense of the underlying drama — recalls that of the original *Star Wars*. *Guardians* manages to skillfully tread a fine line, employing silly gags and outrageous characters, like a genetically engineered, talking raccoon, without falling into farce. The film's climax, in which the planet Xander is threatened with destruction by the warlord Ronan, has an earnest, suspenseful tone and moments of character pathos, as when the talking tree Groot (another seemingly absurd character) sacrifices himself to save his friends. At a time when many contemporary SF blockbusters — such as *After Earth* (2012) and *Man of Steel* (2013) — deflect a camp response by taking an unrelentingly grim, humorless approach to their material, critics hailed *Guardians* for its refreshingly light air. Wesley Morris writes, "The trouble with what George Lucas has done to the movies is that so many writers and directors and companies have learned the wrong lessons. They're building myths and monuments and worlds. But they're not having any fun. . . . Gunn appears to remember the high of certain kinds of moviegoing, where when the credits are over, all you want to do is get back in line and enjoy the whole thing again."[22]

Other tried-and-true legitimating strategies, namely the use of political allegory and scientific realism, are concerned less with avoiding camp and more with building an aura of prestige. We can see these strategies in recent SF films that have been nominated for Best Picture by the Academy. Taking advantage of the Best Picture category's expansion to as many as ten nominees, in 2010 two SF films received nominations. One was James Cameron's *Avatar*, which cost a staggering $280 million, plus another $150 in marketing costs.[23] The other was *District 9* (2009), a programmer independently financed by QED International and purchased for worldwide theatrical release by Sony in 2007.[24] *Avatar*, released in December 2009, quickly became the highest-grossing film in history with a worldwide theatrical gross of $2.7 billion.[25] This extraordinary return was due in large part to its immersive use of 3-D, which attracted audiences and allowed theaters to add a surcharge to each ticket. *District 9*'s box office take was much less than *Avatar*'s, but arguably nearly as impressive in terms of profitability. The film, produced by Peter Jackson, cost only $30 million but made $205 million worldwide.[26]

Popular critics played up the David vs. Goliath dynamic between the two films, but from a wider historical perspective, the similarities between the two are more striking than their differences. Both are spectacular action films that legitimate their pulp SF narratives through allegorical sociopolitical critique, just as *Planet of the Apes* did forty years earlier. Set in a contemporary Johannesburg populated by a million stranded aliens, *District 9* was intended by writer-director Neill Blomkamp as a critique of the forced evictions and ghettoization policies that characterized apartheid. Critics remarked that *District 9*'s political consciousness elevated it above the typical contemporary SF film: "It's been aeons since a sci-fi film made a point larger than Monday morning's grosses," noted *Entertainment Weekly*.[27] Likewise, *Avatar* is an environmentalist critique of American imperialism in which the nature-worshipping alien Na'vi triumph over the mechanized forces of the capitalist humans, who thoughtlessly seek to destroy Pandora's natural beauty in search of a precious mineral. But despite its ostensibly left-wing attitudes, *Avatar*, like all contemporary blockbusters, carefully avoids alienating any audience segment. It therefore contains multiple, often contradictory appeals that blunt the impact of its environmentalist message. For instance, although it seems to condemn the advanced military technology of the human invaders, it also fetishizes it during its prolonged action sequences. Regardless of this deliberate incoherence, the political content of *Avatar* lent it prestige and helped to attract the attention of the middlebrow Academy voters, notorious for ignoring genre films.

In 2014 an SF film finally won a major Academy Award, with Alfonso Cuarón receiving the Best Director Oscar for *Gravity* (2013). The story of a disastrous shuttle mission to repair the Hubble Space Telescope, *Gravity* was remarkable for its use of extreme long takes (the entire film is only 156 shots) and immersive use of 3-D, largely computer-generated cinematography. And while some creative license was used, overall the film strives to adhere to contemporary scientific knowledge. Cuarón "worked very closely with several people and [had] conversations with astronauts to try to really make everything be as plausible and realistic as we could."[28] The intention, in Cuarón's words, was to give "the experience of an IMAX documentary gone wrong."[29] Cuarón's words bring us full circle to George Pal and Robert A. Heinlein in 1950. Indeed, Cuarón knows his SF film history: "There are a lot of films set in space that I am a fan of. . . . In the '50s there was *Destination Moon*, which was very serious in how they tried to convey space travel."[30] Like *Destination Moon* and later space program films like *Marooned* (another Cuarón favorite), *Gravity* positions itself as a docudrama rather than the space fantasy that has come to define SF. This enhances the cultural legitimacy of the film to the point where it not only won five technical Oscars (not unusual for an SF blockbuster), but received Best Picture and Best Actress nominations, as well as the award for Best Director.

Pal and Heinlein's commitment to scientific realism may have gotten swept away by the exploitation wave of the 1950s, but, as *Gravity* vividly demonstrates, it remains a viable approach to the SF genre today. In general, SF's extraordinary variety and ability to blend with different genres have given it a unique flexibility that has allowed it to adapt to the changing demands of the marketplace over the last sixty-five years. In the 1950s it drew from pulp SF in order to thrill exploitation audiences. In the 1970s those same tropes were rejected or adapted into new, more complex forms in order to appeal to more sophisticated adult moviegoers. The resulting cultural legitimation of the genre set the stage for the rise of the '80s SF "super-grosser."

Today, when movies have arguably been overtaken in cultural significance by television, and audiences have begun to favor home exhibition methods such as online streaming, the film industry has focused even more strongly on spectacle and immersion as a means to promote the theatrical experience. This suggests that SF cinema may only be beginning to realize its potential in the marketplace. The contemporary mainstreaming of "geek" culture, such as comic book superheroes, *Doctor Who*, and J. R. R. Tolkien, has inspired cultural critics to argue that "clever people have won at last,"[31] and comic book fans to proclaim, "Nerds won . . . it's our world now. It's time for us to stop feeling marginalized; our culture is bigger and better than ever."[32] The history of SF film in America suggests that it is less that the nerds won, and more that artists have, over the years, adapted SF to reach beyond the boundaries of its original niche appeal. With its cultural and industrial legitimacy well established, the SF genre continues to appeal to our love of spectacle, our deep-seated desire for escapism, and our simultaneous fear and excitement about the future that awaits us.

Notes

Introduction. SF and the American Film Industry

1. J. W. Rinzler, *The Making of "Star Wars"* (New York: Ballantine Books, 2007), 292.

2. "'Wars' Returns to Chinese, Only Such Booking in Half Century," *Variety*, August 3, 1977, 24.

3. Lee Grant, "'Star Wars' out of This World," *Los Angeles Times*, June 4, 1977, B8.

4. "'Star Wars' Ousts 'Jaws' as Champ of U.S. Box Office," *Variety*, November 23, 1977, 1.

5. "Box Office Mojo," www.boxofficemojo.com.

6. Alex Ben Block, "Disney to Buy Lucasfilm for $4.05 Billion; New 'Star Wars' Movie Set for 2015," *Hollywood Reporter*, October 30, 2012, http://www.hollywoodreporter.com/news/disney-buy-lucasfilm-405-billion-384448.

7. Rinzler, *Making of "Star Wars,"* 11.

8. Michael Pye and Linda Myles, *The Movie Brats* (New York: Holt, Rinehart and Winston, 1979), 133.

9. Rinzler, *Making of "Star Wars,"* 301.

10. J. W. Rinzler, *The Making of "The Empire Strikes Back"* (New York: Ballantine Books, 2010), 10.

11. Richard Maltby, *Hollywood Cinema*, 2nd ed. (Malden, MA: Blackwell, 2003), 179.

12. Annette Kuhn, "Introduction: Cultural Theory and Science Fiction Cinema," in *Alien Zone: Cultural Theory and Contemporary Science Fiction Cinema*, ed. Kuhn (London: Verso, 1990), 10.

13. Susan Sontag, "The Imagination of Disaster," *Commentary*, October 1965, 42–48.

14. Kevin Heffernan, *Ghouls, Gimmicks, and Gold: Horror Films and the American Movie Business, 1953–1968* (Durham, NC: Duke University Press, 2004).

15. Blair Davis, *The Battle for the Bs: 1950s Hollywood and the Rebirth of Low-Budget Cinema* (New Brunswick, NJ: Rutgers University Press, 2012); Richard Nowell, *Blood Money: A History of the First Teen Slasher Film Cycle* (New York: Continuum, 2011); James Chapman and Nicholas J. Cull, *Projecting Tomorrow: Science Fiction and Popular Cinema* (New York: IB Tauris, 2013).

16. Barbara Klinger, *Melodrama and Meaning: History, Culture, and the Films of Douglas Sirk* (Bloomington: Indiana University Press, 1994), 70.

17. Ibid.

18. Lea Jacobs, *The Decline of Sentiment: American Film in the 1920s* (Berkeley: University of California Press, 2008), 18.

19. Amanda Ann Klein, *American Film Cycles: Reframing Genres, Screening Social Problems, and Defining Subcultures* (Austin: University of Texas Press, 2011), 5.

20. David Bordwell, *Making Meaning: Inference and Rhetoric in the Interpretation of Cinema* (Cambridge, MA: Harvard University Press, 1989), 148.

21. Rick Altman, *Film/Genre* (London: British Film Institute, 1999), 102.

22. Robin Wood, *Hollywood from Vietnam to Reagan* (New York: Columbia University Press, 1986), 165.

23. Ibid., 166.

24. Quoted in Bill Davidson, "King of Schlock," *New York Times*, December 28, 1975, 128.

25. Influential on my approach was Michael Z. Newman and Elana Levine's *Legitimating Television: Media Convergence and Cultural Status* (New York: Routledge, 2011), which explores the legitimating strategies used by television producers and studios.

Chapter 1. Realizing the Future: SF in the Postwar American Marketplace

1. Brog., "Destination Moon," *Variety*, June 18, 1950, 6.

2. Patrick Lucanio, *Them or Us: Archetypal Interpretations of Fifties Alien Invasion Films* (Bloomington: Indiana University Press, 1987), 1.

3. Victoria O'Donnell, "Science Fiction Films and Cold War Anxiety," in *The Fifties: Transforming the Screen, 1950–1959*, ed. Peter Lev (Berkeley: University of California Press, 2003), 171.

4. Drew Casper, *Postwar Hollywood: 1946–1962* (Malden, MA: Blackwell, 2007), 43.

5. Thomas Schatz, *Boom and Bust: American Cinema in the 1940s* (Berkeley: University of California Press, 1997), 291.

6. Tino Balio, "Introduction to Part I," in *Hollywood in the Age of Television*, ed. Balio (Cambridge, MA: Unwin Hyman, 1990), 3.

7. Ernest Borneman, "United States versus Hollywood: The Case Study of an Antitrust Suit," in *The American Film Industry*, rev. ed., ed. Tino Balio (Madison: University of Wisconsin Press, 1985), 449–462.

8. Schatz, *Boom and Bust*, 14–15.

9. "Majors Mull Prod. Cutback," *Variety*, July 19, 1950, 5.

10. Peter Lev, *The Fifties: Transforming the Screen, 1950–1959* (Berkeley: University of California Press, 2003), 107.

11. Casper, *Postwar Hollywood*, 93.

12. "Hollywood Swings to Exploitation Pix in Bid for New Patrons," *Variety*, July 20, 1949, 7.

13. For more on the classical exploitation film see Eric Schaefer, *"Bold! Daring! Shocking! True!" A History of Exploitation Films, 1919–1959* (Durham, NC: Duke University Press, 1999).

14. "Hollywood Swings to Exploitation Pix in Bid for New Patrons."

15. "'Gimmick Pix' Beat B.O. Nix," *Variety*, March 8, 1950, 1.

16. "Hollywood Swings to Exploitation Pix in Bid for New Patrons."

17. Whitney Williams, "'Exploitation Pictures' Paid Off Big for Majors, Also Indie Producers," *Variety*, January 9, 1946, 36.

18. Paul S. Boyer, "Sixty Years and Counting: Nuclear Themes in American Culture, 1945 to the Present," in *The Atomic Bomb and American Society: New Perspectives*, ed. Rosemary B. Mariner and G. Kurt Piehler (Knoxville: University of Tennessee Press, 2009), 6.

19. Carroll Pursell, *Technology in Postwar America: A History* (New York: Columbia University Press, 2007), 65.

20. "Rocket to the Moon," *Life*, January 17, 1949, 67.

21. Pursell, *Technology in Postwar America*, 99, 103.

22. Patrick Lucanio and Gary Coville, *Smokin' Rockets: The Romance of Technology in American Film, Radio and Television, 1945–1962* (Jefferson, NC: McFarland, 2002), 102.

23. Fred Nadis, *The Man from Mars: Ray Palmer's Amazing Pulp Journey* (New York: Penguin, 2013), 122.

24. Sidney Shalett, "What You Can Believe about Flying Saucers (Part One)," *Saturday Evening Post*, April 30, 1949, 20–21, 136–139; Shalett, "What You Can Believe about Flying Saucers (Part Two)," *Saturday Evening Post*, May 7, 1949, 36, 184–196.

25. Nadis, *Man from Mars*, 135.

26. H. B. Darrach Jr. and Robert Ginna, "Have We Visitors from Space?," *Life*, April 7, 1952, 80–82, 94, 89–92, 94, 96.

27. Lucanio and Coville, *Smokin' Rockets*, 24. Supporting this connection between the flying saucer scare and the Cold War is the first UFO film of the '50s, a minor, low-budget independent called *The Flying Saucer* (1950). The film is actually more an espionage picture than SF; the titular vehicle is an earthly invention over which American and Soviet forces battle.

28. Erin A. Smith, "How the Other Half Read: Advertising, Working-Class Readers, and Pulp Magazines," *Book History* 3 (2000): 204–230.

29. James E. Gunn, *The Road to Science Fiction: From Wells to Heinlein* (Lanham, MD: Scarecrow, 2002), 348.

30. Mike Ashley, *The Time Machines: The Story of the Science-Fiction Pulp Magazines from the Beginning to 1950* (Liverpool: Liverpool University Press, 2000), 175.

31. Ibid., 107.

32. Ibid., 197.

33. Mike Ashley, *Transformations: The Story of the Science-Fiction Magazines from 1950 to 1970* (Liverpool: Liverpool University Press, 2005), 4.

34. Harrison Smith, "The Rise of Fantasy in Literature," *American Scholar* 17, no. 3 (Summer 1948): 305–312.

35. Orville Prescott, "Books of the Times," *New York Times*, June 7, 1946, 29.

36. Fredric Brown, *The Office* (New York: Dutton Press, 1958).

37. Richard B. Gehman, "Imagination Runs Wild," *New Republic*, January 17, 1949, 17.

38. "Science Fiction Delegates Discuss Needs of Writers," *New Orleans Times-Picayune*, September 3, 1951, 11.

39. "Science Fiction Is Often Prophecy, Asserts Writer," *New Orleans Times-Picayune*, September 4, 1951, 2.

40. For the history of the term see David G. Hartwell and Kathyrn Cramer, eds., *The Space Opera Renaissance* (New York City: Orb Books, 2007), 9–18.

41. Quoted ibid., 10. Hartwell and Cramer note that Tucker originally used the term to refer to poor SF stories of any variety and did not attach the label to work by "Doc" Smith, for instance.

42. See Robert Barshay, "Ethnic Stereotypes in *Flash Gordon*," *Journal of Popular Film* 3, no. 1 (1974): 15–30.

43. Harvey Breit, "Talk with Mr. Bradbury," *New York Times*, August 5, 1951, 182.

44. Ashley, *Time Machines*, 124.

45. In the 1960s, Superman's origin was changed to make his powers reliant on the rays of Earth's yellow sun, versus the red sun of Krypton.

46. Bradford W. Wright, *Comic Book Nation: The Transformation of Youth Culture in America* (Baltimore: Johns Hopkins University Press), 56–57.

47. "A Sound of Thunder," *Weird Science-Fantasy* 25 (EC Comics, September 1954), and "There Will Come Soft Rains," *Weird Fantasy* 17 (EC Comics, January–February 1953).

48. "The Superwoman from Space," *Superman* 81 (DC Comics, March–April 1953), and "Judgment Day," *Weird Fantasy* 18 (EC Comics, March–April 1953).

49. Maria Reidelbach, *Completely MAD: A History of the Comic Book and Magazine* (New York: Little, Brown, 1992), 22.

50. Raymond William Stedman, *The Serials* (Norman: University of Oklahoma Press, 1971), 191.

51. Cocomalt advertisement, unknown date, http://www.gono.com/museum2003/museum%20collect%20info/cocomalt/cc6.jpg.

52. Robert C. Dille, ed., *The Collected Works of Buck Rogers in the 25th Century* (New York: Chelsea Books, 1969), 16. Quoted in Lucanio and Coville, *Smokin' Rockets*, 37.

53. Rafael A. Vela, "With the Parents' Consent: Film Serials, Consumerism and

the Creation of a Youth Audience, 1913–1938" (PhD diss., University of Wisconsin–Madison, 2000), 166.

54. Ibid., 260–262.

55. Roy Kinnard, "The Flash Gordon Serials," *Films in Review* 39, no. 4 (April 1988): 195.

56. Wear., "Flash Gordon," *Variety*, March 11, 1936, 27.

57. Kinnard, "Flash Gordon Serials," 198.

58. "*Flash Gordon's Trip to Mars*," *Variety*, February 16, 1938, 17.

59. Gary Johnson, "The Serials: An Introduction," *Images: A Journal of Film and Popular Culture*, http://www.imagesjournal.com/issue04/infocus/introduction5.htm.

60. CBS press release, October 10, 1951, http://home.earthlink.net/~joesarno/tvscifi/out.htm.

61. David Weinstein, "Captain Video: Television's First Fantastic Voyage," *Journal of Popular Film and Television* 30, no. 3 (Fall 2002): 150.

62. Ibid., 150, 155.

63. Ibid., 156.

64. "Captain Video," TV Digest, August 2, 1952, 12, cited in Weinstein, "Captain Video," 148.

65. Schatz, *Boom and Bust*, 183–188.

66. "Eagle-Lion Is Dropping All 'B' Picture Plans," *Motion Picture Herald*, September 28, 1946, 42.

67. Tino Balio, *United Artists: The Company That Changed the Film Industry* (Madison: University of Wisconsin Press, 1987), 18, 21.

68. "PRC Schedules 42 Features for 1946–47 Season," *Motion Picture Herald*, August 24, 1946, 47.

69. "Eagle-Lion Plans 12 Major Films," *Los Angeles Times*, May 16, 1947, 7.

70. "Bryan Foy Sets Dizzy Pace in New Key Post," *Los Angeles Times*, August 18, 1946, C3.

71. Mark Minett, "Eagle-Lion: A Brief History," unpublished manuscript, Department of Communication Arts, University of Wisconsin–Madison, 2004.

72. Balio, *United Artists*, 24.

73. Ibid., 23–24.

74. Unless noted, box office numbers are film rentals, which are the box office gross minus the exhibitors' share, which is typically about 50 percent.

75. "Pathe Industries, Inc. Summary of Outside Producers' Accounts," December 31, 1948, United Artists Collection: Robert Benjamin Papers 1946–1951, Wisconsin Center for Film and Theater Research, Madison, WI (hereafter WCFTR).

76. Thomas F. Brady, "The Hollywood Wire," *New York Times*, November 14, 1948, X5.

77. "Eagle Lion a Distributing Company Beginning Jan. 1," *Motion Picture Herald*, October 15, 1949, 16.

78. Balio, *United Artists*, 32.

79. Borneman, "United States versus Hollywood," 451–452.

80. Brian Taves, "The B Film: Hollywood's Other Half," in *Grand Design: Hollywood as a Modern Business Enterprise, 1930–1939*, ed. Tino Balio (Berkeley: University of California Press, 1993), 317–318. Historically, the term "programmer" has been used by the trade press to refer to low-budget films, or, more generally, any unremarkable film.

81. *Eagle-Lion Studios, Inc. et al. v. Loew's Inc., et al.*, 248 F.2d 438. 1957 U.S. App. LEXIS 5260, Lexis-Nexis.

82. Gail Morgan Hickman, *The Films of George Pal* (Cranbury, NJ: A. S. Barnes, 1977), 17–29.

83. Ibid., 36.

84. "Eagle-Lion Arranges Finances of Films," *New York Times*, August 26, 1949, 14.

85. Undated ledger, Benjamin Papers, WCFTR. The MPCC provided "secondary financing," which meant they received their money only after the initial bank loan was repaid. This high level of risk justified the large percentage of profits they demanded.

86. Ibid.

87. "Revised Abstract of Financial Interests in 'Destination Moon,'" UA Corporation Records, Eagle-Lion Legal File.

88. Letter from Norman Freeman to D. J. Melamed, November 20, 1950, United Artists Corporation Records, Eagle-Lion Legal File.

89. In a promotional interview, Pal argues that the two "stars" of his film are "one of the most unusual stories ever filmed, and Technicolor." "Fact Sheet," May 17, 1950, Accessions, United Artists Collection, WCFTR.

90. Jan Alan Henderson, "Lunar Ambition," *American Cinematographer*, March 2000, 110–111.

91. Robert A. Heinlein, "Shooting *Destination Moon*," in *Focus on the Science Fiction Film*, ed. William Johnson (Englewood Cliffs, NJ: Prentice Hall, 1972), 53.

92. "Pal to N.Y. for Parleys on 500G 'Moon' Drive," *Hollywood Reporter*, May 5, 1950, 4.

93. "Space-Men Invade Show Business," *Motion Picture Herald*, November 11, 1950, 44; memo from Ben Babb to Branch and District Managers, January 25, 1951, United Artists Corporation Records, Unprocessed Accession.

94. Louis Berg, "Reaching for the Moon," *Los Angeles Times*, April 23, 1950, G18.

95. Thomas E. Stimson Jr. "Rocket to the Moon: No Longer a Fantastic Dream," *Popular Mechanics*, May 1950, 89–94, 230, 236.

96. Berg, "Reaching for the Moon," G18.

97. “Fact Book,” United Artists Corporation Records, Unprocessed Accession, 4.

98. “Publicity Approach,” Leon Brandt, undated memo, United Artists Corporation Records, Unprocessed Accession.

99. “Destination Moon,” *Destination Moon* #1 (1950), Fawcett Comics; “Destination: Moon,” *Strange Adventures* #1 (August–September 1950), National Comics Publications, 39–46.

100. Advertisement, *Screen Guide*, September 1950, 13.

101. Sonia Stein, “The Rocket Overloaded, Who Stays on the Moon?,” *Washington Post*, August 19, 1950, 4.

102. Advertisement, *Daily Mirror*, July 27, 1950, 84.

103. “Picture Grosses Pages,” *Variety*, June 28, 1950, 9. Eagle-Lion went into the red by $6,000 at the Mayfair in an effort to establish *Destination Moon* in the first-run market. “‘Destination Moon’ Mayfair, New York City,” Benjamin Papers, WCFTR.

104. “What the Picture Did for Me,” *Motion Picture Herald*, January 17, 1951, 45.

105. “Destination Moon,” *Hollywood Reporter*, June 26, 1950, 3.

106. Bosley Crowther, “The Year’s Best,” *New York Times*, December 31, 1950, X1.

107. “Top Grosses of 1950,” *Variety*, January 3, 1951, 58.

108. “Eagle Lion Classics Asks $15,000,000 from RKO, Loew’s in Anti-Trust Suit,” *Variety*, October 4, 1950, 7.

109. “ELC Seeks Immediate N.Y. Injunction Aimed at Majors’ Booking, Run Setup,” *Variety*, October 11, 1950, 6.

110. *Eagle-Lion Studios, Inc. et al. v. Loew’s Inc., et al.*, 141 F. Supp. 658; 1956 U.S. Dist. LEXIS 3349, Lexis-Nexis.

111. *Eagle-Lion Studios, Inc. et al. v. Loew’s Inc., et al.*, 248 F.2d 438, 1957 U.S. App. LEXIS 5260, Lexis-Nexis.

112. “ELC Tights Its Belt in Pitch for Product,” *Motion Picture Herald*, March 31, 1951, 16.

113. Undated ledger, United Artists Corporation Records, Unprocessed Accession.

114. “Scramble for ELC’s Market,” *Variety*, April 18, 1951, 5.

115. “Upped Sked of 30 Films Reported by Par for 1951,” *Variety* October 18, 1950, 7.

116. Casper, *Postwar Hollywood*, 373–374, 380, 384.

117. Louis Berg, “Reaching for the Moon,” *Los Angeles Times*, April 23, 1953, G18.

118. Schatz, *Boom and Bust*, 379.

119. Jason Mittell, *Genre and Television: From Cop Shows to Cartoons in American Culture* (New York: Routledge, 2004), 131.

120. Casper, *Postwar Hollywood*, 369.

121. William Lafferty, “A Reappraisal of the Semi-Documentary in Hollywood, 1945–1948,” *Velvet Light Trap* 20 (Summer 1983): 24.

122. Aubrey Solomon, *Twentieth Century-Fox: A Corporate and Financial History* (Lanham, MD: Scarecrow, 2002), 243.

123. Tom Weaver, *Science Fiction Stars and Horror Heroes* (Jefferson, NC: McFarland, 1991), 88.

124. "Producer Tor Made His Own Breaks in TV," *Chicago Tribune*, November 22, 1959, WA2.

125. "Science Fiction Indie," *Variety*, August 20, 1952, 5.

126. Bill Warren, *Keep Watching the Skies! American Science Fiction Movies of the Fifties, the 21st Century Edition* (Jefferson, NC: McFarland, 2010), xviii.

127. Vivian Sobchack, *The Limits of Infinity: The American Science Fiction Film, 1950–1975* (New York: Ungar, 1980), 143–144.

128. For instance, *The Magnetic Monster* headlined with UA's *Bandits Corsica* in Los Angeles, where it opened to a "mild" $12,000. "Picture Grosses," *Variety*, March 18, 1953, 8. Budget information from interview with Curt Siodmak in Tom Weaver, *Interviews with B Science Fiction and Horror Movie Makers* (Jefferson, NC: McFarland, 1988), 307.

129. "The Magnetic Monster," *Variety*, February 11, 1953, 6.

130. Interview with Herbert L. Strock, in Weaver, *Interviews with B Science*, 313.

131. "Ziv Preparing Adult Science Fiction Series," *Billboard*, February 5, 1955, 8.

132. "Sees Science Fiction Name Spelling Mud," *Variety*, August 13, 1958, 5.

133. Weaver, *Interviews with B Science*, 316.

134. Solomon, *Twentieth Century-Fox*, 246.

135. Philip K. Scheuer, "Flying Saucer Film Dishes Up Choices," *Los Angeles Times*, May 20, 1951, D3.

136. Rudy Behlmer, ed., *Memo from Darryl F. Zanuck: The Golden Years at Twentieth Century-Fox* (New York: Grove, 1993), 191.

137. Philip K. Scheuer, "Realism Gives Reelism Trial Filming 'When Worlds Collide,'" *Los Angeles Times*, February 4, 1951, D1.

138. Press book for *When Worlds Collide*, Paramount Pictures Pressbooks Collection, Academy of Motion Picture Arts and Sciences (hereafter AMPAS).

139. Steve Rubin, "The War of the Worlds," *Cinefantastique* 5, no. 4 (Spring 1977): 9.

140. "War of the Worlds General Meeting Notes," November 9, 1951, *War of the Worlds* file, Paramount Production Records, AMPAS.

141. Steve Rubin, "Retrospect: *Them!*," *Cinefantastique* 3, no. 4 (Winter 1974): 26.

142. Lucanio, *Them or Us*, 71

143. Tom Weaver, Michael Brunas, and John Brunas, *Universal Horrors: The Studio's Classic Films, 1931–1946*, 2nd ed. (Jefferson, NC: MacFarland, 2007), 561.

144. Davis, *Battle for the Bs*, 177.

Chapter 2. The Pulp Paradox: SF Films of the 1950s

1. For instance, see Cyndy Hendershot, *Paranoia, the Bomb, and 1950s Science Fiction Films* (Bowling Green, KY: Bowling Green University Press, 2000).

2. "Predict More Science-Fiction Pix, Sparked by Increasingly Big Grosses," *Variety*, October 3, 1951, 22.

3. "A Slight Case of Mistaken Identity," undated Eagle-Lion press release, United Artists Collection — Accessions, WCFTR.

4. "Top-Grosses of 1950," *Variety*, January 3, 1951, 58.

5. Stephen Keane, *Disaster Movies: The Cinema of Catastrophe* (London: Wallflower, 2001), 12.

6. Edwin Schallert, "Pal Buys World's End Story," *Los Angeles Times*, October 10, 1949, A7.

7. Helen Gould, "The Trick Men Take Over," *New York Times*, March 25, 1951, 81.

8. Letter from Norman Freeman to D. J. Melamed, Robert Benjamin Papers, WCFTR.

9. Hickman, *Films of George Pal*, 100.

10. Ibid., 51–52.

11. Ledger, November 10, 1951, *When Worlds Collide* file, Paramount Production Records, Special Collections, Margaret Herrick Library, AMPAS.

12. "Top Grossers of 1951," *Variety*, January 2, 1952, 70.

13. "Pal's Option Renewed," *Motion Picture Herald*, July 7, 1951, 56.

14. See Howard Koch, *The Panic Broadcast* (New York: Avon, 1970), for a first-person account from the radio play's writer.

15. Rubin, "War of the Worlds," 6; Sergei Eisenstein, *The Film Sense* (San Diego: Harcourt Brace, 1947), 223.

16. William R. Weaver, "Hollywood Scene," *Motion Picture Herald*, February 14, 1952, 32.

17. Ledger, September 23, 1954, *War of the Worlds* file, Paramount Production Records, AMPAS.

18. Hickman, *Films of George Pal*, 67, and Brog., "War of the Worlds," *Variety*, March 4, 1953, 18.

19. Ledger, September 23, 1954, *War of the Worlds* file, Paramount Production Records, AMPAS, and "Top Grossers of 1953," *Variety*, January 13, 1954, 10.

20. Warren, *Keep Watching*, 299.

21. Frederick S. Clarke and Steve Rubin, "Making Forbidden Planet," *Cinefantastique* 8, nos. 2–3 (Spring 1979): 9.

22. "The Day the Earth Stood Still," *Motion Picture Herald*, September 8, 1951, 1005.

23. Casper, *Postwar Hollywood*, 79.

24. Todd McCarthy, *Howard Hawks: The Grey Fox of Hollywood* (New York: Grove, 1997), 473.

25. Peter Biskind, *Seeing Is Believing: How Hollywood Taught Us to Stop Worrying and Love the Fifties* (New York: Owl Books, 2000), 133–134. Today, it is a critical commonplace for '50s SF films to be interpreted as anticommunist, even if the films were not originally intended to be received that way. For instance, Jeff Smith has shown that the correlation between Communists and the giant mutant ants of *Them!* is an ex post facto interpretation by later critics, not something that was part of the original production or marketing process. See Jeff Smith, *Film Criticism, the Cold War, and the Blacklist: Reading the Hollywood Reds* (Berkeley: University of California Press, 2014), 256–257.

26. Al LaValley, ed., *Invasion of the Body Snatchers* (New Brunswick, NJ: Rutgers University Press, 1989).

27. Mark Jancovich, *Rational Fears: American Horror in the 1950s* (Manchester: Manchester University Press, 1996), 64.

28. "When Worlds Collide," *Hollywood Reporter*, August 28, 1951, 3.

29. Gilb., "When Worlds Collide," *Variety*, September 29, 1951, 6.

30. Bosley Crowther, "The Screen in Review," *New York Times*, February 7, 1952, 30.

31. Philip K. Scheuer, "'Id' Key to Terrifying Menace on Far Planet," *Los Angeles Times*, March 30, 1956, 23.

32. Rubin, "War of the Worlds," 10.

33. George Pal, "Filming *War of the Worlds*," *Astounding Science Fiction*, October 1953, 102.

34. Pal claimed that Hartman wanted him to eliminate the killer ants entirely. Rubin, "War of the Worlds," 16.

35. "Conquest of Space," *Variety*, April 15, 1955.

36. See Vincent Canby, "The Beast from 20,000 Fathoms," *Motion Picture Herald*, June 20, 1953, 1878; "War of the Worlds," *Variety*, March 4, 1953, 18.

37. "Science-Fiction Films Will Stay," *Springfield (MA) Union*, January 12, 1954, 12.

38. Ledger, November 10, 1951, *When Worlds Collide* file, Paramount Production Records, AMPAS.

39. For instance, Betty Grable demanded $150,000 per picture in the early '50s. Todd McCarthy, *Howard Hawks: The Grey Fox of Hollywood* (New York: Grove, 1997), 503.

40. Tom Weaver, *They Fought in the Creature Features* (Jefferson, NC: McFarland, 1995), 2.

41. McCarthy, *Howard Hawks*, 480.

42. Ibid., 482. *The Thing* went over budget by 25 percent, primarily because it took nineteen weeks rather than the originally scheduled nine weeks to shoot. McCarthy notes that this is a good indication that Hawks and not Nyby was in charge.

43. "Top Grossers of 1951," *Variety*, January 2, 1952, 70, and McCarthy, *Howard Hawks*, 484.

44. Richard Hodgens, "A Brief, Tragical History of the Science Fiction Film," *Film Quarterly* 13, no. 2 (Winter 1959): 33.

45. "The Exhibitor Has His Say about Pictures," *Boxoffice*, August 18, 1956, 11.

46. "Top Grossers of 1953," *Variety*, January 13, 1954, 10.

47. "Top Grossers of 1951," *Variety*, January 2, 1952, 70; "Top Grossers of 1953," *Variety*, January 13, 1954, 10.

48. "Appendix: RKO Financial Data," *Historical Journal of Film, Radio and Television* 14, no. 1 (1994): microfiche supplement.

49. Solomon, *Twentieth Century-Fox*, 97.

50. Budget, November 17, 1955, *Conquest of Space* file, Paramount Production Records, AMPAS; "1955's Top Film Grossers," *Variety*, January 25, 1956, 15.

51. Clarke and Rubin, "Making Forbidden Planet," 62; "Top Film Grossers of 1956," *Variety*, January 2, 1957, 4.

52. For instance, *Variety* reports that Warner Bros.' *Them!* "dipped rather abruptly in first holdover sessions." "Picture Grosses," *Variety*, June 20, 1954, 3. Similar reports exist for Warner Bros.' *The Beast from 20,000 Fathoms*, Universal-International's *It Came from Outer Space*, and other fifties SF films that received a first-run release. "Picture Grosses," *Variety* July 8, 1953, 3. Paramount's Jack Karp, via a conversation with Fox's Sid Rogell, confirms the same pattern for *The War of the Worlds*. Solomon, *Twentieth Century-Fox*, 97.

53. "Mae Tinee," "Space Movie Will Delight Rocket Boys," *Chicago Tribune*, April 25, 1955, B14.

54. "The Exhibitor Has His Say about Pictures," *Boxoffice Booking Guide*, December 19, 1953, 1.

55. Dave S. Klein, "What the Picture Did for Me," *Motion Picture Herald*, April 27, 1957, 355.

56. Moz Burles, "What the Picture Did for Me," *Motion Picture Herald*, September 15, 1956, 67.

57. Bosley Crowther, "The Screen in Review," *New York Times*, September 19, 1951, 37.

58. Ibid.

59. Brog., "Forbidden Planet," *Variety*, March 24, 1956, 6.

60. Taves, "B Film," 317.

61. Davis, *Battle for the Bs*, 166.

62. United Artists functioned only as a distributor.

63. Schatz, *Boom and Bust*, 464–465.

64. Film titles and run times taken from Clive Hirschhorn, *The Universal Story* (New York: Crown, 1983), 109–114.

65. Film titles and run times taken from John Douglas Eames, *The MGM Story* (New York: Crown, 1976), 146–154.

66. Thomas Schatz, *The Genius of the System: Hollywood Filmmaking in the Studio Era* (New York: Metropolitan Books, 1988), 239.

67. "'B' Pix B.O. Chasers — Schenck," *Variety*, May 18, 1949, 3, 18.

68. "B's Buzzing out of Business," *Variety*, March 26, 1952, 13.

69. "No Profit Anymore in B (for Bad) Pictures, Warner Tells Guild," *Variety*, November 22, 1953, 1.

70. "U.S. 70% Dual, But B's Vanishing," *Variety*, February 24, 1954, 3.

71. Davis, *Battle for the Bs*, 47.

72. Douglas Gomery, *The Hollywood Studio System: A History* (London: British Film Institute, 2005), 161.

73. Hirschhorn, *Universal Story*, 157.

74. Bernard F. Dick, *City of Dreams: The Making and Remaking of Universal Pictures* (Lexington: University Press of Kentucky, 1997), 145–146.

75. Taves, "B Film," 318.

76. Lev, *Fifties*, 108.

77. Ibid.

78. "Picture Grosses," *Variety*, July 9, 1952, 9.

79. Kevin Heffernan has noted the narrative influences of *The Thing* on *Creature from the Black Lagoon*. Heffernan, *Ghouls, Gimmicks, and Gold*, 39.

80. For an account of the development of Bradbury's lengthy treatment into a screenplay see Jonathan Eller, "Bradbury's Web of Fear: The Lost Metaphor behind the Screen Treatment," in *It Came from Outer Space*, ed. Donn Albright (Colorado Springs, CO: Gauntlet, 2004), 27–41.

81. Heffernan, *Ghouls, Gimmicks, and Gold*, 18.

82. Beth Kleid, "'Bwana Devil' Comin' at Ya in 3-D," *Los Angeles Times*, July 7, 1990, http://articles.latimes.com/1990-07-07/entertainment/ca-296_1_bwana-devil.

83. Lev, *Fifties*, 110.

84. Heffernan, *Ghouls, Gimmicks, and Gold*, 21.

85. Heffernan argues that 3-D horror films are a mix of conventional Hollywood narrative and the presentationalist style of the early silent cinema of attractions. Ibid., 10–12.

86. "Top Grossers of 1953," *Variety*, January 13, 1954, 10.

87. Brog., "It Came from Outer Space," *Variety*, May 27, 1953, 6.

88. Philip K. Scheuer, "Science-Fiction Shocker Loosed in Wide-Screen 3D," *Los Angeles Times*, May 27, 1953, B6.

89. "Picture Grosses," *Variety*, June 3, 1953, 11.

90. *Creature from the Black Lagoon* Production Budget, January 26, 1954, Universal Collection, University of Southern California, Los Angeles (hereafter USC).

91. Rick Altman suggests that *Creature from the Black Lagoon* was a horror film

rebranded as SF by Universal's publicity department to capitalize on current interest in the genre. It seems much more likely that the film was intended as an SF/horror hybrid from its inception. Universal had abandoned classic horror production years earlier, and with the same producer, director, and star, *Creature* was a clear follow-up to *It Came from Outer Space*, which was unambiguously SF. Rick Altman, *Film/Genre* (London: British Film Institute, 1999), 78.

92. "1954 Boxoffice Champs," *Variety*, January 5, 1955, 50.

93. "3-D Looks Dead in United States," *Variety*, May 26, 1954, 1.

94. Casper, *Postwar Hollywood*, 116.

95. Warren, *Keep Watching*, 703.

96. For a summary of New York reviews see Richard Griffith, "'Sea Chase' Called Dull by Critics in New York," *Los Angeles Times*, June 22, 1955, B9.

97. Anonymous critic quoted ibid.

98. "1955's Top Film Grossers," *Variety*, January 25, 1956, 15; Ray Harryhausen and Tony Dalton, *Ray Harryhausen: An Animated Life* (New York: Billboard Books, 2003), 73.

99. *The Deadly Mantis* Production Budget, August 23, 1957, Universal Collection, USC; *It Came from Outer Space* Production Budget, November 25, 1953, ibid.

100. Richard Maltby, *Hollywood Cinema* (Malden, MA: Blackwell, 2003), 182.

101. Warren, *Keep Watching*, 10.

102. Richard B. Jewell, *The Golden Age of Cinema: Hollywood 1929–1945* (Malden, MA: Blackwell, 2007), 143.

103. Ibid., 262.

104. "'King Kong,' 'Leopard Man' Booked in 400 Theaters," *Boxoffice*, May 31, 1952, 20.

105. "RKO Tests a Real Old One, Using Saturation Campaign," *Boxoffice*, June 21, 1952, 22.

106. "'King Kong' Air Campaigns Set for Both East, West," *Boxoffice*, July 19, 1952, 27.

107. "RKO's King Kong Reissue Rolls Up Big Grosses," *Motion Picture Herald*, August 2, 1952, 17.

108. "No New Reissues Rush despite 'Kong' Success; Special Type Seen Needed," *Variety*, July 2, 1952, 7.

109. Harryhausen and Dalton, *Ray Harryhausen*, 58.

110. Ibid., 51.

111. Distribution Agreement, February 27, 1953, *Beast from 20,000 Fathoms* file, Warner Bros. Archive, Special Collections, USC.

112. Vincent Canby, "Top Films Out to Lick Summer 'Doldrums,'" *Motion Picture Herald*, June 27, 1953, 12.

113. "WB Sets Up 1422 Saturation Dates for '20,000 Fathoms,'" *Hollywood Reporter*, June 16, 1953, 6.

114. Ibid.

115. "Ballyhooable 'B's' Glow in Today's Feature Famine," *Variety*, March 3, 1954, 7.

116. "Top Grossers of 1953," *Variety*, January 13, 1954, 10.

117. "2,000 Playdates for WB's 'Them' within a Month!," *Variety*, June 2, 1954, 5.

118. "Ballyhooable 'B's Glow in Today's Feature Famine."

119. Matthew Bernstein, *Walter Wanger, Hollywood Independent* (Berkeley: University of California Press, 1994), 299–300.

120. "Ballyhooable 'B's' Glow in Today's Feature Famine."

121. Heffernan, *Ghouls, Gimmicks, and Gold*, 7–8, 66.

122. Maltby, *Hollywood Cinema*, 164.

123. Kristin Thompson and David Bordwell, *Film History: An Introduction*, 3rd ed. (New York: McGraw-Hill, 2010), 307.

124. "3 Majors Thrive on 'B' Pix," *Variety*, January 12, 1955, 5.

125. Bernard F. Dick, *The Merchant Prince of Poverty Row: Harry Cohn of Columbia Pictures* (Lexington: University Press of Kentucky, 1993), 134.

126. "Jungle Sam," *Time*, December 1, 1952, http://www.time.com/time/magazine/article/0,9171,817485,00.html.

127. "Science Fiction Combo," *Variety*, June 15, 1955, 21.

128. "1955's Top Film Grossers," *Variety*, January 25, 1956, and Harryhausen and Dalton, *Ray Harryhausen*, 73.

129. Clive Hirschhorn, *The Columbia Story* (New York: Crown, 1989), 195.

130. Ibid., 193–199.

131. Davis, *Battle for the Bs*, 104.

132. Sam Arkoff with Richard Trubo, *Flying through Hollywood by the Seat of My Pants* (New York: Birch Lane Press, 1992), 40.

133. Mark Thomas McGee, *Faster and Furiouser: The Revised and Fattened Fable of American International Pictures* (Jefferson, NC: McFarland, 1996), 20.

134. Arkoff, *Flying through Hollywood*, 41.

135. McGee, *Faster and Furiouser*, 43.

136. Arkoff, *Flying through Hollywood*, 46–47.

137. McGee, *Faster and Furiouser*, 49.

138. Ibid., 63.

139. "Picture Grosses," *Variety*, September 2, 1936, 10.

140. "Picture Grosses," *Variety*, June 11, 1952, 8, and "Picture Grosses," *Variety*, July 9, 1952, 8.

141. Scott MacGillivray and Ted Okuda, "Play It Again, Jack: Remembering Realart, the Re-Releasing Company," *Filmfax* 39 (June/July 1993): 41.

142. Arkoff, *Flying through Hollywood*, 41.

143. Ibid., 58.

144. Maltby, *Hollywood Cinema*, 164.

145. Philip K. Scheuer, "Shocker Pioneers Tell How to Make Monsters," *Los Angeles Times*, September 21, 1958, E2.

146. Arkoff, *Flying through Hollywood*, 85.

147. "20–29 Age Group Biggest Filmgoers," *Variety*, July 18, 1956, 1.

148. Thomas Doherty, *Teenagers and Teenpics: The Juvenilization of American Movies in the 1950s*, rev. ed. (Philadelphia: Temple University Press, 2002), 54.

149. "Teens Tend to Double Bills," *Motion Picture Herald*, February 4, 1956, 18.

150. Davis, *Battle for the Bs*, 107.

151. Doherty, *Teenagers and Teenpics*, 7.

152. Ibid., 131.

153. "Douglas Attacks Horror Films," *Washington Post*, February 3, 1958, B1.

154. Irvine Rubine, "Boys Meet Ghouls, Make Money," *New York Times*, March 16, 1958, X7.

155. Joel W. Finler, *The Hollywood Story* (London: Wallflower, 2003), 376.

156. "'Gimmicks' Did Well in 1957," *Variety*, November 6, 1957, 3.

157. "Blockbusters vs. Main Street," *Variety*, February 6, 1957, 5.

158. "Increased Flow of 'B' Indie Films No Cure for Biz — Say 'A' Distribs," *Variety*, August 15, 1956, 7.

159. Lisa Dombrowski, *The Films of Samuel Fuller: If You Die, I'll Kill You!* (Middletown, CT: Wesleyan University Press, 2008), 103.

160. Ibid.

161. Ibid., 108.

162. Memo from Sid Rogell to Buddy Adler, December 19, 1957, *The Fly* file, Twentieth Century-Fox Collection, Special Collections, University of California–Los Angeles (hereafter UCLA).

163. Memo from Frank H. Ferguson to Lew Schreiber, February 25, 1958, *The Fly* file, Twentieth Century-Fox Collection, Special Collections, UCLA.

164. "Preliminary Cost Estimate," undated, *The Fly* file, Twentieth Century-Fox Collection, Special Collections, UCLA; Solomon, *Twentieth Century-Fox*, 227.

165. "'Gimmicks' Did Well in 1957."

166. Interview with William Alland, in Tom Weaver, *Monsters, Mutants, and Heavenly Creatures* (Baltimore: Midnight Marquee Press, 1996), 60.

167. Interview with Irwin S. Yeaworth Jr., ibid., 253.

168. "Par's 'Blob' No Slob," *Variety*, October 15, 1953, 3.

169. "'Gimmicks' Did Well in 1957."

170. Production budget, February 17, 1958, *Island of Lost Women* file, Warner Bros. Archive, Special Collections, USC.

171. Heffernan, *Ghouls, Gimmicks, and Gold*, 70–72.

172. Interview with Jacques Marquette in Tom Weaver, *Attack of the Monster Movie Makers* (Jefferson, NC: McFarland, 1994), 198.

173. "Don't Kill Thrill-Chill Mill," *Variety*, March 26, 1958, 5.

174. "Cheap 'n' Quick No Longer Goes in Horrorfiers," *Variety*, May 20, 1959, 4.

175. Arkoff, *Flying through Hollywood*, 91.

176. Corman claims that *House of Usher* cost about $270,000, and its follow-up *Pit and the Pendulum* cost approximately $200,000. Roger Corman with Jim Jerome, *How I Made a Hundred Movies in Hollywood and Never Lost a Dime* (New York: Delta Books, 1990), 78, 83.

177. Davis, *Battle for the Bs*, 128.

178. Heffernan, *Ghouls, Gimmicks, and Gold*, 44; "'Gimmicks' Did Well in 1957."

179. Quoted in McGee, *Faster and Furiouser*, 185.

180. "Rental Potentials of 1960," *Variety*, January 4, 1961, 47.

Chapter 3. From Parody to Profundity: *2001: A Space Odyssey* and the Critical Legitimation of SF Film

1. McGee, *Faster and Furiouser*, 148.

2. Powe., "4D Man," *Variety*, October 7, 1959, 6.

3. Warren, *Keep Watching*, 11.

4. "Rental Potentials of 1960," *Variety*, January 4, 1961, 47.

5. Stephen Rebello, *Alfred Hitchcock and the Making of "Psycho"* (New York: Harper Perennial, 1991), 22.

6. Drew Casper, *Postwar Hollywood, 1945–1962* (Malden, MA: Blackwell, 2007), 208.

7. Tim Lucas, *Mario Bava: All the Colors of the Dark* (Cincinnati: Video Watchdog, 2007), 207.

8. Ibid.

9. Heffernan, *Ghouls, Gimmicks, and Gold*, 135.

10. Robert Skotak, *Ib Melchior: Man of Imagination* (Baltimore: Midnight Marquee Press, 2000), 145.

11. Nowell, *Blood Money*, 44.

12. Herbert F. Solow and Robert H. Justman, *Inside Star Trek: The Real Story* (New York: Pocket Books, 1996), 299–307.

13. Quoted in Marc Scott Zicree, *The Twilight Zone Companion* (Los Angeles: Silman-James, 1989), 15.

14. David J. Schow, *The Outer Limits Companion* (Hollywood: GNP/Crescendo, 1998), 241.

15. John Brosnan, Kim Newman, and Peter Nicholls, "Irwin Allen," *The Encyclopedia of Science Fiction*, ed. John Clute and Peter Nicholls (New York: St. Martin's Griffin, 1995), 20.

16. "Voyage to the Bottom of the Sea," *Variety*, September 20, 1967, 40.

17. Altman, *Film/Genre*, 62.

18. Raphaëlle Moine, *Cinema Genre*, trans. Alistair Fox and Hilary Radner (Malden MA: Blackwell, 2008), 119.

19. Rick Altman, "A Semantic/Syntactic Approach to Film Genre," in *Film Genre Reader III*, ed. Barry Keith Grant (Austin: University of Texas Press, 2003), 36.

20. "1955's Top Film Grossers," *Variety*, January 25, 1956, 1.

21. Solomon, *Twentieth Century-Fox*, 138.

22. Related films include Irwin Allen's *Voyage to the Bottom of the Sea* (1961), a modern retelling of *20,000 Leagues under the Sea*; Disney's non-SF Verne adaptation *In Search of the Castaways* (1962); and the Czech part-animated feature *Vynález zkázy* (1958), released in America as *The Fabulous World of Jules Verne* in 1961.

23. Tino Balio, *United Artists*, 93–94.

24. Ibid. 261.

25. Ibid., 260.

26. Klein, *American Film Cycles*, 15.

27. Warren, *Keep Watching*, 752.

28. Loren G. Buchanan, "Wild Wild Planet," *Motion Picture Herald*, May 17, 1967, 686.

29. "1961: Rentals and Potential," *Variety*, January 10, 1962, 13.

30. "Rental Potentials of 1960," *Variety*, January 4, 1961, 47; "Top Rental Films of 1963," *Variety*, January 8, 1964, 37.

31. Richard Maibaum, "James Bond's 39 Bumps," *New York Times*, December 13, 1964, X9.

32. "Big Rental Pictures of 1966," *Variety*, January 4, 1967, 8.

33. Thomas Schatz, *Hollywood Genres* (New York: Random House, 1981), 36–41.

34. Ibid., 37–38.

35. Altman, *Film/Genre*, 21–22.

36. Steve Neale, *Genre and Hollywood* (London: Routledge 2000), 213–214.

37. Tag Gallagher, "Shoot-Out at the Genre Corral: Problems in the 'Evolution' of the Western," in Grant, *Film Genre Reader III*, 262, 266.

38. Vincent LoBrutto, *Stanley Kubrick: A Biography* (New York: Da Capo, 1999), 269.

39. Ibid., 269, 306.

40. Ibid., 306. See Herb A. Lightman, "Front Projection for 2001: A Space Odyssey," and Douglas Trumbull, "Creating Special Effects for 2001: A Space Odyssey," in *American Cinematographer* 49, no. 6: 158–166.

41. John Douglas Eames, *The MGM Story* (New York: Crown, 1975), 336.

42. "Big Rental Films of 1967," *Variety*, January 3, 1968, 23.

43. "Big Rental Films of 1968," *Variety*, January 8, 1969, 15.

44. R. Barton Palmer, "2001: The Critical Reception and the Generation Gap," in *Stanley Kubrick's "2001: A Space Odyssey": New Essays*, ed. Robert Kolker (Oxford: Oxford University Press, 2006), 14.

45. David Bordwell, *Narration in the Fiction Film* (Madison: University of Wisconsin Press, 1985), 32.

46. John Belton, "Glorious Technicolor, Breathtaking CinemaScope, and Stereophonic Sound," in *Hollywood in the Age of Television*, ed. Tino Balio (Boston: Unwin Hyman, 1990), 187–188.

47. Thompson and Bordwell, *Film History*, 473.

48. "Metro Roadshows to Cost Millions," *Dallas Morning News*, March 11, 1967, 5C.

49. Michael Coate, "1968: A Roadshow Odyssey," http://in70mm.com/news/2004/2001_in_70mm/engagements/index.htm.

50. Thompson and Bordwell, *Film History*, 303–304.

51. Ibid., 205.

52. Thomas E. Brown, "*2001*'s Original Projection Format," http://www.visual-memory.co.uk/amk/doc/brown1.html.

53. Herbert Shuldiner, "How They Filmed *2001: A Space Odyssey*," *Popular Science*, June 1968, 62.

54. Richard F. Dempewolff, "Backstage Magic for a Trip to Saturn," *Popular Mechanics*, April 1967, 218.

55. Arthur C. Clarke, "Next: On Earth, the Good Life?," *Vogue*, April 15, 1968, 86.

56. "2001: A Space Odyssey Program," http://www.visual-memory.co.uk/2001/contact/scans/page10.jpg.

57. Advertisement, *New York Times*, April 24, 1968, D12.

58. Hollis Alpert, "Is It Strangelove? Is It Buck Rogers? Is It the Future? Offbeat Director in Outer Space," *New York Times*, January 17, 1966, SM8.

59. Quoted in Chapman and Cull, *Projecting Tomorrow*, 95.

60. Arthur C. Clarke, *The Lost Worlds of 2001* (New York: Signet, 1972).

61. Robert Kolker, *A Cinema of Loneliness*, 3rd ed. (London: Oxford University Press, 2000), 129.

62. Stuart Byron, "'Space': Boxoffice Moon-Shot," *Variety*, January 29, 1969, 3.

63. Andrew Sarris, "2001: A Space Odyssey," in *The Village Voice Film Guide*, ed. Dennis Lim (Hoboken, NJ: John Wiley & Sons, 2007), 278.

64. Robe., "2001: A Space Odyssey," *Variety*, April 3, 1968, 6.

65. Stanley Kauffmann, "Lost in the Stars," *New Republic*, May 4, 1968, 24.

66. Judith Crist, "Stanley Kubrick, Please Come Down," *New York*, April 22, 1968, 52–53.

67. Renalta Adler, "'2001' Is Up, Up, and Away," *New York Times*, April 4, 1968, 58.

68. Pauline Kael, "Trash, Art, and the Movies," *Harper's*, February 1, 1969, 81.

69. Ibid.

70. David Bordwell, *Making Meaning: Inference and Rhetoric in the Interpretation of Cinema* (Cambridge, MA: Harvard University Press, 1989), 158.

71. Hollis Alpert, "Offbeat Director in Outer Space," *New York Times*, January 16, 1966, 46, 51.

72. Russell Baker, "Observer: A Machine for All Seasons," *New York Times*, April 7, 1968, E12.

73. Clifford Terry, "A Pair of Films Take 'Way Out Trips between the Monkeys and Monoliths," *Chicago Tribune*, April 21, 1968, F17.

74. A. H. Weiler, "Kazan, Kubrick, and Keaton," *New York Times*, April 28, 1968, D19.

75. Jim Watters, "2001: A Space Odyssey," *Boxoffice*, April 8, 1968, 10.

76. Cited in Jerome Agel, *The Making of Kubrick's "2001"* (New York: Signet, 1970), 230, 233.

77. Penelope Gilliatt, "After Man," *New Yorker*, April 13, 1968, 150–152.

78. Greg Taylor, *Artists in the Audience: Cults, Camp, and American Film Criticism* (Princeton, NJ: Princeton University Press, 1999), 134.

79. Gene Youngblood, "Stanley Kubrick's 2001: A Masterpiece," *Los Angeles Free Press*, March 19, 1968, 29, cited in Paul Monaco, *The Sixties* (Berkeley: University of California Press, 2001), 195; Gene Youngblood, *Expanded Cinema* (New York: E. P. Dutton, 1970).

80. Youngblood, *Expanded Cinema*, 139.

81. Ibid., 156.

82. Tim Hunter, with Stephen Kaplan and Peter Jaszi, "2001: A Space Odyssey," in *The Making of "2001: A Space Odyssey,"* ed. Stephanie Schwam (New York: Modern Library, 2000), 151.

83. Marshall McLuhan, *Understanding Media: The Extensions of Man* (New York: Signet, 1964).

84. The McLuhan connection continued with the April 1970 publication of *The Making of Kubrick's "2001,"* a collection of interviews, reviews, and photographs edited by Jerome Agel, who previously edited McLuhan's and Quentin Fiore's *The Medium Is the Massage*.

85. "'Visual' Mod & 'Verbal' Crix," *Variety*, April 10, 1968, 5.

86. William Kloman, "'2001' and 'Hair': Are They the Groove of the Future?" *New York Times*, May 12, 1968, D15.

87. "'Visual' Mod & 'Verbal' Crix," 5.

88. Rob Latham, "'A Journey beyond the Stars': *2001: A Space Odyssey* and the Psychedelic Revolution in 1960s Science Fiction," in *Science Fiction and the Prediction of the Future: Essays in Foresight and Fallacy*, ed. Gary Westfahl, Wong Kin Yuen, and Amy Kit-sze Chan (Jefferson, NC: McFarland, 2011), 128–134.

89. J. G. Ballard, "Which Way to Inner Space?," in *A User's Guide to the Millennium: Essays and Reviews* (London: Harper Collins, 1996), 197.

90. Adam Roberts, *The History of Science Fiction* (New York: Palgrave Macmillan, 2005), 231.

91. Samuel R. Delany, "2001: A Space Odyssey," *Fantasy & Science Fiction*, August 1968, 63.

92. Ray Bradbury, "Space Odyssey 2001," *Psychology Today* 2, no. 1 (June 1968): 10.

93. Frederik Pohl, "2001: A Second Look," *Film Society Review* 5, no. 6 (February 1970): 27.

94. Lester del Rey, "2001: A Space Odyssey," *Galaxy* 26, no. 6 (July 1968): 194.

95. Latham, "'Journey beyond the Stars,'" 129.

96. Byron, "'Space,'" 5.

97. Ibid., 5, 19.

98. Ibid., 19, and Bob McClay, "2001: A Space Odyssey," in Schwam, *Making of 2001*, 162.

99. Advertisement, *New York Times*, April 18, 1968, 57.

100. Advertisement, *Spokane Daily Chronicle*, October 10, 1968, 25.

101. "Playboy Interview: Stanley Kubrick," in *The Making of 2001: A Space Odyssey*, ed. Stephanie Schwam (New York: Modern Library, 2000), 291.

102. Peter Krämer, *"2001: A Space Odyssey"* (London: British Film Institute, 2010), 90.

103. "Test Revival of '2001' a Smash," *Variety*, August 7, 1974, 23.

104. Agel, *Making of Kubrick's "2001,"* 263–268.

105. Andrew Sarris, "Films in Focus," *Village Voice*, May 7, 1970, 62.

106. "Top Ten 72," *Sight & Sound* 41, no. 1 (Winter 1972): 12.

107. Carolyn Geduld, *Filmguide to "2001: A Space Odyssey"* (Bloomington: Indiana University Press, 1973).

108. Hodgens, "Brief, Tragical History," 30.

109. Ibid., 39.

110. Ibid., 32.

111. Pohl, "2001: A Second Look," 23.

112. Neale, *Genre and Hollywood*, 10.

113. "Carlos Clarens Is Dead at 56; Movie Historian and Author," *New York Times*, February 10, 1987.

114. J. Hoberman, introduction to *An Illustrated History of Horror and Science-Fiction Films*, by Carlos Clarens (New York: Da Capo, 1997), ix.

115. John Baxter, *Science Fiction in the Cinema* (New York: Paperback Library, 1970), 106.

116. Clarens, *Illustrated History*, 171.

117. Baxter, *Science Fiction*, 183.

118. William Johnson, "Journey into Science Fiction," in *Focus on the Science Fiction Film*, ed. Johnson (Englewood Cliffs, NJ: Prentice Hall, 1972), 11–12.

119. Martin Rubin, "The Incredible Shrinking Man," *Film Comment* 10, no. 4 (July/August 1974): 52.

120. Baxter, *Science Fiction*, 128.

121. Andrew Sarris, *The American Cinema: Directors and Directions, 1929–1968* (New York: Da Capo, 1996), 137.

122. Charles T. Gregory, "The Pod Society versus the Rugged Individualists," *Journal of Popular Film* 1, no. 1 (1972): 13.

123. Raymond Durgnat, *Films and Feelings* (Cambridge, MA: MIT Press, 1971), 268.

124. Ibid., 256.

125. Ibid., 257.

126. Ibid., 262–263.

127. Margaret Tarratt, "Monsters from the Id," in Grant, *Film Genre Reader III*, 347.

128. Ibid., 361–362.

129. Vivian C. Sobchack, "*The Leech Woman*'s Revenge, or a Case for Equal Misrepresentation," *Journal of Popular Film* 4, no. 3 (January 1975): 236–257.

130. "77 Films over $1 Mil in U.S.," *Variety*, May 9, 1973, 44.

131. Philip Strick, "Zardoz and John Boorman," *Sight and Sound* 43, no. 2 (Spring 1974): 75.

132. Solomon, *Twentieth Century-Fox*, 257.

133. John Boorman, *Adventures of a Suburban Boy* (London: Faber & Faber, 2003), 209.

134. Solomon, *Twentieth Century-Fox*, 232.

135. "N.Y. Critics Opinions," *Variety*, February 20, 1974, 23.

136. Gary Arnold, "In the Land of 'Zardoz,'" *Washington Post*, March 15, 1974, B8.

137. Murf., "Zardoz," *Variety*, January 30, 1974, 30.

138. John Boorman director commentary, *Zardoz* (Beverly Hills, CA: Twentieth Century Fox, 2001), DVD.

139. Gene Siskel, "Gloom and Doom Infect 'Zardoz,'" *Chicago Tribune*, March 19, 1974, B4.

140. Pauline Kael, "O Consuella!," *New Yorker*, February 18, 1974, 98.

141. "Fox Ire Re: 'Zardoz,'" *Variety*, February 20, 1974, 23.

142. Siskel, "Gloom and Doom," B4.

143. Marsha Kinder, "Zardoz," *Film Quarterly* 27, no. 4 (Summer 1974): 49–57.

144. Fredric Jameson, "History and the Death Wish: Zardoz as Open Form," *Jump Cut* 3 (1974), http://www.ejumpcut.org/archive/onlinessays/JC03folder/ZardozJameson.html.

145. Deborah Painter, *Forry: The Life of Forrest J. Ackerman* (Jefferson, NC: McFarland, 2010), 60.

146. Matt Yockey, "Monster Mashups: At Home with *Famous Monsters of Filmland*," *Journal of Fandom Studies* 1, no. 1 (November 2012): 66.

147. Bob Rehak, "Materializing Monsters: Aurora Models, Garage Kits, and the Object Practices of Horror Fandom," *Journal of Fandom Studies* 1, no. 1 (November 2012): 35–36.

148. Quoted in Richard Klemensen, "A History of Horror Film Fanzines: *Photon*," *Little Shop of Horrors* 26 (April 2011): 15.

149. David MacDowall, "2001: A Critique," *Photon* 24 (1974): 25.

150. Dale Winogura, "The Auteur in Science Fiction," *Photon* 24 (1974): 46.

151. Ibid., 17.

152. Tim Lucas, "Citizen Clarke: A Memoir of Frederick S. Clarke, *Cinefantastique*'s Founding Father," *Little Shop of Horrors* 31 (October 2013): 12.

153. Pat H. Broeske, "The Little Magazine That Could," *Los Angeles Times*, March 16, 1986, P23.

154. Frederick S. Clarke, "How's Your Sense of Wonder?," *Cinefantastique* 1, no. 1 (Fall 1970): 3.

155. Paul M. Sammon, "Inside *The Black Hole*," *Cinefantastique* 9, nos. 3/4 (Spring 1980): 5–65.

156. Frederick S. Clarke, "Sense of Wonder," *Cinefantastique* 9, nos. 3/4 (Spring 1980): 3.

157. "Letters," *Cinefantastique* 9, no. 1 (Fall 1979): 47.

158. Jeffrey Sconce, "'Trashing' the Academy: Taste, Excess, and an Emerging Politics of Cinematic Style," *Screen* 36, no. 4 (Winter 1995): 371–393.

159. "Film Ratings," *Cineafantastique* 12, nos. 5/6 (July–August 1982): 87.

160. Broeske, "Little Magazine That Could," P42, P44.

161. In 2005 the online Classic Horror Film Board began hosting a discussion of Clarke's legacy, wherein many contributors to *Cinefantastique* expressed their ambivalence toward Clarke — gratitude for the opportunity he gave them, admiration of his enthusiasm for cinema, but also distaste for his antisocial behavior. See http://monsterkidclassichorrorforum.yuku.com/topic/6493/.

162. Frederick S. Clarke, "Sense of Wonder," *Cinefantastique* 1, no. 2 (Winter 1971): 3.

163. Frederick S. Clarke and Steve Rubin, "Making *Forbidden Planet*," *Cinefantastique* 8, nos. 2/3 (Spring 1979): 4–84.

164. David Sanjek, "Fans' Notes: The Horror Film Fanzine," *Literature/Film Quarterly* 18, no. 3 (July 1990): 152.

165. Michele Pierson, *Special Effects: Still in Search of Wonder* (New York: Columbia University Press, 2002), 100.

166. Sobchack, *Limits of Infinity*, 12.

167. Ibid., 223.

168. "Letters," *Cinefantastique* 9, no. 1 (Fall 1979): 47.

Chapter 4. Return to Relevance: Art, Exploitation, and Politics in SF Film, 1968–1976

1. Tino Balio, "Introduction to Part II," in Balio, *Hollywood in the Age of Television*, 259.

2. "1956–87 Big-Buck Scorecard," *Variety*, January 20, 1988, 64.

3. Solomon, *Twentieth Century-Fox*, 256.

4. Ibid., 231, 256.

5. Ibid., 165–166.

6. David A. Cook, *Lost Illusions: American Cinema in the Shadow of Watergate and Vietnam, 1970–1979* (Berkeley: University of California Press, 2000), 302–303.

7. Ibid., 315.

8. Finler, *Hollywood Story*, 379.

9. Ibid., 376–377, and Cook, *Lost Illusions*, 491.

10. Solomon, *Twentieth Century-Fox*, 174.

11. For a history of grind-house exhibition see David Church, "From Exhibition to Genre: The Case of Grind-House Films," *Cinema Journal* 50, no. 4 (Summer 2011): 1–25.

12. Cook, *Lost Illusions*, 31, and Solomon, *Twentieth Century-Fox*, 256; "Beatty 'Shampoo' Terms Rock Majors," *Variety*, February 20, 1974, 22.

13. Cook, *Lost Illusions*, 159.

14. Solomon, *Twentieth Century-Fox*, 256.

15. Ibid., 232, 256.

16. Ibid. 232, 257.

17. Peter Bart, *Fade Out: The Calamitous Final Days of MGM* (New York: Anchor Books, 1990), 38–40.

18. Ibid., 40.

19. "Making the Movies into a Business," *Business Week*, June 23, 1973, 117.

20. Janet Wasko, *Movies and Money: Financing the American Film Industry* (Norwood, NJ: Albex, 1982), 190, cited in Mark Shiel, "American Cinema 1970–1975," in *Contemporary American Cinema*, ed. Linda Ruth Williams and Michael Hammond (London: McGraw-Hill, 2006), 126; "1956–87 Big Buck Scorecard," 64.

21. Joe Russo and Larry Landsman with Edward Gross, *"Planet of the Apes" Revisited* (New York: St. Martin's Press 2001), 10–13.

22. Ibid., 21.

23. Solomon, *Twentieth Century-Fox*, 254.

24. Ibid., 230.

25. Russo, Landsman, and Gross, *"Planet of the Apes" Revisited*, 35.

26. Kevin Thomas, "'Planet of Apes' out of This World," *Los Angeles Times*, March 24, 1968, D18.

27. Pauline Kael, "Apes Must Be Remembered, Charlie," *New Yorker*, February 17, 1968, 108.

28. "Honored Show-A-Rama Exhibitor Lays Out 'Planet of the Apes' Campaign," *Boxoffice*, March 11, 1968, 37.

29. Solomon, *Twentieth Century-Fox*, 255.

30. "Planet of the Apes," *Motion Picture Herald*, February 21, 1968, 776-A.

31. "Big Rental Films of 1968," *Variety*, January 8, 1969, 15.

32. Kubrick's film would substantially increase its box office total with successful reissues in 1971 and 1972.

33. Quoted in Dale Winogura, "Dialogues on Apes, Apes, and More Apes," *Cinefantastique* 2, no. 2 (Summer 1972): 21.

34. Peter Bellamy, "'Planet of Apes' Soars," *Cleveland Plain Dealer*, April 7, 1968, G1.

35. Murf., "Planet of the Apes," *Variety*, February 7, 1968, 6.

36. "20th Century Fox Showmanship Showcase," *Boxoffice*, April 1, 1968, A3.

37. Eric Greene, *"Planet of the Apes" as American Myth: Race and Politics in the Films and Television Series* (Jefferson, NC: McFarland, 1996), 9.

38. Ibid., 35, 38.

39. Russo, Landsman, and Gross, *"Planet of the Apes" Revisited*, 182.

40. Quoted ibid., 199.

41. Ted Mahar, "Planet of the Apes Goes On and On," *Oregonian*, July 29, 1972, 20.

42. Ibid., 182.

43. "Big Rental Films of 1968."

44. Kael, "Trash, Art, and the Movies," 66–67.

45. James M. Naughton, "Nixon Proposes 2 New Agencies on Environment," *New York Times*, July 10, 1970, 1.

46. Paul R. Erlich, "The Population Bomb," *New York Times*, November 4, 1970, 47.

47. John G. Cawelti, "*Chinatown* and Generic Transformation in Recent American Films," in Grant, *Film Genre Reader III*, 250.

48. Ibid., 260.

49. Joan F. Dean, "Between 2001 and Star Wars," *Journal of Popular Film and Television* 7, no. 1 (1978): 34.

50. Wayne Kinsey, *Hammer Films: The Elstree Studio Years* (Sheffield, UK: Tomahawk, 2007), 115.

51. Ibid., 116.

52. Herb A. Lightman, "Filming 'Planet of the Apes,'" *American Cinematographer* 49, no. 4 (April 1968): 258.

53. Ibid., 259.

54. Independent exploitation films remained popular in the United States in the early seventies, but the trendy genres at the time were horror, blaxploitation, martial arts films, and pornography. SF exploitation consisted largely of a steady stream of Japanese imports like *Yog: Monster from Space* (1970) and the occasional AIP release like *The Incredible Two-Headed Transplant* (1971).

55. Glenn Lovell, *Escape Artist: The Life and Films of John Sturges* (Madison: University of Wisconsin Press, 2008), 272.

56. Howard Thompson, "Screen: 'Marooned,' Space Film, Opens the New Zigfield," *New York Times*, December 19, 1969, 65.

57. Murf., "Westworld," *Variety*, August 15, 1973, 12.

58. Judy Klemesrud, "Feminists Recoil at Film Designed to Relate to Them," *New York Times*, February 26, 1975, 29.

59. "Big Rental Films of 1975," *Variety*, January 7, 1976, 13.

60. Solomon, *Twentieth Century-Fox*, 232, 257.

61. Russo, Landsman, and Gross, *"Planet of the Apes" Revisited*, 197.

62. Ibid., 198.

63. Cook, *Lost Illusions*, 67.

64. "Big Rental Films of 1969," *Variety*, January 7, 1970, 15.

65. Mel Gussow, "Movies Leaving 'Hollywood' Behind," *New York Times*, May 17, 1970, 36, and "New King of MGM's Jungle Cracking Whip," *Los Angeles Times*, February 15, 1970, Q1.

66. Gussow, "Movies Leaving 'Hollywood' Behind," 36.

67. Gene D. Phillips, *Godfather: The Intimate Francis Ford Coppola* (Lexington: University Press of Kentucky, 2004), 67.

68. Ibid., 90.

69. William Whittington, *Sound Design and Science Fiction* (Austin: University of Texas Press, 2007), 72–76.

70. Charles Champlin, "New World of Tyranny in 'THX,'" *Los Angeles Times*, March 11, 1971, F1.

71. Vincent Canby, "Wanda's a Wow, So's THX," *New York Times*, March 21, 1971, 11.

72. Philip Wuntch, "Screen: 'THX 1138' Takes Chilling Look at Future," *Dallas Morning News*, April 1, 1971, 23A.

73. Stanley Kauffmann, "THX 1138," *New Republic*, April 10, 1971, 31–32.

74. Murf., "THX 1138," *Variety*, March 17, 1971.

75. Dale Pollock, *Skywalking: The Life and Films of George Lucas*, updated ed. (New York: Da Capo, 1999), 97.

76. Michael Pye and Linda Myles, *The Movie Brats: How the Film Generation Took Over Hollywood* (New York: Holt, Reinhart and Winston 1979), 89.

77. "351 Films above $100,000 Gross," *Variety*, May 3, 1972, 32.

78. Cook, *Lost Illusions*, 303.

79. *Esquire*, April 1971.

80. "Teen Power Fading at B.O.," *Variety*, February 24, 1971, 1.

81. Noel King, "'The Last Good Time We Ever Had': Remembering the New Hollywood Cinema," in *The Last Great American Picture Show: New Hollywood Cinema in the 1970s*, ed. Thomas Elsaesser, Alexander Horwath, and Noel King (Amsterdam: Amsterdam University Press 2004), 100, 104.

82. Paul Burkhart Ramaeker, "A New Kind of Movie: Style and Form in Hollywood Cinema, 1965–1988" (PhD diss., University of Wisconsin-Madison, 2002), 141.

83. Robert B. Ray, *A Certain Tendency of the Hollywood Cinema, 1930–1980* (Princeton, NJ: Princeton University Press), 294.

84. David Bordwell, Janet Staiger, and Kristin Thompson, *The Classical*

Hollywood Cinema: Film Style and Mode of Production to 1960 (New York: Columbia University Press, 1985), 72–74.

85. Gerald Jonas, "S.F.," *New Yorker*, July 29, 1972, 36.

86. Helen Merrick, "Fiction, 1964-1979," in *The Routledge Companion to Science Fiction*, ed. Mark Bould et al. (New York: Routledge, 2011), 106.

87. John Maginnis, "Science Fiction Joins College Lists," *Dallas Morning News*, November 29, 1970, 16B.

88. Rob Latham, "The New Wave," in *A Companion to Science Fiction*, ed. David Seed (Malden, MA: Blackwell, 2005), 203–204.

89. Jonas, "S.F.," 44.

90. Ibid., 49.

91. Pressbook, *Slaughterhouse-Five* (1972), Margaret Herrick Library, AMPAS.

92. Charles Champlin, "Vonnegut Novel on the Screen," *Los Angeles Times*, March 24, 1972, G1.

93. Judith Crist, "Billy Pilgrim's Progress," *New York*, April 3, 1972, 59.

94. "Big Rental Films of 1972," *Variety*, January 3, 1973, 36.

95. Ray, *Certain Tendency*, 294.

96. Jan-Christopher Horak, *Saul Bass: Anatomy of Film Design* (Lexington: University Press of Kentucky, 2014), 351.

97. King, "'Last Good Time,'" 19–36.

98. Eric Schaefer, *"Bold! Daring! Shocking! True!" A History of Exploitation Films, 1919–1959* (Durham, NC: Duke University Press, 1999), 336.

99. Cook, *Lost Illusions*, 71.

100. Joan Hawkins, *Cutting Edge: Art-Horror and the Horrific Avant-Garde* (Minneapolis: University of Minnesota Press, 2000), 22.

101. Heffernan, *Ghouls, Gimmicks, and Gold*, 336.

102. Balio, *United Artists*, 313–314.

103. Ibid., 320.

104. Ibid., 325.

105. Budget July 12, 1974, United Artists Collection, Corporate Records — Accession, WCFTR.

106. Balio, *United Artists*, 325.

107. "Big Rental Films of 1973," *Variety*, January 9, 1974, 19.

108. Promo Sheet, United Artists Collection, Corporate Records — Accession, WCFTR.

109. Advertisement, *Variety*, May 21, 1975, 11–14.

110. Norman Jewison, audio commentary, *Rollerball* (Santa Monica, CA: MGM, 1998), DVD.

111. Barry Salt sampled a group of 101 films from 1970 to 1975 and came up with an average shot length of 7.0 seconds. Barry Salt, *Film Style and Technology* (London: Starwood, 1992), 283.

112. Kevin Kelly, "Rollerball at Cinema 57," *Boston Globe*, July 10, 1975, 50.

113. Dominique Pail Noth, "Rollerball Misses Out," *Milwaukee Journal*, July 11, 1975, 6.

114. Stephen Farber, "'Rollerball' in Retrospect," *Los Angeles Times*, August 17, 1975, 32.

115. Hollis Alpert, "Future Jack," *Saturday Review*, August 9, 1975.

116. Jan Dawson, "Caan-age," *Listener*, September 18, 1975, UA Collection, Corporate Records — Accession, WCFTR.

117. Pauline Kael, "A Clockwork Orange: Stanley Strangelove," *New Yorker*, January 1, 1972, 137, and Roger Ebert, "A Clockwork Orange," *Chicago Sun-Times*, February 11, 1972, http://rogerebert.suntimes.com/apps/pbcs.dll/article?AID=/19720211/REVIEWs/202110301/1023.

118. Janet Staiger, "The Cultural Productions of *A Clockwork Orange*," in *Stanley Kubrick's "A Clockwork Orange*," ed. Stuart Y. McDougal (Cambridge: Cambridge University Press, 2003), 37–60.

119. Cook, *Lost Illusions*, 271.

120. "A Newspaper Says No to 'Orange,'" *New York Times*, April 23, 1972, D11.

121. Ibid.

122. "Facesaver: Dr. Stern or Dr. Kubrick?," *Variety*, August 30, 1972, 4.

123. "Big Rental Films of 1972," *Variety*, January 3, 1973, 7.

124. Arthur Knight, "Knight at the Movies," *Hollywood Reporter*, June 27, 1975, UA Collection, Corporate Records — Accession, WCFTR.

125. "Appeal and Re-Appeal Fix R on 'Rollerball'; UA Chagrined," *Variety*, July 16, 1975, 5.

126. Philip Puntch, "Jewison Carries the Ball," *Dallas Morning News*, June 25, 1975, E14.

127. Ibid.

128. Charles Champlin, "'Rollerball' — Second Try for PG," *Los Angeles Times*, July 23, 1975, F15.

129. Arthur Krim to Richard Heffner, July 31, 1975, UA Collection, Corporate Records — Accession, WCFTR.

130. Richard Heffner to Norman Jewison, April 24, 1975, UA Collection, Corporate Records — Accession, WCFTR.

131. Champlin, "'Rollerball' — Second Try for PG," F15.

132. "'Rollerball' Still R," *Variety*, July 30, 1975, 4.

133. Champlin, "'Rollerball' — Second Try for PG," F15.

134. "Big Rental Films of 1975," *Variety*, January 7, 1976, 13.

135. Ibid.

136. Gary Arnold, "It's a Game, But Is It a Movie?," *Washington Post*, July 2, 1975, D1.

137. Murray Smith, "Gangsters, Cannibals, Aesthetes, or Apparently Perverse

Allegiances," in *Passionate Views: Film, Cognition, and Emotion*, ed. Carl Plantinga and Greg M. Smith (Baltimore: Johns Hopkins University Press, 1999), 217–238.

138. William Gildea, "'Rollerball' Get-Together: A Glimpse of the Future," *Washington Post*, June 20, 1975, B1, B3.

139. "Jewison's New 'Rollerball' Introduced on ABC Sports," *Boxoffice*, March 24, 1975, 7.

140. "'Rollerball' Touted in Sports Illustrated," *Boxoffice*, May 19, 1975, 25.

141. Advertisement, *Variety*, May 21, 1975, 11–14.

142. Pauline Kael, "*A Clockwork Orange*: Stanley Strangelove," *New Yorker*, January 1, 1972, 138.

143. William Hall, "Mankind Plays Out Its Option in 'Rollerball,'" *Los Angeles Times*, September 25, 1974, 26.

Chapter 5. Revenge of the Nerds: The Pulp SF Blockbuster, 1977–1982

1. For instance, Thomas Schatz, "The New Hollywood," in *Film Theory Goes to the Movies*, ed. Jim Collins, Hilary Radner, and Ava Preacher Collins (New York: Routledge, 1993), 17.

2. "Big Rental Films of 1975," *Variety*, January 7, 1976, 13.

3. Sheldon Hall and Steve Neale, *Epics, Spectaculars, and Blockbusters: A Hollywood History* (Detroit: Wayne State University Press, 2010), 210–212.

4. "Saturation for 'Westworld' Hits 845G in 5 Days," *Variety*, October 10, 1973, 7.

5. Cook, *Lost Illusions*, 42–43.

6. Gomery, *Hollywood Studio System*, 213.

7. Cook, *Lost Illusions*, 42.

8. "Big Rental Films of 1970," *Variety*, January 6, 1971, 11.

9. "'King Kong' Is Launched in over 1,000 Locations," *Boxoffice*, January 3, 1977, 3.

10. Richard Eder, "At the Movies," *New York Times* December 24, 1976, 40; Lee Grant, "Biggest Bite: Ape or Shark?," *Los Angeles Times*, December 27, 1976, E12.

11. "G&W Disappointed by B.O. Action of 'Kong,' 'Marathon,'" *Variety*, February 9, 1977, 3.

12. "'Kong,' in 984, $35,105,052," *Variety*, January 12, 1977, 5.

13. Carl Gottlieb, *The "Jaws" Log* (New York: New Market Press, 2001), 53.

14. "1956–1987 Big-Buck Scorecard," *Variety*, January 20, 1988, 64.

15. Jeffrey Kaye, "Epic Price Tags for Epic Films," *Washington Post*, November 18, 1979, G1.

16. Ralph Kaminsky, "Media Event Boosts 'Meteor,'" *Boxoffice*, October 29, 1979, 1.

17. "Big Rental Films of 1979," *Variety*, January 9, 1980, 70.

18. Aljean Harmetz, "Disaster Strikes Disaster Films," *New York Times*, December 26, 1979, C21.

19. Frederick S. Clarke, Steve Rubin, and Wallace A. Wyss, "Production," *Cinefantastique* 5, no. 2 (Fall 1976): 20.

20. Ibid., 20–21.

21. Gene Siskel, "'Logan's Run' Takes a Wrong, Winding Road," *Chicago Tribune*, June 28, 1976, D4.

22. "Logan's Run," *Cinefantastique* 5, no. 2 (Fall 1976): 4.

23. "Whitlock, Taylor Join Danforth in Exile over 'Kong' Award," *Variety*, April 20, 1977, 30.

24. Rinzler, *Making of "Star Wars,"* 12.

25. Ibid., 83.

26. Ibid., 82, 93.

27. Ibid., 84.

28. Pollock, *Skywalking*, 184; Solomon, *Twentieth Century-Fox*, 301.

29. Sheldon Hall, "Blockbusters in the 1970s," in *Contemporary American Cinema*, ed. Linda Ruth Williams and Michael Hammon (London: McGraw-Hill, 2006), 165.

30. Pollock, *Skywalking*, 184.

31. A. D. Murphy, "'Star Wars' Best Start since 'Jaws,'" *Variety* June 1, 1977, 1; Rinzler, *Making of "Star Wars,"* 284. Aubrey Solomon argues that the more limited initial release actually helped *Star Wars* at the box office, as media reports of the long lines of patrons waiting to see the film helped give it an "event" status. Solomon, *Twentieth Century-Fox*, 180–181.

32. "Big Rental Films of 1977," *Variety*, January 4, 1978, 21, and "Big Rental Films of 1978," *Variety*, January 3, 1979, 17.

33. Joseph McBride, *Steven Spielberg: A Biography*, 2nd ed. (Jackson: University Press of Mississippi, 2010), 287.

34. Douglas Trumbull claims that the true cost of the special effects ($3.3 million) was withheld from Columbia until the production was well under way. McBride, *Steven Spielberg*, 273.

35. Ibid., 271, 273.

36. Frank Segers, "Levy Foresees $24-Mil Guarantees for Columbia's Close Encounters," *Variety*, July 13, 1977, 4; McBride, *Steven Spielberg*, 270–271.

37. Segers, "Levy Foresees," 4.

38. "Big Rental Films of 1977," *Variety*, January 4, 1978, 21; "Big Rental Films of 1978," *Variety*, January 3, 1979, 17. "Big Rental Films of 1980," *Variety*, January 14, 1981, 29.

39. Murphy, "'Star Wars' Best Start," 6. After Fox had made its various deductions, Lucas was left with approximately $40 million. See Pollock, *Skywalking*, 188.

40. Pollock, *Skywalking*, 188.

41. Solomon, *Twentieth Century-Fox*, 181. Notoriously, Fox signed away all sequel and merchandising rights to Lucas in his 1976 contract; when it came time to

negotiate a new deal for the first sequel, *The Empire Strikes Back*, Lucas demanded (and received) 77 percent of the net profits. Pollock, *Skywalking*, 199.

42. Quoted in Gregg Kilday, "'Close Encounters': Go or No Go?," *Los Angeles Times*, November 5, 1977, B9.

43. "'Close Encounters' Sends Columbia Profits into Orbit," *Los Angeles Times*, May 12, 1978, H18.

44. Sally Kline, ed. *George Lucas Interviews* (Jackson: University Press of Mississippi, 1999), 102.

45. Pollock, *Skywalking*, 17–18.

46. Quoted in David J. Skal, *The Monster Show: A Cultural History of Horror* (New York: Penguin Books, 1993), 272.

47. McBride, *Steven Spielberg*, 262.

48. Chuck Kleinhans, "Taking Out the Trash: Camp and the Politics of Parody," in *The Politics and Poetics of Camp*, ed. Moe Meyer (London: Routledge, 2004), 186.

49. Susan Sontag, "Notes on 'Camp,'" in *The Cult Film Reader*, ed. Ernest Mathijs and Xavier Mendik (Berkshire, UK: Open University Press, 2008), 47.

50. Ibid., 43, 48.

51. This camp response was about more than simply mocking comic-book tropes. Matt Yockey argues that the camp hyperbole of *Batman* provided a space for audiences to deal with their ambivalence about postwar American culture. Matt Yockey, *Batman* (Detroit: Wayne State University Press, 2014).

52. Sasha Torres, "The Caped Crusader of Camp: Pop, Camp, and the Batman Television Series," in *Camp — Queer Aesthetics and the Performing Subject: A Reader*, ed. Fabio Cleto (Ann Arbor: University of Michigan Press, 1999), 334–335.

53. Andrew Ross, "Uses of Camp," in *The Cult Film Reader*, ed. Ernest Methijs and Xavier Mendik (Berkshire, UK: Open University Press, 2008), 58.

54. Dan Bates, "Barbarella," *Film Quarterly* 22, no. 3 (Spring 1969): 58.

55. Murf., "Barbarella," *Variety*, October 9, 1968, 6.

56. Charles Champlin, "'Barbarella' — a Spicy Space Oddity Starring Jane Fonda," *Los Angeles Times*, October 6, 1968, S16.

57. Quoted in Steven Paul Davies, *Get Carter and Beyond: The Cinema of Mike Hodges* (London: Batsford Books, 2002), 102.

58. "KCOP Goes Camp via 'Flash' and 'Buck' Serials and Pics," *Variety*, February 16, 1966, 34.

59. Ken Feil, *Dying for a Laugh: Disaster Movies and the Camp Imagination* (Middletown, CT: Wesleyan University Press, 2005), 46.

60. Ibid., 97.

61. "Big Rental Films of 1980," *Variety*, January 14, 1981, 29.

62. Feil, *Dying for a Laugh*, 97.

63. Ibid., xxv.

64. Ray, *Certain Tendency*, 367.

65. Quoted in Grant, "'Star Wars' out of This World," B8. This atmosphere was reproduced twenty years later when the original *Star Wars* trilogy was reissued to theaters. The extremely successful rerelease (the first film was the eighth-highest-grossing film of 1997) was propelled in part by nostalgia. But the reissue was not a camp revival, as when the Batman serials were shown to laughing audiences in the mid-1960s. On the contrary, Lucas discouraged a camp response by using computer-generated imagery to update the special effects of each film to conform to contemporary standards.

66. Pollock, *Skywalking*, 164.

67. Vincent Canby, "'Star Wars'—a Trip to a Far Galaxy That's Fun and Funny," *New York Times*, May 26, 1977, 66.

68. Stanley Kauffmann, "Innocences," *New Republic*, June 18, 1977, 22.

69. Julie A. Turnock, *Plastic Reality: Special Effects, Technology, and the Emergence of 1970s Blockbuster Aesthetics* (New York: Columbia University Press, 2015), 49–50, 167.

70. Ibid., 220.

71. Ibid., 130, 139–140.

72. Rinzler, *Making of "Star Wars,"* 74.

73. For a scholarly study of world-building across media see Mark J. P. Wolf, *Building Imaginary Worlds: The Theory and History of Subcreation* (New York: Routledge, 2012).

74. David Seed, "Introduction: Approaching Science Fiction," in *A Companion to Science Fiction*, ed. Seed (Malden, MA: Blackwell, 2005), 4.

75. Gary Westfahl, "Hard Science Fiction," in Seed, *Companion to Science Fiction*, 194–195.

76. Quoted in Kline, *George Lucas Interviews*, 48.

77. For an analysis of the "richly realized world" of Peter Jackson's *Lord of the Rings* trilogy, which is rooted in nearly subliminal levels of detail, see Kristin Thompson, *The Frodo Franchise: The Lord of the Rings and Modern Hollywood* (Berkeley: University of California Press, 2007), 92.

78. Charles Champlin, "Futurist Film's Tricks to Treat the Eye," *Los Angeles Times*, June 20, 1976, K1.

79. Rinzler, *Making of "Star Wars,"* 65.

80. Ibid., 99.

81. Henry Ladson, "Alien," *Cineaste* 9, no. 4 (Fall 1979): 46.

82. David Baron, "Excess Violence Only One of Flaws of 'Blade Runner,'" *New Orleans Times-Picayune*, June 29, 1982, 4–6.

83. Pauline Kael, "Baby, the Rain Must Fall," *New Yorker*, July 12, 1982, 82, 84–85.

84. Tom Figenshu, "Screams of a Summer Night," *Film Comment* 15, no. 5 (September–October 1979): 53.

85. Janet Maslin, "What's Happened to Movies That You See for Fun?," *New York Times*, June 8, 1979, C8.

86. David Denby, "High Tech Blob," *New York*, June 4, 1979, 71.

87. Richard Martin, "An Evil Movie," *Los Angeles Times*, July 15, 1979, O2.

88. David Denby, "Battle of the Stereotypes," *New York*, June 28, 1982, 53.

89. Stephen Prince, *A New Pot of Gold: Hollywood under the Electronic Rainbow, 1980–1989* (Berkeley: University of California Press, 2000), 352.

90. Elliot Stein, "Have Horror Films Gone Too Far?," *New York Times*, June 20, 1982, H1.

91. Pauline Kael, "Why Are Movies So Bad? Or, the Numbers," *New Yorker*, June 23, 1980, 93.

92. William Paul, *Laughing Screaming: Modern Hollywood Horror and Comedy* (New York: Columbia University Press, 1994), 10.

93. Ibid., 32–33.

94. Aljean Harmetz, "Fox's 'Alien' Grosses $4.7 Million in Its First Week," *New York Times*, June 2, 1979, 12.

95. "Big Rental Films of 1979," *Variety*, January 9, 1980, 21.

96. "'Alien' Film Earns Profit of $4 Million, Fox Reports," *Los Angeles Times*, August 10, 1980, R29.

97. "Big Rental Films of 1982," *Variety*, January 12, 1983, 13.

98. Quoted in David J. Hogan, "I Don't Know What It Is, But It's Weird and Pissed Off," *Cinefantastique* 13, nos. 2/3 (November–December, 1982), 74.

99. Dale Pollock, "Carpenter: Doing His 'Thing' Despite Critics," *Los Angeles Times*, July 9, 1982, G8.

100. "1956–1987 Big-Buck Scorecard," *Variety*, January 20, 1988, 62, 64.

101. Lawrence Cohn, "Gore Perpetual Fave of Young Film Fans," *Variety*, August 26, 1981, 42.

102. Kevin Thomas, "Well-Made But Routine 'Galaxy,'" *Los Angeles Times*, October 19, 1981, G5.

103. Christopher T. Koetting, *Mind Warp! The Fantastic True Story of Roger Corman's New World Pictures* (Baltimore: Midnight Marquee Press, 2003), 194.

104. "Big Rental Films of 1981," *Variety*, January 13, 1982, 42.

105. Murf., "Star Wars," *Variety*, May 25, 1977.

106. Jack Kroll, "Fun in Space," *Newsweek*, May 30, 1977, 60.

107. Pete Hamill, "'Star Wars'—Dumb Good Times Here Again?," *Chicago Tribune*, June 8, 1977, A13.

108. "Star Wars: The Year's Best Movie," *Time*, May 30, 1977, 57.

109. Quoted in Kline, *George Lucas Interviews*, 53.

110. Quoted in Donald Goddard, "From 'American Graffiti' to Outer Space," *New York Times*, September 12, 1976, 89.

111. Quoted in Kline, *George Lucas Interviews*, 48.

112. Gary Arnold, "Star Wars: A Spectacular Intergalactic Joyride," *Washington Post*, May 25, 1977, B1.

113. Charles Champlin, "Futurist Film's Tricks to Treat the Eye," *Los Angeles Times*, June 20, 1976, K1.

114. Philip Wuntch, "'Star Wars' Pure Adventure," *Dallas Morning News*, May 26, 1977, 51.

115. John Simon, "Star Dust," *New York*, June 20, 1977, 71.

116. Pauline Kael, "Contrasts," *New Yorker*, September 26, 1977, 123.

117. Kauffmann, "Innocences," 22.

118. Jonathan Rosenbaum, "The Solitary Pleasures of Star Wars," *Sight & Sound* 46 (Autumn 1977): 209.

119. See Robin Wood, *Hollywood from Vietnam to Reagan* (New York: Columbia University Press, 1986), 162–174.

120. Ruth McCormick, "Star Wars," *Cineaste* 8, no. 3 (1978): 60.

121. Andrew Gordon, "Star Wars: A Myth for Our Time," *Literature/Film Quarterly* 6, no. 4 (Fall 1978): 314.

122. Quoted in Kline, *George Lucas Interviews*, 53.

123. Joanne Waterman Williams, "George Lucas Believes in the Force of Myths, Fairy Tales," *Chicago Sun-Times*, May 18, 1980.

124. Gordon, "Star Wars: A Myth," 325.

125. "'Star Wars' Shunned G Rating as 'Uncool' for Young Crowd," *Variety*, June 1, 1977, 6.

126. Peter Krämer, "'The Best Disney Film Disney Never Made': Children's Films and the Family Audience in American Cinema since the 1960s," in *Genre and Contemporary Hollywood*, ed. Steve Neale (London: British Film Institute, 2002), 192.

127. Peter Krämer, "Disney and Family Entertainment," in *Contemporary American Cinema*, ed. Linda Ruth Williams and Michael Hammond (Berkshire, UK: Open University, 2006), 266.

128. Charles Champlin, "Disney Aims for the Stars," *Los Angeles Times*, October 13, 1978, C1.

129. Sally Ogle Davis, "Wishing upon a Falling Star at Disney," *New York Times*, November 16, 1980, 36.

130. "Big Rental Films of 1980," *Variety*, January 14, 1981, 29.

131. "1956–87 Big-Buck Scorecard," *Variety*, January 20, 1988, 62.

132. Kathryn Harris, "Disney Net Off 25% in Quarter, Blames 'Tron,'" *Los Angeles Times*, November 5, 1982, G1.

133. Deborah Caulfield, "'E.T.' Gossip: The One That Got Away?," *Los Angeles Times*, July 18, 1982, K3.

134. David Sterritt, "Two More Films from Spielberg, a One-Man Fantasy Factory," *Christian Science Monitor*, June 3, 1982, http://www.csmonitor.com/1982/0603/060300.html.

135. "E.T. Smashes Box Office Records in First Month," *Washington Post*, July 13, 1982, C4.

136. Robert Metz, "What 'E.T.' Does for MCA," *New York Times*, November 5, 1982, D6.

137. Richard Corliss, "Steve's Summer Magic," *Time*, May 31, 1982.

138. David Denby, "The Visionary Gleam," *New York*, June 14, 1982, 73–75.

139. Pauline Kael, "The Pure and the Impure," *New Yorker*, June 14, 1982, 119, 122.

140. Bryce Nelson, "The Alien Already Here: Insights into E.T.'s Power," *New York Times*, December 21, 1982, C1, C4.

141. Wayne Maser, "The Long Voyage Home: Steven Spielberg's Film, *Schindler's List*," *Harper's Bazaar*, February 1994.

142. Cook, *Lost Illusions*, 51.

143. Stephen J. Sansweet, *"Star Wars": From Concept to Screen to Collectible* (San Francisco: Chronicle Books, 1992), 62.

144. Rinzler, *Making of "The Empire Strikes Back,"* 90.

145. "Spielberg's 'E.T.' Out in June with 11 Kiddie Licensing Deals Tied In," *Variety*, April 7, 1982, 26.

146. Advertisement, *Variety*, May 26, 1982, 21.

147. "MCA Ties 43 Licensors to 'E.T.,'" *Variety*, August 11, 1982, 4.

148. Ibid., 28.

149. Quoted in McBride, *Steven Spielberg*, 334.

150. Sheila Benson, "A Year of Cheers and the Cheerless," *Los Angeles Times*, January 2, 1983, N3.

151. Lee Beaupre and Anne Thompson, "Industry," *Film Comment* 19, no. 2 (March/April 1983): 63.

152. Dale Pollock, "Spielberg Philosophical over 'E.T.' Oscar Defeat," *Los Angeles Times*, April 13, 1983, K1.

Conclusion. SF Film Today

1. "Big Rental Films of '86," Variety, January 14, 1987, 25.

2. James Kendrick, *Hollywood Bloodshed: Violence in 1980s American Cinema* (Carbondale: Southern Illinois University Press, 2009), 198–199.

3. Ibid., 171, 200.

4. "Box Office Mojo," http://www.boxofficemojo.com/movies/?id=jurassicpark.htm.

5. Quoted in Scott Tobias, "Shane Carruth," *A.V. Club*, October 27, 2004, http://www.avclub.com/article/shane-carruth-13898.

6. Quoted in Lane Brown, "Shane Carruth Explains His Cultural Influences," *Vulture*, April 7, 2013, http://www.vulture.com/2013/04/shane-carruth-explains-his-cultural-influences.html.

7. Gary Wolf, "We've Created a Monster!," *Wired*, October 2004, http://www.wired.com/wired/archive/12.10/scifi.html.

8. Yvonne Villarreal, "'Sharknado 2' Nabs 3.9 Million Viewers, Millions More Than Original," *Los Angeles Times*, July 31, 2014, http://touch.latimes.com/#section/-1/article/p2p-80958040/.

9. Quoted in John Seabrook, "Letter from Skywalker Ranch: Why Is the Force Still with Us?," *New Yorker*, January 6, 1997, 46.

10. Peter Keough, "A Loud Explosion of CGI in 'Transformers: Age of Extinction,'" *Boston Globe*, June 27, 2014, http://www.bostonglobe.com/arts/movies/2014/06/27/transformers-age-extinction-review-loud-explosion-cgi/tZIusWCujRuQgQGRUHZh9j/story.html.

11. Steve Rose, "The U.S. Military Storm Hollywood," *Guardian*, July 6, 2009, http://www.theguardian.com/film/2009/jul/06/us-military-hollywood.

12. Mary Pols, "*Transformers: Revenge of the Fallen* Falls Short," *Time*, June 29, 2009, http://content.time.com/time/arts/article/0,8599,1906689,00.html.

13. Charles Taylor, "Has George Lucas Ruined Hollywood Movies?," *Houston Chronicle*, June 10, 2005, http://www.chron.com/entertainment/movies/article/Has-George-Lucas-ruined-Hollywood-movies-1931706.php.

14. Lewis Beale, "How 'Star Wars' Ruined Sci-Fi," CNN.com, May 5, 2014, http://www.cnn.com/2014/05/02/opinion/beale-star-wars/.

15. Thomas Schatz, "New Hollywood, New Milennium," in *Film Theory and Contemporary Hollywood Movies*, ed. Warren Buckland (New York: Routledge, 2009), 30.

16. Michael V. Copland, "Tell Jabba I've Got His Money," *Wired*, May 25, 2012, http://www.wired.com/2012/05/tell-jabba-ive-got-his-money-star-wars-revenue-throughout-our-galaxy/.

17. Marc Graser, "Disney Buys LucasFilm, New 'Star Wars' Planned," *Variety*, October 30, 2012.

18. Quoted in Tara Lachapelle and Christopher Palmieri, "Disney's Marvel-Like Lucasfilm Deal Sees Many Avengers," *Bloomberg*, November 1, 2012, http://www.bloomberg.com/news/2012-11-01/disney-s-marvel-like-lucasfilm-deal-sees-many-avengers.html.

19. Kamila Kocialkowska, "Star Wars: A Sale or a Sell-Out?," *New Statesman*, October 31, 2012, http://www.newstatesman.com/culture/culture/2012/10/star-wars-sale-or-sell-out.

20. Peter Travers, "The Avengers," *Rolling Stone*, April 30, 2012, http://www.rollingstone.com/movies/reviews/the-avengers-20120430.

21. For an analysis of how Marvel's synergistic strategies work on the level of marketing and merchandising as well as film and transmedia production, see Matthias Stork, "Assembling the Avengers: Reframing the Superhero Movie through Marvel's Cinematic Universe," in *Superhero Synergies: Comic Book*

Characters Go Digital, ed. James N. Gilmore and Matthias Stork (Lanham, MD: Rowman & Littlefield, 2014), 77–96.

22. Wesley Morris, "I Feel Groot!," *Grantland*, August 1, 2014, http://grantland.com/features/guardians-of-the-galaxy-get-on-up-review/.

23. Rebecca Keegan, "How Much Did *Avatar* Really Cost?," *Vanity Fair*, December 22, 2009, http://www.vanityfair.com/online/oscars/2009/12/how-much-did-avatar-really-cost.html.

24. Patrick Frater, "Sony to Release Jackson's 'District,'" *Variety*, November 4, 2007, http://www.variety.com/article/VR1117975365.html?categoryid=13&cs=1.

25. "Avatar," *Box Office Mojo*, http://www.boxofficemojo.com/movies/?id=avatar.htm.

26. "District 9," *Box Office Mojo*, http://boxofficemojo.com/movies/?id=district9.htm.

27. Adam B. Vary, "Out of this World!," *Entertainment Weekly*, August 13, 2009, http://www.ew.com/ew/article/0,,20297858,00.html.

28. Quoted in Gavin Smith, "Interview: Alfonso Cuarón," *Film Comment*, February 27, 2014, http://www.filmcomment.com/entry/interview-alfonso-cuaron.

29. Quoted in Dan P. Lee, "Alfonso Cuaron on Making Gravity," *Vulture*, September 22, 2013, http://www.vulture.com/2013/09/director-alfonso-cuaron-on-making-gravity.html.

30. Quoted in Devin Feraci, "Alfonso Cuaron Talks Putting Science Back in SciFi with Gravity," *Badass Digest*, September 30, 2013, http://badassdigest.com/2013/09/30/alfonso-cuaron-talks-putting-science-back-in-scifi-with-gravity/.

31. Andrew Harrison, "Rise of the New Geeks: How the Outsiders Won," *Guardian*, September 2, 2013, http://www.theguardian.com/fashion/2013/sep/02/rise-geeks-outsiders-superhero-movies-dork.

32. Jared Cornelius, "We Won the Culture War: Celebrating the Reach of Fandom," *Bleeding Cool*, May 6, 2014, http://www.bleedingcool.com/2014/05/06/we-won-the-culture-war-celebrating-the-reach-of-fandom/.

Selected Bibliography

Periodicals

Billboard, 1955
Boxoffice, 1952–1953, 1968, 1975–1977
Business Week, 1973
Chicago Sun-Times, 1972, 1980
Chicago Tribune, 1955, 1959, 1968, 1974–1976
Cinefantastique, 1972–1982
Cleveland Plain Dealer, 1968
Dallas Morning News, 1967, 1970, 1975, 1977
Esquire, 1971
Fantasy & Science Fiction, 1968
Galaxy, 1968
Harper's, 1969
Hollywood Reporter, 1950–1955
Life, 1949, 1952
Little Shop of Horrors, 2011, 2013
Los Angeles Times, 1946–1983, 1986, 1990
Milwaukee Journal, 1975
Motion Picture Herald, 1946–1957, 1967–1968
New Orleans Times-Picayune, 1951
New Republic, 1949, 1968, 1977
New York, 1968, 1972, 1977, 1979, 1982
New York Times, 1946–1983
New Yorker, 1968, 1972, 1974, 1980, 1982
Newsweek, 1977
Oregonian (Portland, OR), 1972
Photon, 1974
Popular Mechanics, 1950, 1967
Psychology Today, 1968
Saturday Evening Post, 1949
Saturday Review, 1975
Screen Guide, 1950
Spokane Daily Chronicle, 1968
Time, 1977
Variety, 1936, 1938, 1946, 1949–1983
Washington Post, 1950, 1975, 1977

Books and Journal Articles

Agel, Jerome. *The Making of Kubrick's "2001."* New York: Signet, 1970.

Allen, Robert C., and Douglas Gomery. *Film History: Theory and Practice*. New York: McGraw-Hill, 1985.

Altman, Rick. *Film/Genre*. London: British Film Institute, 1999.

———. "A Semantic/Syntactic Approach to Film Genre." In *Film Genre Reader III*, edited by Barry Keith Grant, 27–41. Austin: University of Texas Press, 2003.

"Appendix: RKO Financial Data." *Historical Journal of Film, Radio and Television* 14, no. 1 (1994): microfiche supplement.

Arkoff, Sam, with Richard Trubo. *Flying through Hollywood by the Seat of My Pants*. New York: Birch Lane Press, 1992.

Ashley, Mike. *The Time Machines: The Story of the Science-Fiction Pulp Magazines from the Beginning to 1950*. Liverpool: Liverpool University Press, 2000.

———. *Transformations: The Story of the Science-Fiction Magazines from 1950 to 1970*. Liverpool: Liverpool University Press, 2005.

Balio, Tino. "Introduction to Part I." In *Hollywood in the Age of Television*, edited by Tino Balio, 3–40. Cambridge, MA: Unwin Hyman, 1990.

———. *United Artists: The Company That Changed the Film Industry*. Madison: University of Wisconsin Press, 1987.

Ballard, J. G. "Which Way to Inner Space?" In *A User's Guide to the Millennium: Essays and Reviews*, 195–198. London: Harper Collins, 1996.

Barshay, Robert. "Ethnic Stereotypes in *Flash Gordon*." *Journal of Popular Film* 3, no. 1 (1974): 15–30.

Bart, Peter. *Fade Out: The Calamitous Final Days of MGM*. New York: Anchor Books, 1990.

Bates, Dan. "Barbarella." *Film Quarterly* 22, no. 3 (Spring 1969): 58.

Baxter, John. *Science Fiction in the Cinema*. New York: Paperback Library, 1970.

Beaupre, Lee, and Anne Thompson. "Industry." *Film Comment* 19, no. 2 (March/April 1983): 62–80.

Behlmer, Rudy, ed. *Memo from Darryl F. Zanuck: The Golden Years at Twentieth Century-Fox*. New York: Grove Press, 1993.

Belton, John. "Glorious Technicolor, Breathtaking CinemaScope, and Stereophonic Sound." In *Hollywood in the Age of Television*, edited by Tino Balio, 185–212. Boston: Unwin Hyman, 1990.

Bernstein, Matthew. *Walter Wanger, Hollywood Independent*. Berkeley: University of California Press, 1994.

Biskind, Peter. *Seeing Is Believing: How Hollywood Taught Us to Stop Worrying and Love the Fifties*. New York: Owl Books, 2000.

Boorman, John. *Adventures of a Suburban Boy*. London: Faber & Faber, 2003.

Bordwell, David. *Making Meaning: Inference and Rhetoric in the Interpretation of Cinema*. Cambridge, MA: Harvard University Press, 1989.

———. *Narration in the Fiction Film*. Madison: University of Wisconsin Press, 1985.

———. *Poetics of Cinema*. New York: Routledge, 2008.

Bordwell, David, Janet Staiger, and Kristin Thompson. *The Classical Hollywood Cinema: Film Style and Mode of Production to 1960*. New York: Columbia University Press, 1985.

Borneman, Ernest. "United States versus Hollywood: The Case Study of an Antitrust Suit." In *The American Film Industry*, rev. ed., edited by Tino Balio, 449–462. Madison: University of Wisconsin Press, 1985.

Boyer, Paul S. "Sixty Years and Counting: Nuclear Themes in American Culture, 1945 to the Present." In *The Atomic Bomb and American Society: New Perspectives*, edited by Rosemary B. Mariner and G. Kurt Piehler, 3–18. Knoxville: University of Tennessee Press, 2009.

Bradbury, Ray. "Space Odyssey 2001." *Psychology Today* 2, no. 1 (June 1968): 10.

Brosnan, John, Kim Newman, and Peter Nicholls. "Irwin Allen." In *The Encyclopedia of Science Fiction*, edited by John Clute and Peter Nicholls, 20. New York: St. Martin's Griffin, 1995.
Brown, Fredric. *The Office*. New York: Dutton, 1958.
Casper, Drew. *Postwar Hollywood: 1946–1962*. Malden, MA: Blackwell, 2007.
Cawelti, John G. "*Chinatown* and Generic Transformation in Recent American Films." In *Film Genre Reader III*, edited by Barry Keith Grant, 243–261. Austin: University of Texas Press, 2003.
Chapman, James, and Nicholas J. Cull. *Projecting Tomorrow: Science Fiction and Popular Cinema*. New York: IB Tauris, 2013.
Church, David. "From Exhibition to Genre: The Case of Grind-House Films." *Cinema Journal* 50, no. 4 (Summer 2011): 1–25.
Clarens, Carlos. *An Illustrated History of Horror and Science-Fiction Films*. New York: Da Capo, 1997.
Clarke, Arthur C. *The Lost Worlds of 2001*. New York: Signet, 1972.
Cook, David A. *Lost Illusions: American Cinema in the Shadow of Watergate and Vietnam, 1970–1979*. Berkeley: University of California Press, 2000.
Corman, Roger, with Jim Jerome. *How I Made a Hundred Movies in Hollywood and Never Lost a Dime*. New York: Delta Books, 1990.
Davies, Steven Paul. *Get Carter and Beyond: The Cinema of Mike Hodges*. London: Batsford Books, 2002.
Davis, Blair. *The Battle for the Bs: 1950s Hollywood and the Rebirth of Low-Budget Cinema*. New Brunswick, NJ: Rutgers University Press, 2012.
Dean, Joan F. "Between 2001 and *Star Wars*." *Journal of Popular Film and Television* 7, no. 1 (1978): 32–41.
Dick, Bernard F. *City of Dreams: The Making and Remaking of Universal Pictures*. Lexington: University Press of Kentucky, 1997.
———. *The Merchant Prince of Poverty Row: Harry Cohn of Columbia Pictures*. Lexington: University Press of Kentucky, 1993.
Dille, Robert C., ed. *The Collected Works of Buck Rogers in the 25th Century*. New York: Chelsea Books, 1969.
Doherty, Thomas. *Teenagers and Teenpics: The Juvenilization of American Movies in the 1950s*. Rev. ed. Philadelphia: Temple University Press, 2002.
Dombrowski, Lisa. *The Films of Samuel Fuller: If You Die, I'll Kill You!* Middletown, CT: Wesleyan University Press, 2008.
Durgnat, Raymond. *Films and Feelings*. Cambridge, MA: MIT Press, 1971.
Eames, John Douglas. *The MGM Story*. New York: Crown, 1975.
Eisenstein, Sergei. *The Film Sense*. San Diego: Harcourt Brace, 1947.
Eller, Jonathan. "Bradbury's Web of Fear: The Lost Metaphor behind the Screen Treatment." In *It Came from Outer Space*, edited by Donn Albright, 27–41. Colorado Springs, CO: Gauntlet, 2004.

Feil, Ken. *Dying for a Laugh: Disaster Movies and the Camp Imagination*. Middletown, CT: Wesleyan University Press, 2005.

Figenshu, Tom. "Screams of a Summer Night." *Film Comment* 15, no. 5 (September–October 1979): 49–53.

Finler, Joel W. *The Hollywood Story*. London: Wallflower, 2003.

Gallagher, Tag. "Shoot-Out at the Genre Corral: Problems in the 'Evolution' of the Western." In *Film Genre Reader III*, edited by Barry Keith Grant, 262–276. Austin: University of Texas Press, 2003.

Geduld, Carolyn. *Filmguide to "2001: A Space Odyssey."* Bloomington: Indiana University Press, 1973.

Gomery, Douglas. *The Hollywood Studio System: A History*. London: British Film Institute, 2005.

Gottlieb, Carl. *The "Jaws" Log*. New York: New Market Press, 2001.

Greene, Eric. *"Planet of the Apes" as American Myth: Race and Politics in the Films and Television Series*. Jefferson, NC: McFarland, 1996.

Gregory, Charles T. "The Pod Society versus the Rugged Individualists." *Journal of Popular Film* 1, no. 1 (1972): 2–14.

Gunn, James E. *The Road to Science Fiction: From Wells to Heinlein*. Lanham, MD: Scarecrow Press, 2002.

Hall, Sheldon, and Steve Neale. *Epics, Spectaculars, and Blockbusters: A Hollywood History*. Detroit: Wayne State University Press, 2010.

Harryhausen, Ray, and Tony Dalton. *Ray Harryhausen: An Animated Life*. New York: Billboard Books, 2003.

Hartwell, David G., and Kathyrn Cramer, eds. *The Space Opera Renaissance*. New York: Orb Books, 2007.

Hawkins, Joan. *Cutting Edge: Art-Horror and the Horrific Avant-Garde*. Minneapolis: University of Minnesota Press, 2000.

Heffernan, Kevin. *Ghouls, Gimmicks, and Gold: Horror Films and the American Movie Business, 1953–1968*. Durham, NC: Duke University Press, 2004.

Heinlein, Robert A. "Shooting *Destination Moon*." In *Focus on the Science Fiction Film*, edited by William Johnson, 52–65. Englewood Cliffs, NJ: Prentice Hall, 1972.

Hendershot, Cyndy. *Paranoia, the Bomb, and 1950s Science Fiction Films*. Bowling Green, KY: Bowling Green University Press, 2000.

Hickman, Gail Morgan. *The Films of George Pal*. Cranbury, NJ: A. S. Barnes, 1977.

Hirschhorn, Clive. *The Columbia Story*. New York: Crown, 1989.

———. *The Universal Story*. New York: Crown, 1983.

Hoberman, J. Introduction to *An Illustrated History of Horror and Science-Fiction Films*, by Carlos Clarens, vii–xi. New York: Da Capo, 1997.

Hodgens, Richard. "A Brief, Tragical History of the Science Fiction Film." Film Quarterly 13, no. 2 (Winter 1959): 30–39.

Horak, Jan-Christopher. *Saul Bass: Anatomy of Film Design*. Lexington: University Press of Kentucky, 2014.

Hunter, Tim, with Stephen Kaplan and Peter Jaszi. "2001: A Space Odyssey." In *The Making of "2001: A Space Odyssey,"* edited by Stephanie Schwam, 151–158. New York: Modern Library, 2000.

Jacobs, Lea. *The Decline of Sentiment: American Film in the 1920s*. Berkeley: University of California Press, 2008.

Jameson, Fredric. "History and the Death Wish: *Zardoz* as Open Form." *Jump Cut* 3 (1974). http://www.ejumpcut.org/archive/onlinessays/JC03folder/ZardozJameson.html.

Jewell, Richard B. *The Golden Age of Cinema: Hollywood 1929–1945*. Malden, MA: Blackwell, 2007.

Johnson, Gary. "The Serials: An Introduction." *Images: A Journal of Film and Popular Culture*. http://www.imagesjournal.com/issue04/infocus/introduction5.htm.

Johnson, William. "Journey into Science Fiction." In *Focus on the Science Fiction Film*, edited by William Johnson, 1–12. Englewood Cliffs, NJ: Prentice Hall, 1972.

Keane, Stephen. *Disaster Movies: The Cinema of Catastrophe*. London: Wallflower, 2001.

Kendrick, James. *Hollywood Bloodshed: Violence in 1980s American Cinema*. Carbondale: Southern Illinois University Press, 2009.

Kinder, Marsha. "Zardoz." *Film Quarterly* 27, no. 4 (Summer 1974): 49–57.

King, Noel. "'The Last Good Time We Ever Had': Remembering the New Hollywood Cinema." In *The Last Great American Picture Show: New Hollywood Cinema in the 1970s*, edited by Thomas Elsaesser, Alexander Horwath, and Noel King, 19–36. Amsterdam: Amsterdam University Press, 2004.

Kinnard, Roy. "The Flash Gordon Serials." *Films in Review* 39, no. 4 (April 1988): 195–203.

Kinsey, Wayne. *Hammer Films: The Elstree Studio Years*. Sheffield, UK: Tomahawk, 2007.

Klein, Amanda Ann. *American Film Cycles: Reframing Genres, Screening Social Problems, and Defining Subcultures*. Austin: University of Texas Press, 2011.

Kleinhans, Chuck. "Taking Out the Trash: Camp and the Politics of Parody." In *The Politics and Poetics of Camp*, edited by Moe Meyer, 182–201. London: Routledge, 2004.

Klinger, Barbara. *Melodrama and Meaning: History, Culture, and the Films of Douglas Sirk*. Bloomington: Indiana University Press, 1994.

Koch, Howard. *The Panic Broadcast*. New York: Avon, 1970.

Koetting, Christopher T. *Mind Warp! The Fantastic True Story of Roger Corman's New World Pictures*. Baltimore: Midnight Marquee Press, 2003.

Kolker, Robert. *A Cinema of Loneliness*. 3rd ed. London: Oxford University Press, 2000.

Krämer, Peter. *"2001: A Space Odyssey."* London: British Film Institute, 2010.
———. "'The Best Disney Film Disney Never Made': Children's Films and the Family Audience in American Cinema since the 1960s." In *Genre and Contemporary Hollywood*, edited by Steve Neale, 185–200. London: British Film Institute, 2002.
———. "Disney and Family Entertainment." In *Contemporary American Cinema*, edited by Linda Ruth Williams and Michael Hammond, 265–279. Berkshire, UK: Open University, 2006.
Kuhn, Annette, ed. *Alien Zone: Cultural Theory and Contemporary Science Fiction Cinema*. London: Verso, 1990.
Ladson, Henry. "Alien." *Cineaste* 9, no. 4 (Fall 1979): 46.
Lafferty, William. "A Reappraisal of the Semi-Documentary in Hollywood, 1945–1948." *Velvet Light Trap* 20 (Summer 1983): 24.
Latham, Rob. "'A Journey beyond the Stars': *2001: A Space Odyssey* and the Psychedelic Revolution in 1960s Science Fiction." In *Science Fiction and the Prediction of the Future: Essays in Foresight and Fallacy*, edited by Gary Westfahl, Wong Kin Yuen, and Amy Kit-sze Chan, 128–134. Jefferson, NC: McFarland, 2011.
———. "The New Wave." In *A Companion to Science Fiction*, edited by David Seed, 202–216. Malden, MA: Blackwell, 2005.
Lev, Peter. *The Fifties: Transforming the Screen, 1950–1959*. Berkeley: University of California Press, 2003.
Lightman, Herb A. "Filming 'Planet of the Apes.'" *American Cinematographer* 49, no. 4 (April 1968): 256–259, 278.
———. "Front Projection for *2001: A Space Odyssey*." *American Cinematographer* 49, no. 6 (June 1968): 158–166.
Lim, Dennis, ed. *The Village Voice Film Guide*. Hoboken, NJ: John Wiley & Sons, 2007.
LoBrutto, Vincent. *Stanley Kubrick: A Biography*. New York: Da Capo, 1999.
Lovell, Glenn. *Escape Artist: The Life and Films of John Sturges*. Madison: University of Wisconsin Press, 2008.
Lucanio, Patrick. *Them or Us: Archetypal Interpretations of Fifties Alien Invasion Films*. Bloomington: Indiana University Press, 1987.
Lucanio, Patrick, and Gary Coville. *Smokin' Rockets: The Romance of Technology in American Film, Radio and Television, 1945–1962*. Jefferson, NC: McFarland, 2002.
Lucas, Tim. *Mario Bava: All the Colors of the Dark*. Cincinnati: Video Watchdog, 2007.
Maltby, Richard. *Hollywood Cinema*. 2nd ed. Malden, MA: Blackwell, 2003.
McCarthy, Todd. *Howard Hawks: The Grey Fox of Hollywood*. New York: Grove, 1997.
McGee, Mark Thomas. *Faster and Furiouser: The Revised and Fattened Fable of American International Pictures*. Jefferson, NC: McFarland, 1996.
McLuhan, Marshall. *Understanding Media: The Extensions of Man*. New York: Signet, 1964.
Merrick, Helen. "Fiction, 1964–1979." In *The Routledge Companion to Science Fiction*, edited by Mark Bould et al., 102–111. New York: Routledge, 2011.

Michelson, Annette. "Bodies in Space: Films as 'Carnal Knowledgment.'" *Artforum* 7, no. 6 (February 1969): 54–63.

Minett, Mark. "Eagle-Lion: A Brief History." Unpublished manuscript, Department of Communication Arts, University of Wisconsin–Madison, 2004.

Mittell, Jason. *Genre and Television: From Cop Shows to Cartoons in American Culture.* New York: Routledge, 2004.

Moine, Raphaëlle. *Cinema Genre*. Translated by Alistair Fox and Hilary Radner. Malden, MA: Blackwell, 2008.

Monaco, Paul. *The Sixties*. Berkeley: University of California Press, 2001.

Nadis, Fred. *The Man from Mars: Ray Palmer's Amazing Pulp Journey*. New York: Penguin, 2013.

Neale, Steve. *Genre and Hollywood*. London: Routledge, 2000.

Nowell, Richard. *Blood Money: A History of the First Teen Slasher Film Cycle.* New York: Continuum, 2011.

O'Donnell, Victoria. "Science Fiction Films and Cold War Anxiety." In *The Fifties: Transforming the Screen, 1950–1959*, edited by Peter Lev, 169–196. Berkeley: University of California Press, 2003.

Painter, Deborah. *Forry: The Life of Forrest J. Ackerman*. Jefferson, NC: McFarland, 2010.

Palmer, R. Barton. "2001: The Critical Reception and the Generation Gap." In *Stanley Kubrick's "2001: A Space Odyssey": New Essays*, edited by Robert Kolker, 14–27. Oxford: Oxford University Press, 2006.

Paul, William. *Laughing Screaming: Modern Hollywood Horror and Comedy.* New York: Columbia University Press, 1994.

Phillips, Gene D. *Godfather: The Intimate Francis Ford Coppola*. Lexington: University Press of Kentucky, 2004.

Pierson, Michele. *Special Effects: Still in Search of Wonder*. New York: Columbia University Press, 2002.

Pohl, Frederik. "2001: A Second Look." *Film Society Review* 5, no. 6 (February 1970): 27.

Pollock, Dale. *Skywalking: The Life and Films of George Lucas*. New York: Da Capo, 1999.

Prince, Stephen. *A New Pot of Gold: Hollywood under the Electronic Rainbow, 1980–1989*. Berkeley: University of California Press, 2000.

Pursell, Carroll. *Technology in Postwar America: A History*. New York: Columbia University Press, 2007.

Pye, Michael, and Linda Myles. *The Movie Brats: How the Film Generation Took Over Hollywood*. New York: Holt, Reinhart and Winston, 1979.

Ramaeker, Paul Burkhart. "A New Kind of Movie: Style and Form in Hollywood Cinema, 1965–1988." PhD diss., University of Wisconsin–Madison, 2002.

Ray, Robert B. *A Certain Tendency of the Hollywood Cinema, 1930–1980*. Princeton, NJ: Princeton University Press, 1985.

Rebello, Stephen. *Alfred Hitchcock and the Making of "Psycho."* New York: Harper Perennial, 1991.

Rehak, Bob. "Materializing Monsters: Aurora Models, Garage Kits, and the Object Practices of Horror Fandom." *Journal of Fandom Studies* 1, no. 1 (November 2012): 27–45.

Reidelbach, Maria. *Completely MAD: A History of the Comic Book and Magazine.* New York: Little, Brown, 1992.

Rinzler, J. W. *The Making of "Star Wars."* New York: Ballantine Books, 2007.

———. *The Making of "The Empire Strikes Back."* New York: Ballantine Books, 2010.

Roberts, Adam. *The History of Science Fiction.* New York: Palgrave Macmillan, 2005.

Ross, Andrew. "Uses of Camp." In *The Cult Film Reader*, edited by Ernest Methijs and Xavier Mendik, 53–66. Berkshire, UK: Open University Press, 2008.

Rubin, Martin. "The Incredible Shrinking Man." *Film Comment* 10, no. 4 (July/August 1974): 52–53.

Russo, Joe, and Larry Landsman, with Edward Gross. *"Planet of the Apes" Revisited.* New York: St. Martin's Press, 2001.

Salt, Barry. *Film Style and Technology.* London: Starwood, 1992.

Sanjek, David. "Fans' Notes: The Horror Film Fanzine." *Literature/Film Quarterly* 18, no. 3 (July 1990): 150–159.

Sansweet, Stephen J. *Star Wars: From Concept to Screen to Collectible.* San Francisco: Chronicle Books, 1992.

Sarris, Andrew. *The American Cinema: Directors and Directions, 1929–1968.* New York: Da Capo, 1996.

Schaefer, Eric. *"Bold! Daring! Shocking! True!" A History of Exploitation Films, 1919–1959.* Durham, NC: Duke University Press, 1999.

Schatz, Thomas. *Boom and Bust: American Cinema in the 1940s.* Berkeley: University of California Press, 1997.

———. *Hollywood Genres.* New York: Random House, 1981.

———. "The New Hollywood." In *Film Theory Goes to the Movies*, edited by Jim Collins, Hilary Radner, and Ava Preacher Collins, 8–36. New York: Routledge, 1993.

———. "New Hollywood, New Milennium." In *Film Theory and Contemporary Hollywood Movies*, edited by Warren Buckland, 19–46. New York: Routledge, 2009.

Schow, David J. *The Outer Limits Companion.* Hollywood: GNP/Crescendo, 1998.

Sconce, Jeffrey. "'Trashing' the Academy: Taste, Excess, and an Emerging Politics of Cinematic Style." *Screen* 36, no. 4 (Winter 1995): 371–393.

Seed, David. "Introduction: Approaching Science Fiction." In *A Companion to Science Fiction*, edited by David Seed, 1–8. Malden, MA: Blackwell, 2005.

Shiel, Mark. "American Cinema, 1970–1975." In *Contemporary American Cinema*, edited by Linda Ruth Williams and Michael Hammond, 124–157. London: McGraw-Hill, 2006.

Skotak, Robert. *Ib Melchior: Man of Imagination*. Baltimore: Midnight Marquee Press, 2000.

Smith, Erin A. "How the Other Half Read: Advertising, Working-Class Readers, and Pulp Magazines." *Book History* 3 (2000): 204–230.

Smith, Harrison. "The Rise of Fantasy in Literature." *American Scholar* 17, no. 3 (Summer 1948): 305–312.

Smith, Jeff. *Film Criticism, the Cold War, and the Blacklist: Reading the Hollywood Reds*. Berkeley: University of California Press, 2014.

Smith, Murray. "Gangsters, Cannibals, Aesthetes, or Apparently Perverse Allegiances." In *Passionate Views: Film, Cognition, and Emotion*, edited by Carl Plantinga and Greg M. Smith, 217–238. Baltimore: Johns Hopkins University Press, 1999.

Sobchack, Vivian C. "*The Leech Woman*'s Revenge, or a Case for Equal Misrepresentation." *Journal of Popular Film* 4, no. 3 (January 1975): 236–257.

———. *The Limits of Infinity: The American Science Fiction Film, 1950–1975*. South Brunswick, NJ: A. S. Barnes, 1980.

Solomon, Aubrey. *Twentieth Century-Fox: A Corporate and Financial History*. Lanham, MD: Scarecrow, 2002.

Solow, Herbert F., and Robert H. Justman. *Inside Star Trek: The Real Story*. New York: Pocket Books, 1996.

Sontag, Susan. "Notes on 'Camp.'" In *The Cult Film Reader*, edited by Ernest Mathijs and Xavier Mendik, 41–52. Berkshire, UK: Open University Press, 2008.

Staiger, Janet. "The Cultural Productions of *A Clockwork Orange*." In *Stanley Kubrick's "A Clockwork Orange,"* edited by Stuart Y. McDougal, 37–60. Cambridge: Cambridge University Press, 2003.

Stedman, Raymond William. *The Serials*. Norman: University of Oklahoma Press, 1971.

Stork, Matthias. "Assembling the Avengers: Reframing the Superhero Movie through Marvel's Cinematic Universe." In *Superhero Synergies: Comic Book Characters Go Digital*, edited by James N. Gilmore and Matthias Stork, 77–96. Lanham, MD: Rowman & Littlefield, 2014.

Strick, Philip. "Zardoz and John Boorman." *Sight and Sound* 43, no. 2 (Spring 1974): 73–77.

Tarratt, Margaret. "Monsters from the Id." In *Film Genre Reader III*, edited by Barry Keith Grant, 346–365. Austin: University of Texas Press, 2003.

Taves, Brian. "The B Film: Hollywood's Other Half." In *Grand Design: Hollywood as a Modern Business Enterprise, 1930–1939*, edited by Tino Balio, 313–350. Berkeley: University of California Press, 1993.

Taylor, Greg. *Artists in the Audience: Cults, Camp, and American Film Criticism*. Princeton, NJ: Princeton University Press, 1999.

Thompson, Kristin. *The Frodo Franchise: "The Lord of the Rings" and Modern Hollywood*. Berkeley: University of California Press, 2007.

Thompson, Kristin, and David Bordwell. *Film History: An Introduction*. 2nd ed. New York: McGraw-Hill, 2003.

"Top Ten 72." *Sight & Sound* 41, no. 1 (Winter 1972): 12–16.

Torres, Sasha. "The Caped Crusader of Camp: Pop, Camp, and the Batman Television Series." In *Camp — Queer Aesthetics and the Performing Subject: A Reader*, edited by Fabio Cleto, 330–343. Ann Arbor: University of Michigan Press, 1999.

Trumbull, Douglas. "Creating Special Effects for *2001: A Space Odyssey*." *American Cinematographer* 49, no. 6: 158–166.

Turnock, Julie A. *Plastic Reality: Special Effects, Technology, and the Emergence of 1970s Blockbuster Aesthetics*. New York: Columbia University Press, 2015.

Vela, Rafael A. "With the Parents' Consent: Film Serials, Consumerism and the Creation of a Youth Audience, 1913–1938." PhD diss., University of Wisconsin-Madison, 2000.

Warren, Bill. *Keep Watching the Skies! American Science Fiction Movies of the Fifties: The 21st Century Edition*. Jefferson, NC: McFarland, 2010.

Wasko, Janet. *Movies and Money: Financing the American Film Industry*. Norwood, NJ: Albex, 1982.

Weaver, Tom. *Attack of the Monster Movie Makers*. Jefferson, NC: McFarland, 1994.

———. *Interviews with B Science Fiction and Horror Movie Makers*. Jefferson, NC: McFarland, 1988.

———. *Monsters, Mutants, and Heavenly Creatures*. Baltimore: Midnight Marquee Press, 1996.

———. *Science Fiction Stars and Horror Heroes*. Jefferson, NC: McFarland, 1991.

———. *They Fought in the Creature Features*. Jefferson, NC: McFarland, 1995.

Weaver, Tom, Michael Brunas, and John Brunas. *Universal Horrors: The Studio's Classic Films, 1931–1946*. 2nd ed. Jefferson, NC: McFarland, 2007.

Weinstein, David. "Captain Video: Television's First Fantastic Voyage." *Journal of Popular Film and Television* 30, no. 3 (Fall 2002): 148–157.

Westfahl, Gary. "Hard Science Fiction." In *A Companion to Science Fiction*, edited by David Seed, 197–208. Malden, MA: Blackwell, 2005.

Whittington, William. *Sound Design and Science Fiction*. Austin: University of Texas Press, 2007.

Wood, Robin. *Hollywood from Vietnam to Reagan*. New York: Columbia University Press, 1986.

Wright, Bradford W. *Comic Book Nation: The Transformation of Youth Culture in America*. Baltimore: Johns Hopkins University Press, 2001.

Yockey, Matt. *Batman*. Detroit: Wayne State University Press, 2014.

———. "Monster Mashups: At Home with *Famous Monsters of Filmland*." *Journal of Fandom Studies* 1, no. 1 (November 2012): 65–86.

Youngblood, Gene. *Expanded Cinema*. New York: E. P. Dutton, 1970.

Zicree, Marc Scott. *The Twilight Zone Companion*. Los Angeles: Silman-James, 1989.

Archival Collections

Benjamin, Robert. Papers. Wisconsin Center for Film and Theater Research, Madison.

Paramount Production Records. Margaret Herrick Library, Academy of Motion Picture Arts and Sciences, Beverly Hills, CA.

Twentieth Century-Fox Collection. Arts Library Special Collections. Young Library, University of California–Los Angeles.

United Artists Corporation Records. Wisconsin Center for Film and Theater Research, Madison.

Universal Studios Collection. Cinematic Arts Library, University of Southern California, Los Angeles.

Warner Bros. Archive. Special Collections. University of Southern California, Los Angeles.

Index

Page numbers in italics refer to the illustrations.

Wesleyan Film

A SERIES FROM WESLEYAN UNIVERSITY PRESS

Edited by Lisa Dombrowski and Scott Higgins

ORIGINATING EDITOR: Jeanine Basinger

Anthony Mann
by Jeanine Basinger

It's the Pictures That Got Small
Hollywood Film Stars on 1950s Television
by Christine Becker

The South Korean Film Renaissance
Local Hitmakers, Global Provocateurs
by Jinhee Choi

The Art of Comedy
The Films of Frank Tashlin
by Ethan de Seife

The Films of Samuel Fuller
If You Die, I'll Kill You!
by Lisa Dombrowski

Kazan Revisited
edited by Lisa Dombrowski

The Lives of Robert Ryan
by J. R. Jones

Physical Evidence
Selected Film Criticism
by Kent Jones

The New Entrepreneurs
An Institutional History of
Television Anthology Writers
by Jon Kraszewski

Action Speaks Louder
Violence, Spectacle,
and the American Action Movie
by Eric Lichtenfeld

Hollywood Ambitions
Celebrity in the Movie Age
by Marsha Orgeron

Brutal Intimacy
Analyzing Contemporary French Cinema
by Tim Palmer

The Cinema of Errol Morris
by David Resha

Escape Velocity
American Science Fiction Film,
1950–1982
by Bradley Schauer

Soul Searching
Black-Themed Cinema
from the March on Washington
to the Rise of Blaxploitation
by Christopher Sieving

Paul on Mazursky
by Sam Wasson

A Splurch in the Kisser
The Movies of Blake Edwards
by Sam Wasson

BRADLEY SCHAUER is an assistant professor of film studies at the University of Arizona. His articles have appeared in *Film History*, *The Velvet Light Trap*, and *The Quarterly Review of Film and Video*.